THE GREEN MARINE

Graham Dale is a computer systems analyst, volunteer fire-fighter and an emergency medical technician who now lives in Austin, Texas. He is a single man born in Dublin in 1978. Graham has been both a former Irish defence force reservist rifleman and a US Marine reserve mortarman who served in Iraq during Operation Iraqi Freedom. He has also cross trained with the Royal Moroccan army in operation African Lion.

Neil Fetherstonhaugh is a thirty-seven-year-old author and a journalist with the Dublin People group of newspapers. He is married and lives in Dublin. *The Green Marine* is the fourth book he has worked on.

THE GREEN MARINE

Graham Dale

with

Neil Fetherstonhaugh

HACHETTE
BOOKS
IRELAND

First published in 2008 by Hachette Books Ireland

A CIP catalogue record for this title is available from the British Library.

ISBN 978 0 340 96027 1

Hachette Books Ireland's policy is to use papers that are
natural, renewable and recyclable products and made from wood grown in
sustainable forests. The logging and manufacturing processes are expected to
conform to the environmental regulations of the country of origin.

Typeset in Adobe Garamond and Bodini by Hachette Books Ireland
Cover design by Anú Design, Tara

Printed and bound in Great Britain by Mackays of Chatham Ltd,
Chatham, Kent

Hachette Books Ireland
8 Castlecourt Centre, Castleknock, Dublin 15, Ireland

A division of Hachette Livre
338 Euston Road, London NW1 3BH, England

Contents

This book is dedicated to
my first love Aoife, my Irish Rose.

It is also dedicated to the men and women
of the US armed forces who have fallen in
Iraq and Afghanistan.

Prologue

11 September 2001

You can never know when you go to bed at night that the following day, nothing will ever be the same again.

The morning everything changed for me started out like many others. I was woken early by a voice over the PA system in the fire department where I volunteered alerting us to our first call-out of the day. It took a few moments for my eyes to focus as I emerged into the truck bay where the rest of the crew was already getting into the fire engine. The dispatcher gave us the address and we were soon on our way to assist an elderly patient who was suffering from breathing difficulties. This was nothing new. For some reason, we tended to get a lot of geriatric-related calls first thing in the morning.

It was another beautiful late summer's day and the sun was shining from the brilliant blue sky as we raced through the streets of Anderson Mill, a quiet suburban neighbourhood in northwest Austin, Texas. We got to the house and went in to see how the patient was doing.

We were in the middle of attending to him when an unusual message came in over the radio. I caught something about a plane crashing into the World Trade Center in New York. I'd never heard of it and when the paramedics arrived to take over, I asked my lieutenant what the World Trade Center was. He said he wasn't sure.

We got back to the fire station and switched on the TV to see if there was any more news about the plane crash. It took a few moments for the stations to pick up on what we had already heard over the emergency radio channel but, soon enough, the early-morning talk shows were interrupted with the newsflashes coming from Manhattan.

There, in front of our astonished eyes, were images of a skyscraper, the north tower of the World Trade Center, with smoke billowing from a huge gash in its side. 'Holy shit,' I gasped, as we all crowded around watching the live footage that, at that moment, was being beamed across the world.

And as we watched in awe, we caught the flicker of a shadow in the corner of the screen.

In the instant that the second plane hit, we knew it was no accident. When the reports started coming in of other planes crashing out of the same blue sky I had admired only hours before, we knew we were under attack.

There were no more doubts. This was war, and we felt like we were in the front line. We were only fifteen miles from the Texas state capitol building. Was that going to be a target too? Calmly, we readied our gear and waited by the trucks, waiting for the inevitable rash of emergency calls. It was one of those situations when you don't know what to say to the people near you, so we sat silently, waiting and listening as the world fell apart around us.

I decided to call my mum back home in Dublin. She answered on the first ring, up the wall with worry. I tried to reassure her and explained that I was just about as far away from New York as she was, but it didn't work. The truth was that neither of us knew what was going on.

I hung up and walked outside to have a smoke and clear my head. I gazed up at the Stars and Stripes on the firehouse flagpole, billowing in a gentle breeze. I was still thinking of my family and hadn't noticed the biker pulling up on his Harley Davidson behind me. I glanced at him as he walked over to me. We just kind of looked at each other and, without a word, walked towards the flag and grabbed a hold of the guide ropes.

I gave it a tug and, slowly, it came down. At half-mast, I tied it up and we stood there staring at it. As the realisation of what was happening started to sink in, I began to get angry.

And the longer I stood there, the angrier I got.

I had to do something. I decided there and then that I had to stand up and be counted.

Without much more thought, I jumped in my car and drove to the nearest armed forces recruitment centre. Within an hour, I was filling out the paperwork that would change my life for ever.

***

On the afternoon of 11 September 2001, I volunteered to join the United States Marine Corps.

I was twenty-three years old at the time, an Irishman living in America. Three years later, I would find myself fighting for my life in the barren desert wastes of western Iraq.

My life-changing decision has had repercussions that I'm still battling with today. Since 2001, many people, especially at home in

Ireland, have asked me why I chose to fight for another country's military in a war that has divided the world. It's easier now, with the benefit of hindsight, to have an informed opinion about the bitter conflict that is still raging in the Middle East but, in those first frightening hours of 9/11, nothing was that clear.

Although I didn't know who had just sucker-punched us in the back, I took it personally and I wanted revenge – for the firemen, for the people who worked in those buildings, for America and for humanity.

I was not an American, but I couldn't remain impartial and say that this horrific act against my adopted home had nothing to do with me. I lived in America, my friends were American and I was pretty sure my kids would be too. I may not have been a citizen, but I was an immigrant, like all the other immigrants who helped build the country I now called home.

I couldn't sit by on the sidelines and watch these terrible events unfold like it was a daytime TV drama. We were under attack and I felt it was my duty to step up to the plate, roll up my sleeves and fight to defend a way of life that was now mine.

I could have turned a blind eye and just been relieved that it hadn't happened in Ireland. But if I did that, I'd be letting the scumbags win. And who was to say they wouldn't turn around the next day and bomb my hometown and my family?

As I walked through the door of the recruiting office, I had resolved to offer my help, to fight back against whoever had attacked us.

Part I

THE US MARINES

Chapter 1

Even though it sounds rash – running off to join the Marines immediately after what had happened in New York – it wasn't entirely a spur-of-the-moment decision.

If the truth be told, the 9/11 attacks merely provided me with the ultimate reason to finally go and do something I had always wanted to do. Ever since I was a kid, I had wanted to be a Marine.

At home, we grew up with the memory of my great-grandfather who had faced the Germans in the trenches of the First World War. As a rifleman in the Royal Dublin Fusiliers, he had been wounded in combat and died of his wounds. On the other side of my family, my mother's relatives had fought against the English to free Ireland, one of them had died on hunger strike when he was captured. I had two uncles who served in the US army during the Cuban Missile Crisis and, later on in life, I found out that I had a second cousin from England who had been a Royal Marine in the Falklands War, although I did not know anything about him until I saw him in a documentary about training Royal Marine Commandos. I respected the hell out of each of them and the fact that, despite the turmoil of the times, they had the courage to fight for their convictions.

I was brought up with the same belief – to fight for what I thought was right. One important thing I took with me from my childhood was that I should always stand up for myself.

I came home from school with black eyes, bloodied noses and swollen lips so many times that I couldn't even begin to count them all, but the aul fella would only ever ask two simple questions – who started it and why. If I could convince him that it was someone else and that they were out of line, well, he would back me 100 per cent. It didn't really matter who won or lost, what mattered was that I had held my ground, drawn a line in the sand and refused to back down.

There was a lot of that typical bullshit in my school. Kids were picked on all the time and, sometimes, it was those who were defending themselves from the bullies who got into trouble. Of course, the teachers didn't see it that way. They didn't care why people were fighting, only that it was wrong and deserved to be punished no matter what. As a result, I spent a lot of time at school standing outside the principal's office waiting for yet another bollocking. But my schooldays helped me develop a sense of fairness and a belief that the weak needed protection from aggression.

At the age of thirteen, I watched in horrified fascination as all the terrible drama of the first Gulf War unfolded live on our television at home. I couldn't understand why Iraq had invaded this small country, Kuwait. As I got older, all the news seemed to be about war. I found it even harder to explain what was happening in Yugoslavia, Somalia and all the other troubled places. To me, it felt like the world was in turmoil, terrorised by evil dictators, psychopaths and warlords, and I was moved by the injustice of it all. Tens of thousands of people were being exterminated in these countries, and I felt that we in Ireland appeared to have stuck our heads in the sand, pretending that nothing was happening. Instead, we stuck a few pence in a Trócaire box to make it all better.

In my innocence, I asked my dad why we didn't send an army to help the people in Kuwait or Kosovo. He told me we couldn't because we were a neutral country. What was this neutrality? I wondered. It was a concept that didn't make any sense to me. After all, from my own family history I knew that Irishmen had always fought for what they believed was right. I resolved that some day I would follow in their footsteps.

Watching old Second World War movies with my older brothers reinforced this ideal of the manner in which men in the past had put everything aside to die for the cause they believed in. We cheered when John Wayne stormed the beaches in the *Sands of Iwo Jima* and laughed at those movies in which angry but overfed German machine-gunners screamed, 'Halt!' as the POWs made their great escape.

Like most kids, I had an active imagination and these war movies inspired the games I played. I spent a lot of time sneaking into the Capuchin monastery, which was just up the road from the house where I grew up in Raheny, with my friends to act out our soldier fantasies. The monastery was my favourite hang-out for years. It had everything a boy could want – wooded areas, open fields, twisting trails and great hiding spots. I climbed every tree and left no stone unturned. We had to be careful, as the monks who dwelled there were rumoured to enjoy catching juvenile intruders and making them peel potatoes as punishment.

It became our pretend battlefield, where we ambushed enemy columns and hid from Nazi or Viet Cong patrols. Sometimes, we engaged in real battles with rival gangs of kids and our play-acting gradually became more serious. It was like actual military training. We would go into the city centre and head down to the army surplus shops on Little Mary Street to buy anything we thought looked useful. We would all wear camouflage fatigues and carry ropes, knives, cammo paint, and even food and water to last a few days.

We thought of ourselves as professionals and we read up on the SAS and US Navy Seals, hoping to learn the little tricks that would give us the upper hand in our war games. One Christmas, I got a survival manual from my brother, which I still have to this day. From that book, I quickly set about experimenting with the simple traps and snares it illustrated before I moved on to more complex tripwires and spiked pits, like the ones I'd seen in Indiana Jones movies and read about in stories from the Vietnam War.

One time, we tied a six-foot Christmas tree to an overhead branch so that it would swing down thirty feet on a rope and smack straight into any poor unfortunate who happened to walk into the trap. It was pretty effective when we tested it and I was really pleased with myself – although, perhaps fortunately, we were smart enough not to try it out on a real person and we dismantled it before we went home.

Things started to change in our little war games around the time we hit puberty. One night, I was up in a tree that overlooked one of our trails, planning an ambush. I had a buddy in another tree about fifty metres along the way and we were talking on our high-speed Scooby Doo walkie-talkies that someone's little brother had been given for Christmas. We were waiting for our enemies from the other end of our road, who were playing the North Vietnamese army. To the south flank, we had two more soldiers armed with heavy machine guns, which were actually just big sticks. We had positioned ourselves carefully so we wouldn't catch ourselves in the crossfire. This, I thought, was the perfect setup.

Darkness fell while we were waiting, which added to our concealment. Our patience finally paid off some time later when I saw three silhouetted figures moving towards my position on the trail. I stayed quiet and hunkered down in silence until they passed right under me, just as I had hoped.

Then, I jumped down from the branch and opened up with my stick-rifle, making loud shooting sounds. My buddies joined in, adding their own shouts to the noise of battle. A high-pitch screeching noise that sounded like a baby pig caught in a fence stopped us in our tracks. We stood there bewildered.

Instead of surprised enemy troops, there were three hysterical girls standing in front of us screaming at the top of their lungs. In fairness to them, four guys had just jumped out of nowhere with green paint on their faces and surrounded them, shaking sticks and shouting like gobshites.

Eventually, we all calmed down and figured out what they were doing there. Apparently, one of the NVA lads had invited them up to hang out with our gang but hadn't told us. I scratched my head and wondered why anyone would want to do that. What use did we have for girls? Surely they didn't want to play soldiers ... unless they wanted to be nurses in our little field hospital. But when I asked them if they would tend to our wounded or cook up some rations, they told me to feck off.

Up to that point, I had never taken any interest in girls. I had a sister but she wasn't a 'real' girl. I was brought up in a male-dominated house and went to an all-boys school. Girls served no obvious purpose and I didn't take too much notice of them.

However, that day would prove to be the beginning of the end of our childhood. Little by little, the soldiering days of my little gang gradually gave way to trips to the cinema to watch soppy movies and walks in the park. I watched, aghast. It seemed to me that everything we had trained so hard for was being left behind. Instead of *Apocalypse Now*, it was *When Harry Met Sally*.

We started going to discos and those with girlfriends would spend the night kissing them or holding their hands. Soon, I'd lost a good radio operator, two machine-gunners, half a platoon of Special Forces commandos and a highly decorated squad leader.

Everything was changing in my little world. I couldn't mentally adjust to growing up – or maybe I simply didn't want to. Either way, I made a conscious effort to delay the rites of passage that marked the average adolescence.

Even when I went on to secondary school, I didn't date anyone, partly because I had no interest but mainly because nobody was interested in me. Instead of chasing girls, I looked elsewhere for distraction. I decided I wanted to become a real soldier when I left school and, in particular, I dreamed of becoming a fighter pilot with the Marines. I studied hard and tried to stay out of trouble as best I could and, for a while, everything was going to plan. Then, one day, I had my bloody eyes tested in school and found out I was short-sighted – which explained why I could never make out the words on the blackboard – and this put an end to my ambitions to be a pilot.

It was a devastating blow. I consoled myself with the thought that I could still join the Marine Corps as a grunt in the infantry. It didn't have the same glamorous appeal as a fighter pilot, but at least I didn't have to continue to be as diligent with my studies as I had been. All I had to do was keep fit and get through my Leaving Cert.

As I considered Shakespeare and so much of the other stuff the education system wanted to teach me to be pretty much pointless, I figured it was a perfect solution.

Just to keep my options open, I applied for various college courses and when I got the results from my final school exams, I actually did better than expected and found I had enough points to get into Dundalk RTC to study computing. When I left school in 1996, I decided to give it a go. I spent the first six weeks half-heartedly trying to figure out where my classes were and quickly found out I had nothing in common with the people who sat around debating the world's woes. They seemed to know everything about everything and could solve international crises over a ten-minute tea break smoking cigarettes.

Whenever we talked about politics or history, one of them would say something like, 'Why can't they all just get along?' Brilliant, I thought, Why didn't anyone else think of that before? I know, why don't we send a letter to the Somali warlords after communications class asking them to 'get along'?

It was enough to convince me that spending the rest of my youth sitting in a classroom wasn't for me.

I dropped out of public college and considered my options. Dublin in the 1990s offered few exciting choices for a disillusioned nineteen-year-old. Most people my age seemed to have limited ambitions that didn't stretch beyond buying a house in some anonymous suburb, getting married, having several kids and working the rest of their lives in a nice, stable job while saving hard to pay for their retirement.

In school, the teachers had encouraged us to aspire to these dull futures, telling us that if we were lucky, then some day we'd get to work for a bank or in the post office. Fuck that, I thought, I'm not licking stamps for the rest of my life. My attitude was that life should be an adventure and, as you only got one chance, you should make the most of it. I decided to follow my own path and see where it took me.

Around this time, I met a beautiful girl who blew me away and it didn't take long for me to fall in love. Aoife was the kind of girl who I could really talk to and, even more surprising, she cared enough to listen to me. We became inseparable and my life took on new meaning as a young man in love for the first time. I finally figured out what had led half of my platoon away from our childhood games and I embraced the change with a new heart.

I eventually got an interview with the Dell Computer Corporation in Bray, just outside Dublin, after completing a computer course in a private college. I got the job and, with a natural knack for computers, was eventually promoted to become a network engineer. Not bad for a twenty-year-old kid. I got the opportunity to fly all around Europe and even once to the United States. I had always wondered about those people who got picked up at airports by guys who stood at the arrivals gate holding cards with their names on them, and now I was one of them. I remember thinking as I sat in my business-class seat during another flight to the continent that this was so much better than being sent to the principal's office or being stuck in detention. An added bonus was the fact that as it was an American company, there was a chance that I could get a transfer to the United States.

In the meantime, as I was still curious about military life, I joined the reserve defence forces in Dublin, known as the FCA – otherwise cruelly referred to as the 'Free Clothes Association'.

One of my friends had brought me up to the historic Cathal Brugha Barracks in Rathmines in south Dublin and, after a look around, I signed up with the 20th Infantry Battalion and was assigned to C Company.

It was a part-time activity but I enjoyed the training that took place every Tuesday night and on Sundays. We'd be brought up to the mountains near Dublin and taught field craft and small-unit warfare. The training was actually really good and I learned field skills that I kept with me and use to this day, but it occurred to me that we only learned small-unit warfare as there were fuck-all people in the reserve, and society, as a whole, had little or no interest in us, so what choice did we have?

Initially, I did quite well – I received the Best New Recruit in the Battalion award that year – but, soon, I became discouraged when I realised that the reserve was treated by the military more like an unwanted stepchild than a functioning arm of the army. The active-duty guys would call us 'Sandbags' which, I have to admit, I thought was hilarious.

I enjoyed my stint in the FCA all the same although my time there was short.

I was still in love with Aoife but when we broke up after a year or so I realised I had to move on. I had spent two previous summers when I was still in secondary school visiting my sister in Austin, Texas, and I had loved it there. I applied for a green card, dousing the application in holy water and saying Hail Marys all the way to the post office. The good Virgin hooked me up and I was soon on my way to the American embassy in Dublin for an interview. I mentioned to the woman quizzing me that I was going to join the Marines, although, to be honest, I had been distracted by the good life at that point and was thinking more along the lines of swimming pools and fancy convertible cars, but it seemed to work for her. When I told her, she smiled, stopped asking me questions and approved my application. As she said, 'Welcome to America,' I had a smile from ear to ear. I skipped out of the place elated.

On the way home, I called everyone I knew on my oversized mobile phone to tell them that I was on my way to America, where I was going to get rich and marry Alicia Silverstone and live happily ever after.

Chapter 2

If only life was so simple. Because I was established with an American company, I thought it would be easy to get a transfer there. I set about getting one approved by the HR department, and then I got the bad news – there was a hiring freeze in Dell America and they couldn't give me a job over there.

Problem was, I had to leave for America by a certain date under the conditions of my green card. I had a choice of staying with my career or jumping ship and taking my chances in America. I decided to grab the opportunity while I still could. I quit work in March 2000 and bid farewell to my family. Several long flights later, I was in my new home – Austin, Texas, USA, the live-music capital of the world. My sister was still living there – although she would eventually move back to Ireland in 2003 – and she put me up for a while after I arrived, but I was determined to strike out on my own.

Of course, I was a bit anxious about facing an unknown future in a country I knew very little about, but I was brimming with confidence, like most cocky twenty-two-year-olds are. As it turned out, it wasn't too hard to find a job. The dot-com boom was in full swing and, within a few weeks, I was working as a consultant for IBM on a software automation team. I started off on a good wage and soon things were going well.

I was living far, far away from home, driving a brand-new Ford Mustang with an engine practically the size of my entire banged-up Ford Fiesta that was still sitting in the mother's garden back home. I got my own apartment, and I'm not talking about renting a room – I had the place to myself. There was a swimming pool in the complex and a hot tub to boot. Enough said!

The best thing, though, was having the money to spend on whatever the hell I wanted. I'd never had that luxury before and I blew loads of cash on lots of stupid stuff. One day, I went out and bought six fake trees. I put them all around my new apartment and then drove to the local pet shop and bought some tropical birds, a cage and all the bits and pieces that went with it. I got home and assembled the cage but left the door open. I decided that my birds would be allowed to fly wherever they wanted. It was my way of exhibiting my independence, or maybe my stupidity.

There were some culture shocks, like the day I walked into Wal-Mart and bought a rifle just like it was a can of Coke. I was bewildered by how easy it was but, there again, it was part and parcel of getting to understand the place. Owning a gun in Texas is not just a right, it's a way of life. Everybody is armed; that's the way it's always been and always will be, and it suited me fine.

The weather was also a major bonus. I would sit out on my balcony on a warm Texan night and reflect that this would have been a great place to grow up. At home, I'd spent a lot of my teenage years sitting on a wall on my road, spitting on the ground in the rain, kicking a football against the wall and pissing off all the neighbours, because I didn't have much else to do. I looked at the kids in Texas and they were all going to theme parks and floating down rivers in rubber tubes in the summer. They had cars and went to the movies and arcades all the time. All I ever did in my late teens, besides studying for my Leaving Certificate and drinking cans of beer from a blue bag in the laneway, was work in a Chinese restaurant at the weekend and try to avoid getting mugged coming back from the local cinema.

Every now and again, I did think about joining the Marines but things were going too well for me to contemplate it seriously. I was enjoying my new life and now that I was well taken care of, the world and its woes seemed far away. Instead, I decided to become a fireman, thinking that it might satisfy my desire for excitement. I had only been in the States a few months when I joined the fire department in Jollyville as a volunteer.

As the months passed, I really settled into the pace of American life. I travelled around a bit, even flying to New York to watch the Wolfe Tones in Queens after seeing an advert in the *Irish Echo* newspaper the night before the concert. I downed pints of Guinness in Bull McCabe's Bar in downtown Austin and started hanging out with new friends. We got into a bit of trouble along the way – just the usual stuff that you'd expect a bunch of young lads to get up to – but for the most part we just partied it up.

By September 2001, I was still at IBM, working away and spending most of my spare time with the fire department in Jollyville, where we attended the car crashes, house fires and other dramas of the job. I had volunteered more for the buzz than anything else, but soon an opportunity came along to train as an EMT – an emergency medical technician. Initially, I didn't think it would be something I would be interested in. As far as I was concerned, these guys were just ambulance drivers who applied plasters to kids' knees after they fell off their bicycles. If anything, I wanted to be at the centre of it all, kicking down doors, cutting up cars and saving all kinds of young maidens from certain fiery deaths.

But I changed my mind as I watched the EMTs in action. I grew to admire the professionalism they displayed on a daily basis. I enrolled in a school to take my Emergency Medical Technician Basic Certificate in August 2001 and from the day I picked up their training manual, I was hooked. I had no idea that the work was so complex and yet so fascinating. Any medical treatment I had learned up to that point involved putting some iodine on a cut and saying a few Hail Marys. In secondary-school science class, I'd had to memorise the differences between an artery and a vein, know where the heart was and what white and red blood cells did, but it didn't really mean anything to me at the time as I had no interest in becoming a nurse or a doctor.

In Emergency Medical Service School, it all started to make more sense, and the training taught me how to use the knowledge I had to help people in the real world. I was sent to a busy hospital to get hands-on experience in an emergency room and I joined the crew of a paramedic ambulance to learn the ropes out on the street. Day by day, I understood a little bit more about the science behind the EMS. What I really liked about the training was that they weren't typical classes where the instructor blabbed his mouth off and you repeated after him. If you couldn't figure something out, they would help you understand, but if you still couldn't get it right and failed your tests, then you were out the door. There was no room for mistakes in the EMS. They are trained to provide the level of care you would want for your own family. I kept that philosophy in my head and thought of it as my mission statement.

I started going to school on Tuesday and Thursday nights, doing my 'clinicals' in the emergency room and riding out on the ambulance at weekends. I was taking it all very seriously and was considering it as a full-time career. Most of my nights off were spent sitting in front of the books, studying for the most part – although I will not lie to you and say I never took a book to the pub. One night, I was sitting alone with a pint in front of me when a girl came walking over to talk to me. Curious to see what I was reading, she glanced down at the page I had open in front of me. I had been studying the chapter on major burning and it featured some nasty-looking pictures of people who had been burned alive. I don't know what she thought I was doing sitting there, drinking a pint on a Saturday night on my own looking at pictures of dead people but, when I tried to say hello, she walked away without a word.

Other nights, I'd study at the firehouse and stay over if it got too late to go home. One night, I crashed out on the couch in the day room as all the beds in the crew room were taken. I brought in a blanket and sat up watching cable television until I got tired. As I reached over to turn off the light, I noticed the time. It was after midnight on the morning of Tuesday, 11 September 2001.

Chapter 3

As I drove to the recruitment office later that terrible day, all manner of thoughts were going through my head. It was frightening, but if there was going to be a war, I wanted to help fight it. I was also excited. This was my chance to take the test and see if I really had what it took to be a United States Marine.

To anyone unversed in the ways of the modern military, the United States Marine Corps represents the very best that the fighting armed services can offer. They are the elite, the toughest of the tough. They are the first in and last out. Over the years, I had read fervently about the history of the Marines and absorbed all the glorious deeds that they had performed. For all those reasons, it proved all the more astonishing to find how relatively easy it was to join.

Signing up for the military in America isn't like it is in Ireland. At home, they only recruit once or twice a year and then you have to go through the whole application procedure, which can take months. In the US, there are recruiting stations all over the place, just like McDonald's, and you can pop in at any time and sign up at the drop of a hat.

A Marine Staff Sergeant sitting behind the desk stood up as I opened the door. In my thick Dublin accent, I told him that I wanted to join. He was pretty helpful, but he kept looking at me as if I was lost, and it took me a while to convince him that I was serious. He seemed unsure whether or not an Irishman could walk in off the street and qualify for recruitment. There's a general misconception that you have to be a citizen to join the American military. That's not the case. All I needed was a green card and I had a letter from the US embassy in Dublin stating that I could join up.

I showed this letter to the staff sergeant and he made a quick phone call. He obviously got the all clear to start processing me, as he hung up, grinned and said, 'You're good to go, son.'

He explained that as I was not actually a US citizen, there were some sensitive units in the Marines I couldn't join. Unfortunately, I wasn't permitted to work in reconnaissance or intelligence, which were some of the jobs that interested me.

We discussed what I wanted to do instead, and he went through what the various options were. He laid down little cards in front of me that had words and phrases written on them, such as 'Personal Development', 'Honor', 'Career', 'Benefits' and 'Education'. I noticed that there wasn't a single one that said anything about fighting or killing, which struck me as funny. After all, surely that was pretty much what this game was all about – or so I thought. Either way, I had no interest in what the little cards offered.

Then he put on a short promotional video that showed all the nice things about being a Marine, with the emphasis on the crisp uniforms and the shiny buttons and medals hanging off them. I really wasn't interested in going through this malarkey, as the guy didn't have to sell me anything. I didn't need any convincing. I told him I didn't care about personal development or college benefits, I just wanted a rifle and someone to shoot. I think he liked that. We never mentioned it, but we both knew it was no accident that I was sitting in front of him that day.

To join up full-time required a minimum of four years' service and I said I didn't want that. I wasn't looking for a career in the military. If the country was invaded the next day, I was prepared to take my place in the ranks but, until then, I wanted to hang on to my job. I didn't want to come back to civilian life after four years and be forced to start from the bottom all over again.

He suggested that I join an Infantry Reserve Unit that was based right there in Austin. He said I could still go to boot camp like everyone else and then on to infantry school. After I was fully trained, I could return home, go to weekend training every month and would be called up if I was really needed. This sounded like the best compromise. I would be ready to fight if there was a war but in between training, I could go back home and live a normal life.

He took out the paperwork, and I took my first step on the road to becoming a US Marine.

We agreed that I should wait until my EMT class was complete and to give me time to take my state EMT exam. Pending the results of my physical tests, which would take place in three days' time, it would be at least January 2002 before I was actually shipped out to boot camp. Satisfied that I had made the right decision, I shook his hand and, later that week, was in San Antonio undergoing my medical screening.

This is also where the US military conducts an aptitude test called the ASVAB. It comprised maths, reading and English, but it was actually easier than the entrance exam for secondary school. They then give applicants a battery of physical examinations from various doctors and technicians. There were hundreds of young men and women there who had obviously rushed in to join any one of the numerous branches of the armed forces in the wake of the 9/11 attacks.

We were herded around like cattle and given the third degree. A military doctor told me to look left, look right and cough while he prodded and probed me. I completed all the tests and was passed as fit. Later that day, I was to take my oath as a new member of the US armed forces and swear the Oath of Enlistment. Scared I was going to make an ass out of myself, I walked over to the lady from the government who was in charge and asked her if she had the words written down somewhere. She smiled and told me not to worry. She said she would say it out loud and that all I had to do was repeat after her. I was thinking to myself, man, it's bloody easy to join this crowd. You don't even need to know what you're doing.

I pledged allegiance to the United States with my right hand held up and took my oath to defend the country. I felt a little weird as I repeated the words 'I, Graham Dale, do solemnly swear that I will support and defend the Constitution of the United States against all enemies, foreign and domestic; that I will bear true faith and allegiance to the same; and that I will obey the orders of the President of the United States and the orders of the officers appointed over me, according to regulations and the Uniform Code of Military Justice, so help me God.' I managed to get all the words out OK and officially became a Poolee, the name given to those who are pooled while waiting in the delayed entry programme to be sent to boot camp.

As I drove back to Austin, I felt a surreal sensation rising in my stomach. I had thought about this moment for a long time and now that it was actually a reality, I had a lot of things to mull over. I thought about how I would tell my parents back in Dublin that I had just joined the Marines when it already seemed inevitable that there would be a military reaction to what had happened on 9/11. Surely, the last thing a mother would want to hear, and would find even harder to understand, was that her son might be going to war. I felt bad as I imagined telling her. I had a vision of her standing there as I came home in a wooden box draped in a flag. I pushed the thought to the back of my mind and drove straight to Razzoo's, my favourite neighbourhood bar. Pints were in order, and I called a few of the boys to tell them to come down and meet me so I could fill them in.

My friends reacted in various ways when I told them – some said they thought I was crazy, others patted me on the back. We drank long into the night while I debated how to tell my parents. In the end, I did what any smart man with a sister would do – I rang her instead. She was surprised when I told her, but supportive. Then I asked her not to tell my parents, knowing full well that as soon as I hung up, she would be on to them straight away. Then I sat back and waited for the inevitable call from Ireland. While I waited, I wondered again how my mother would react. I'm sure many other Irish mothers got surprise calls from sons living abroad, telling them that they were getting married or having a baby or something like that. My poor mother had always wanted the same for me, but it wasn't to be just yet. Instead of announcing that she was going to be a grandmother, I had to tell her I had just signed a contract with the American government to go and fight if needed.

When she finally called a few hours later, it was a nerve-wracking conversation. I could tell she was upset, but she said she respected my decision. I spent the rest of the call trying to calm her as best I could. I'm not proud to admit that I didn't actually tell her I had joined the infantry. I lied and said I was doing computer stuff and would be in a room somewhere buried underneath a mountain looking at monitors, just like in the movies. You can lie all you want to your mother, but she will always know the truth. I think she pretended to believe what I told her and we left it at that.

Then she put my father on. Being a man, he was a little bit more reserved. There was no way he was going to get all emotional on me and he passed it off by joking that the Marines must be crazy to let me join. But then he told me he was proud of me. He said he knew I'd do a good job even if I did get into a few scrapes along the way. My brothers were grand with the idea and it didn't bother them too much. Like most lads, we were just happy to agree to go out and have a pint to discuss the matter further whenever we got the chance. I think my sister leaned a little more on my mother's side, in that she didn't really agree with what I was doing. I never really asked her how she felt about it but, for the moment, there was nothing more to talk about. I was a going to join the Marines and that was that. The only thing left to do now was drink some more pints.

Chapter 4

On 7 October 2001, the US invaded Afghanistan. This marked the beginning of the War on Terror declared by President Bush in response to the 9/11 attacks. The whole country was on a war footing – shops even sold out of bottled water and tinned food. The declared purpose of the invasion was to capture Osama bin Laden, destroy Al-Qaeda and remove the Taliban regime, which had provided support and safe harbour for the terrorists. Together with the Brits, the US launched an aerial bombing campaign to support ground forces that were made up primarily of the Afghan Northern Alliance.

I was still working at IBM but, as soon as I qualified from EMT school in December 2001, I handed in my notice and took a few weeks off before I shipped out to boot camp. I enjoyed a quiet Christmas in Texas and, two days after my twenty-fourth birthday, on 13 January 2002, I was on my way to the Marine Corps Recruit Depot (MCRD) in San Diego. I flew out of San Antonio, Texas, on a regular commercial civilian flight amid the tourists and businessmen. As we took off, I reflected that I had been on similar journeys many times before, but this one was going to be different. That night, I wouldn't be putting my head down on a plump pillow in some four-star hotel – I was headed for what had the potential to be three months of hell.

On the plane, I got talking with a guy sitting beside me. It turned out he was a new recruit on his way to San Diego too. He seemed kind of nervous and at one stage actually asked me if I had ever been on a plane before. When I tried to explain that I was from Ireland, he cut in and said, 'But you came over on one of them boats, right?' Needless to say, we had an interesting conversation as I tried to convince him that Irish people now flew to and from America on a regular basis. He seemed bewildered to be on his way to boot camp and I offered to help him when we got there, but we were separated when we got off the plane at San Diego International Airport, and I never saw him again. The rest of the recruits who had been on the flight, including myself, were directed to a part of the airport where the United Services Organization was based to await the arrival of the buses that would bring us to boot camp.

I stood around with the same stupid, scared look that everyone else had on their face, totally unsure of what to expect. This was the moment when everything was going to change. I would soon be on the bottom rung of a very tall Marine Corps ladder. I had my doubts about what I was about to do but, whatever happened, I knew I had nobody else to blame for this one but myself.

It was dark by the time the buses eventually pulled up to the pavement. When the doors opened, we got our first glimpse of the drill instructors, the infamous DIs. I thought to myself, All right, man, here we go.

I took a last drag on my cigarette, knowing that it would be at least three months before I would be allowed to put another in my mouth. I also noticed that everyone had suddenly stopped talking and a hush fell over the crowd of disorganised kids. Everybody was standing there in silence, peering at the DIs as they got off the bus, not wanting to be the first to draw attention to themselves.

The DIs were imposing figures. I was hardly expecting a happy-go-lucky type with a big silly grin on his face like a Club Med holiday rep, but these guys looked pretty pissed off as they strode purposely towards us. In their iconic Campaign Cover hats and Marine Corps uniforms, they fitted perfectly the image I'd had of them.

They started barking out names and as each one was called out, we were told to get on the bus and were warned not to open our mouths. One by one, we rushed on and sat down without a word. When we were all accounted for, one of the DIs jumped on board and told us to put our heads between our knees. We all glanced nervously around, not knowing if he was serious, then he exploded. 'GET YOUR HEADS DOWN BETWEEN YOUR FRICKING KNEES!' he screamed over the noise of the engine starting up. 'YOU HAVE NO BUSINESS LOOKING OUT THAT WINDOW. YOU ARE DONE WITH THAT SHIT. LOCK IT UP, RIGHT NOW.' I put my head down between my knees and closed my eyes. I had a growing feeling in my heart that this was going to be a very rough ride.

The bus pulled off into the darkness and it seemed like only minutes later when we stopped again. We were already at our destination, but everyone was too afraid to look around. We sat there quietly in the darkness until the lights suddenly came on, and then all hell broke loose.

'GET OFF MY BUS RIGHT NOW!' the DI yelled. Forty clumsy guys jumped up in unison and tried to get out the door. But we didn't move fast enough and the DI started screaming over and over, 'GET OFF MY BUS RIGHT NOW! GET OFF MY BUS RIGHT NOW! GET OFF MY BUS RIGHT NOW!' Some of the lads looked like rabbits caught in the headlights and I'm sure they would have leapt out the windows if they could.

In a panic, the awkward rabble scrambled off the bus. We came tumbling out the door and joined the hundreds of silhouetted shapes milling about all over the place. None of us knew where we were. We were just a frightened herd of cattle bumping into each other as we ran a gauntlet of shouting DIs. We were chased across the tarmac and ordered to line up on the famous yellow steps of MCRD with our hands by our sides. The steps were actually footprints painted on the ground to show raw recruits where to stand. When you took your place on those yellow steps, it was the first time you stood in an official Marine Corps formation. The DIs stalked among us, trying to get us to stand at attention. We were now very disorientated. From the looks on some of their faces, I doubted that many of the other recruits had been screamed at like that in their entire lives. And the funny thing was, we had only been there for about forty-five seconds. This was only the beginning – we had another three months of this. By now, I was pretty sure every one of us was already questioning his reasons for being there. We were all probably thinking the same thing – this wasn't exactly what had been in the brochures.

As I stood there on the yellow steps amid the well-organised confusion that surrounded me, I noticed a massive sign above my head: 'Welcome to MCRD, San Diego'. Some welcome, I thought. That's got to be a joke. But it was no joke. This was boot camp – this was the Marines.

From the steps, we were hurried in single file over to the processing building. The first thing they did was strip us of our clothes and our personal belongings. We were brought into a huge room and told to put everything we had on the tables. I was allowed to keep something like five dollars in cash and a small notepad with some names and addresses in it, but that was it. Everything else was either thrown away or taken from us to be stored until the end of boot camp.

The floor was soon strewn with the debris of civilian life. I couldn't believe some of the things that people had brought with them. One guy had a soap dish. That immediately caught the DIs' attention and they surrounded him in a second. But then they found a packet of condoms in another guy's pocket. In the outside world, carrying a condom is probably a smart thing to do, but showing up with a pack for three months of boot camp in an all-male environment to join an organisation that isn't exactly known for its tolerance of alternative lifestyles was quite possibly the stupidest thing this fella had done in his life up to that point. By the time they were done screaming at him, spraying spit all over his face and calling him some crude names that I couldn't possibly repeat, the poor guy was in tears.

And that's how we spent the next few hours. On the first night at boot camp, they don't let you sleep. Instead, you are berated by the DIs and chased from one station to the next, ordered to sign paper-work, told to draw down the linen for your racks – which I quickly found out was the Marine word for a bed – and issued with your new fatigues. We moved so fast and for so long that the rest of that night passed in a blur. It didn't stop for one second and, as the hours passed, we only seemed to be expected to move faster and faster to the sound of the DIs' shouting. 'Come on you maggots, move, move, move!' 'Why are you here?' 'Why are you looking at me?' 'Do you like me, you scumbag? Is that it? You want my asshole?' 'What makes you think you can become a Marine?'

One of the last inductions was having our hair shaved off – the absolute, final symbolic transformation from civilian to recruit.

After what seemed like years, it had started to get bright outside and we were marched over to the chow hall to get morning chow. We were all tired and hungry, but there was to be no let-up. They pushed us together and told us to walk 'As to Bs' – shuffling along with each guy's balls pressed against the ass of the man in front. Keeping our tight-knit posture the whole time, we approached the long food lines. When it was my turn, I pushed my tray out. Another recruit was standing behind the counter with a ladle in his hand, shouting at me to sound off what I wanted. There were trays of food in front of me, but I didn't recognise any of it. Exhausted, I just asked him to give me anything, I didn't care what.

With a stupid smile on his face, as if he was enjoying all this, he ordered me on down the line and turned to the next man in the queue. I started to protest, but I was dragged onward and soon I was at the end of the line with an empty tray in front of me. My first morning with the Marines would be spent hungry. I locked a mental image of that fucker in my brain and swore that if I ever met him again, I'd break his legs with a hammer.

Chapter 5

No matter how hard you might try, it's almost impossible to imagine how hard boot camp really is.

Of course, I had seen the movies and read the books, but nothing prepared me for the reality of life as a raw recruit in the US Marines. Over the next few months, we would be transformed from a bunch of scared, pampered civilian kids into a tight team of well-trained, well-disciplined killing machines. And the men whose jobs it was to achieve this transformation were the DIs, the frightening figures who had complete control over every second of our existence.

As it turned out, the DIs who had picked us up at the airport were only the welcoming committee. As scary as they had been, we hadn't seen anything yet. After completing all of the administrative tasks, we were divided into groups and marched over to our new 'house', where we would live for the three months of our training.

On our way over, we learned that we were about to get 'picked up' by the DIs who would be in charge of our platoon. First, an officer ordered us to sit motionless on the ground in tightly packed rows with our hands on our knees while he gave us a very stern welcome speech about how this was an excellent opportunity to learn, train and build. Then he said it was time to meet our new DIs and, with that, the door of the duty hut opened. I caught a glimpse of three figures as they walked in but kept my head down and didn't look directly at them. I stared at the ground as they took their positions in front of our little gaggle of recruits and recited the Drill Instructors' Creed in loud and determined voices. 'These recruits are entrusted to my care. I will train them to the best of my ability. I will develop them into smartly disciplined, physically fit, basically trained Marines, thoroughly indoctrinated in love of Corps and country. I will demand of them, and demonstrate by my own example, the highest standards of personal conduct, morality and professional skill.'

With that, the officer told the DIs that we were all theirs and he walked out of the squad bay, leaving us alone with them. I felt like I had just been dropped off by my parents on the first day of school. There was an eerie silence for a few seconds and then the three of them really let us have it. At the top of their voices, they ordered us to get up on our feet. I was absolutely terrified – we all were – and, in our terror, we couldn't even stand up correctly, which made them angrier. When they gave us the order to stand in line by our racks, the stampede left some guys falling over foot lockers and others bouncing off walls. One guy was bleeding after he fell and another was hyperventilating, and the funny thing was that the DIs hadn't touched anyone.

Then they laid down the ground rules. They told us that, from that moment, we were no longer individuals. There was no such thing as 'I' or 'we' any more. From now on, we could only refer to ourselves in the third person. Whenever we were asked a question, we could only reply with 'this recruit' or 'these recruits'. It was our first lesson on a long and painful road to forgetting that we had ever existed outside the Marine Corps. We had to learn a new language with enough words and expressions to fill a small book. We were told to exchange simple expressions such as 'OK' for 'kill'. The Marines are traditionally a naval force and, in their vocabulary, you look through portholes rather than windows, walk on decks, close hatches instead of doors and sleep in racks.

Over the next few days, we were slowly indoctrinated into the ways of the Corps. The DIs demanded 100 per cent of our attention at all times, even when we were asleep and, boy, did they get it. If they had us running from one point to another and wanted us to stop, the DI would bark out 'Zeee-ro!' and, in response, the entire platoon would instantly halt on the spot and reply in one voice, 'Freeze, recruit, freeze!' To resume the activity, the DI would yell, 'As you were,' and our immediate response was to shout, 'Discipline!'

There was a deeply rooted reasoning behind every word, every phrase and every expression and each was designed to generate a particular reaction – and you had to remember the correct response to every order. Trying to achieve this under pressure was a tough feat and, in the early stages, it was more or less impossible to appease the expectations of the DIs. We always fucked up. If it wasn't me who fucked up, it was one of the other seventy in the platoon who did. As far as the DIs were concerned, when one of us fucked up, we all fucked up, and we paid dearly for every mistake. The idea behind it was that we needed to act like a team and in that team, if one messed up, the crime wasn't that he had done something wrong, it was that the rest of us had messed up by not ensuring that he knew what to do and how to do it. We heard this every day, from sun up to sun down, the words 'team', 'platoon' and 'buddy' describing our new priorities as we adapted to the fact that our lives were now in other people's hands.

When the DIs wanted to single out a particular recruit for punishment, they sent him to the dreaded quarterdeck, which was a clear area by the main hatch. The recruit was then ordered through a series of repetitive exercises at a blistering pace that was known as 'killing' or getting 'ITd'. The DIs kept the recruit at it for as long as they deemed fit and, at some point, everybody was sent there – the only difference being for how long and how often.

We had one guy who messed up so many times that the DIs gave him his own little personal quarterdeck. They stuck tape on the ground in the shape of a square where he had to go every time somebody else fucked up, even if he hadn't done anything wrong himself.

I spent a significant period of my time up there, particularly at the beginning, because I didn't have a clue what the DIs were saying. They had really strong, deep voices, which all sounded vaguely similar, as if there was some sort of DI accent. They didn't speak English but used a kind of bastardised version of it.

What was worse for me was the fact that they couldn't understand me. My accent confused them and made me stand out – and the one thing you did not want to do at boot camp was stand out. The DIs looked for any slight chink in someone's personality that they considered a weakness and then they would latch on to it and use it to beat them down. Everyone was singled out for their own particular brand of attention in this way and, for me, it was the fact I spoke with a foreign accent. I knew I was fucked very quickly.

One of my DIs was Sergeant Gannon, a tall, skinny good ol' country boy from southern Texas who spoke with a heavy Texan accent. He was assigned to our platoon after a week or so and was eager to make a good impression on the senior DIs. The first time he asked me a question, we were all standing in a line. I gave him the proper response but, as the words rolled off of my tongue in my Dublin accent, he made the strangest expression. He turned back to me and with the hard edge of his Campaign Cover hat bouncing off the bridge of my nose, he started screaming, 'Boy, what the fuck are you fucking saying, you fucking stupid, boy? Where the fuck are you from?'

I said, 'Sir, this recruit is from Ireland, Sir.'

'I don't give a fuck. What the fuck you doing here in my Marine Corps?'

It was kind of funny because, right at that moment, I was thinking the same thing. He and I would have a communication problem throughout my entire time at boot camp, but I think that, in the long run, it helped me out because he got tired of fucking with me when he realised it was pointless because he would never understand what I said to him.

Staff Sergeant Sanchez was another tough DI who referred to us all as his 'little nasty bitches', but at least he had a sense of humour. He told me that he reckoned I was really in the IRA and the Marine Corps was fucking crazy to be giving me this training for free so I could go back home to train terrorists. He said they should arrest my ass and put me on an aeroplane back to wherever the fuck I was from. Another time, he had me stand in front of all the hundreds of other recruits at morning chow and shout over to the Senior Mess Chief, 'Where's me Lucky Charms, Sir?' in a big, fake Oirish accent. I actually thought that was pretty funny, but nobody laughed in case they were next.

One of the toughest DIs was Staff Sergeant Mireles. He gave everyone a hard time, including me, but I ended up with a lot of respect for him. He had a habit of walking up behind you when you were doing drill and whacking you over the knuckles with a metal clipboard when you least expected it. You'd be standing at attention in formation with your thumbs in the correct position on the trouser seam of your cammies, then you'd start thinking about something else and your hands would start wandering. All of a sudden, you'd get a belt of that clipboard. It scared the bollox out of you, but you had to stay standing there at the position of attention and not flinch despite the stinging pain.

For someone who had always been a hard-headed individual and had a strong personality, my first few experiences with the DIs were pretty hard to take. Initially, I hated them. They could hit me, knowing full well I couldn't hit them back and there were many times in those first few days when I wanted to lose the head and start punching and kicking but, instead, I bit my tongue and, eventually, I learned how to play the game.

Now that I was there, I had to see it through. I wanted to become a Marine and I resolved that the DIs wouldn't break me. Over time, I would grow to respect them and the jobs they did. Their methods may have seemed harsh at the time, but they were teaching us how to get tough so we could fight and survive.

The DIs ruled our days from the moment we woke up to the moment we fell unconscious onto our racks at the end of the brutally tough days. A typical day in boot camp started the night before with firewatch. A list was drawn up and, throughout the night, four recruits were ordered to stand an hour of watch. You dared not sleep on watch, as you could expect a surprise visit by the DIs in the middle of the night. So, when reveille was called the following morning at 05:00, you had already been up for at least an hour during the night. At reveille, the lights would be switched on and the DIs would burst into the squad bay screaming at the top of their lungs. We would all jump up out of our racks and stand in line and to attention.

The first order of the day was to get a count of the number of recruits in the platoon to make sure that nobody had run away or committed suicide during the night. Standing by our racks, we would sound off our number. When the DIs were satisfied that we were all there, it was time to get dressed. This was done by numbers and every movement was directed by the DIs. They would tell you when to put a sock on your left foot, on your right foot, your left leg in your pants and so on until you were fully clothed. They gave you a second to get it done. You held the particular item of clothing out in front of you and the DI would bark, 'Put it on right now, three, two, one, and you are?' and we all would respond in unison, 'Done, Sir!' If anyone failed to get the piece of clothing on in time, he was told to get the sand out of his clit and was accused of trying to fuck with the DI. Then the rest of the platoon would have to take that item of clothing back off and we would all have to start again. If we kept fucking up, we would end up standing there naked all morning until we got it right. One time, we had to put our dirty skivvies into a metal rubbish bin and then had to take out a random pair and put them on. It was disgusting and degrading, but I couldn't help but laugh when one recruit put his hand up and told the DI that the pair of shorts he had picked out was wet. I paid dearly for laughing, but it was so worth it. I spent about thirty minutes on the quarterdeck in a puddle of sweat, wearing another man's underwear, and couldn't stop laughing until the pain of getting 'killed' overwhelmed me.

Once dressed, we had one minute to make up our racks. We slept in bunk beds and you worked with your rack mate on one rack and then the other, always using the buddy system. Once we were squared away, we were given another minute to make a head call. Once the minute started, we'd all run like cheetahs to the toilet, where we had to work as a team to get everyone in and out on time. This was a real challenge, as there were only six toilets and six urinals for seventy guys. It would be a difficult task for civilian minds, but we learned quickly how to bunch up and have three of us at each urinal and toilet pissing simultaneously. It actually worked, and nobody bitched about it. As we would learn, there were very few opportunities to piss during the day, so we appreciated our morning ritual. Most of the time we got it right, but there were always occasions when the guy behind couldn't hold his water any longer as he waited his turn and you'd end up walking around with his piss on your legs.

After the head call, we were told to run downstairs and get into platoon formation before we were marched to the chow hall. The sign on the stairs said 'no running', but nobody pointed that out to the DIs. Every movement was an opportunity for the DIs to improve our skills at drilling and the screaming never stopped. There was a standard ritual to everything at boot camp and we had to learn it all or fall by the wayside. Even when we were eating and drinking, there was a set procedure that had to be followed to the letter. We could only drink water and when we drank it, we had to hold the cup with both hands, close our eyes and tilt our heads back. When we ate, we could only use one hand. The other had to remain firmly in our laps while our feet stayed flat on the floor with heels together and the toes pointing out at a forty-five-degree angle. We had to devour a tray of food in as little as a single minute, as most of the time that's all we had. We would shovel unchewed food down our hungry throats, fearing that, at any moment, the DI would tell the platoon that we were done. On many occasions, we didn't get any food. We would be ordered to go eat chow, but when we got there, we would be signed in as a platoon and marched straight back out again. As far as the official records were concerned, Platoon 3051 ate at 05:30 but, on the whim of our DI, we wouldn't even have sat down.

The rest of the morning was spent attending educational classes or engaging in physical activities. We were taught what it was to be a Marine and were lectured about the Corps' heroes. We learned that General Chesty Puller was the best Marine who had ever lived and how Dan Daly killed two hundred men in China with his bayonet during the Boxer Rebellion and then went on to fight in the First World War. He is a revered figure in the Marine Corps and is best remembered for his famous cry during the Battle of Belleau Wood when, besieged, outnumbered, outgunned and pinned down, he led his men into attack, shouting, 'Come on, you sons of bitches. Do you want to live for ever?' We were told that it was a good thing to die saving your buddy's life and wrong to live if you failed.

But the hardest part about those first few days was the physical training. As an avid marathon runner – I'd completed the Dublin Marathon twice and the London Marathon once with a best time of three hours and seven minutes – I was physically in great shape before I went to boot camp, but nothing could have prepared me for the rigours when I got there. It was intense, and the DIs worked the recruits to the bone. We never actually ran more than three or four miles at a time and that was easy – it was the gruelling exercises they made us do that hurt the most. They pushed us harder and harder each time and expected us to grow stronger and better with each repetitive exercise, known variously as 'Chinese Sit-Ups' or 'Monkey Fuckers'.

'Speed' and 'intensity' were our new watchwords when approaching every task. We couldn't slack off or slow down. We had to complete every challenge using the traits dictated by that philosophy or you'd end up getting the platoon in trouble. If one guy couldn't complete a task, the rest of us paid for it and we did double. This was an ongoing regime and you just ended up fucking hating the bastard who couldn't do his push-ups. You'd think to yourself, What the fuck was he thinking when he signed up for the Marines?, as you sweated in the sand boxes which served the same function as the quarterdecks when you were outside. Sometimes, someone would fuck up so badly that we'd be forced to stand up in the squad bay holding a filled footlocker out in front of us. By far the worst thing about letting your platoon down was having your boys mad at you. I'm not saying that anyone was beaten with a sock filled with bars of soap like you see in the movies, but we policed ourselves and made sure that everybody was putting 100 per cent into every effort.

Some of the activities the DIs subjected us to were designed to fuck with our heads. At some stage during the day, we would conduct a 'field day', which was the term for cleaning our house. When we didn't work fast enough for the DI, we played the inside-outside game, which was a pretty interesting pastime. We would have to take everything from inside the squad bay – all our lockers and racks, uniforms and boots – and bring them outside and lay them on the ground exactly as they had been inside. Then we had to take all the sand bags from outside, bring them in and empty them all over the floor. As we were doing this, the DI would be screaming at us to move faster. When we were almost done scrambling to move everything around, the DI would disappear and another one would show up and go fucking crazy. He would demand to know what the fuck we were doing and, from experience, we knew that the correct response was, 'Sir, these recruits don't know what they are doing, Sir. These recruits are idiots, Sir.' He would tell us to put all the shit back inside and warn us to get all the sand off the floor and make sure it was shining by the time he got back. Then he would walk away while we rushed around trying to put everything back in its proper place. Sure enough, we would be almost done when the original DI would show up once again and scream, 'What the fuck is going on here? I told you to get that shit outside! What the hell? Have you lost your minds?' And we'd have to respond, 'Sir, these recruits are idiots, Sir,' and we'd begin the process all over again.

Another game the DIs enjoyed that sticks out in my memory was the Daytona 500. We would have to get a wet towel, put it on the ground in front of us, place both our hands on it and then use our feet to push our body weight around the room in a big circle. It really hurt, but it was a good way to build up leg-muscle strength. It was called the Daytona 500 because as we were pushing the towels around, we had to make car noises while trying our best not to laugh or bump into each other.

After lunch, which we called 'afternoon chow', there would sometimes be classes on the administrative and garrison aspects of being a Marine. We also learned the basics of the Marine Corps Martial Arts Programme, known as MCMAP, which taught you how to fight efficiently and kill an opponent when you were tired, hungry and about to give up.

If there were no classes after afternoon chow, we were out drilling on the parade deck. The parade deck has an almost religious significance to the Corps and the one at MCRD was steeped in Marine Corps history. Men who had graduated on that deck had served in all the major conflicts of the twentieth century. It was the same hallowed ground that Marines had marched on before being shipped out to such places as Iwo Jima in Japan and Hue in Vietnam. Every time we paraded on that deck, it was with a growing sense of honour. To raw recruits like us, it was a privilege to drill on the same parade ground where we would some day graduate and become US Marines.

Until that day, we marched around the depot for hours in the Californian sun, practising our close-order drill. When it was considered to be too hot outside, we drilled inside in our living quarters, a process known as the mini-grinder. The beds would be pushed to one side to make more room, and we would be ordered to march up and down.

At the end of a long day at boot camp, it was time for a shower. Taking off our clothes was done much the same way as we had put them on in the morning and the process of showering was conducted in the same way too. We were instructed about which part of our 'nasty little body' to scrub, for how long and in what order. Some nights, we'd have to skip the formal showering process and literally had to do a quick run-through instead. We'd all stand in a line naked and when we got to the rain room, we had to put our arms out like we were aeroplanes, trot around the circumference of the room and back out again. You came out wet in some places and dry in others, but it had to do.

With all that completed, we had a hygiene inspection. I was the designated 'witch doctor', as I had my EMT licence, and I would have to accompany the DI as he examined each recruit. It's not a job I wanted, but I had no choice. The DIs paid close attention to the physical well-being of the recruits, as some of them were sometimes too afraid to report an illness or injury.

The process was another well-defined dramatic procedure during which the DI used a flashlight, which he referred to as a 'moonbeam', to look into your ears and under your fingernails. It was quite amusing early on in boot camp to learn how some guys had no standards of hygiene. The DIs not only had to teach us how to be Marines, but they also had to show many of the group how to look after themselves. A lot of the kids walking around had absolutely no idea of the basics of housekeeping, as their parents had done everything for them. There were guys who couldn't use an iron, who had never made a bed and who had never mopped a floor. But the DIs quickly changed all that and, by the time we graduated, we had all become efficient little homemakers.

We settled into military life as best we could. Drilling was continuous and every exhausting day felt like it was never going to end. There was no time off and no easy or short days – they were all long. There was no opportunity to be alone at boot camp and it was impossible to find a place to have some time to yourself. The only downtime was on a Sunday morning when each recruit went to some form of religious service, whether he believed in a god or not. I didn't meet anyone at boot camp who was brave enough to tell the DIs that he didn't want to go to church. Refusing would have meant being left behind in the squad bay, alone with the DIs and the subject of their undivided attention. You went to church and you loved it. For forty-five minutes, you felt like a human being again and you could listen to the service in relative peace and quiet without fear of interruption. When mass was over, we were marched back to the squad bay and permitted to write letters home or take care of our uniforms while we waited for the other denominations to finish their services.

After a few weeks, we were issued with our new weapons. When I took hold of my M-16A2 rifle for the first time, it felt like I had been born with it in my hands. I spent hours wielding it, cleaning it, disassembling it, reassembling it, marching with it, praying with it and sleeping with it. Our rifles became an extra limb and, whenever somebody fucked up, I stood in a line along with the rest of the platoon with my arms straight out and my rifle hanging off my little finger as punishment.

I would learn how to strip down that rifle to its basic components in seconds and then reassemble it just as quickly. We were taught to believe that there was nothing more ferocious than a Marine with a rifle and we learned the Rifleman's Creed to ensure that we did not forget it.

During the second half of boot camp, we were bussed up to Camp Pendleton in north San Diego County, where we spent weeks out in the field humping with our packs, patrolling, sleeping under the stars and learning how to shoot. We were marched out to the firing range and took up positions five hundred yards from the targets. At that distance, I could barely even make it out, but the shooting coaches showed us how to adjust the weapon's sighting controls so that it was a custom fit for your shot. My coach liked to joke that I was in the IRA, which I was getting used to at that stage, and every time I pulled the trigger, he would make me sound off the names of members of the British royal family, saying it would improve my aim. His little plan must have worked, because, eventually, I qualified as a rifle expert.

As the weeks passed, you could tell we were coming together as a team. We had started off as a disorganised rabble, but we were starting to fit the mould. Although we didn't exactly have time to hang out, I gradually got to know my fellow recruits. Each of us looked out for one another and some of us even became friends.

There was a cross-section of all walks of life from various states west of the Mississippi – all those who are recruited east of the river go to Parris Island in South Carolina. There were cowboys from Oklahoma and Wyoming and Latinos from California, all there for many different reasons. Some guys wanted to fight, others wanted the educational benefits and there were those who joined up simply because they didn't have any direction in their lives. We even had one kid who joined to be in the Marine Corps Band.

Most of them had never been outside the US before and some had never even left their home state. As a foreigner, I was the subject of a lot of curiosity. I didn't want to be treated differently just because I was from overseas, but it didn't matter because I stuck out like a priest in a whorehouse. They asked me a million questions about Ireland and I did my best to put them straight on many misconceptions. A common one, of course, was that I had come over on a boat. They also had romantic notions about Ireland and some of them were surprised and a little disappointed to learn that I didn't live in a little white cottage beside a lake and a mountain. One guy was convinced that I rode a horse to work and that we were still living under English rule. They also insisted that I didn't speak the same language because they spoke American.

One of my new buddies, Cannon, was hilarious. He was a white guy from a small town in Mississippi and had the thickest southern drawl you could imagine. He was my rack mate and he slept on the bunk above mine. We were paired together for most things and we always promised that we'd go for a beer together when we finished boot camp, but we never did and I didn't see him again after graduation. The non-white DIs loved taking him to pieces. They would call him out in the chow hall and have him point out the Mississippi flag from all the other state flags that were hanging on the wall. The Mississippi state flag still incorporates the Confederate flag and, to the black DIs, that represented slavery. For the three months of boot camp, they made that guy's life a living hell.

Jones was a six-foot-six goliath from Wisconsin. He was easily the biggest person I have ever known. Although there wasn't much time for chit-chat in recruit training, he became one of my good friends. We worked well together – he watched my back, and I his.

One of my other buddies was a Hispanic guy from Riverside in California called Juan. Both of us could run like Jessie Owens and shoot like Jessie James, but we shared one common problem in that neither of us could swim very well. For some reason, it had never occurred to either of us that the Marines would make us get in the water, but all recruits have to pass a minimum requirement level before they can graduate.

We were brought to a massive swim tank and told to don a flak jacket and helmet and were given a rubber rifle to hold. Then they pushed us into the water one by one. I kicked my legs for all I was worth and, somehow, managed to stay afloat with all the gear on. Then another recruit grabbed on to me and started using me as a floating aid when he decided he couldn't swim any more. The prick dragged me down and the swim instructors had to jump in and pry him off me as we struggled under the water. I lay coughing and spluttering on the cold tiles and had to start the whole process again.

But the one guy who stuck out more than anybody else in my platoon in boot camp by far was the Don't-ask-don't-tell recruit. From the moment he opened his mouth, it was fairly obvious that he was gay. Now, he was a nice guy and he wasn't at boot camp to prove a point or anything like that, he just wanted to be a Marine like his dad, but the DIs really had it in for him. They gave him the name Don't-ask-don't-tell which referred to official Marine policy that banned people from asking if someone was gay or declaring that they were gay themselves.

As we all started to come together as a team, each recruit displayed a specific skill that he may not even have been aware he had. A guy might be particularly good at polishing boots, ironing cammies or cleaning weapons and he would offer to help the others with these particular tasks. There was only one guy in the platoon who could tie a double Windsor knot and he ended up having to do all our ties on graduation day, but Don't-ask-don't-tell declared one day that if anybody needed any help sewing on buttons, then he was their man.

It caused a couple of chuckles at the time – though we never said any-thing to him – but the DIs punished him mercilessly and frequently. I can't remember exactly why, but on one particular occasion, his punishment was that he wasn't permitted to sleep for three days. At night on firewatch, the recruits had to keep him awake. On my watch one night, we found him passed out, sleeping in the corner. I dragged him into the shower with one of the other recruits and we turned on the showers. We pinned him to the ground and let the freezing cold water pour all over him. He was crying and pleading with me to let him go, but I had to tell him it was my orders to keep him awake. I felt a bit bad about it and I think that was when I realised that being a Marine was changing me.

There was no quitting at boot camp. You couldn't just give up when you had enough and say, 'I quit, Sir, I'm going home,' but two guys managed to get out of our platoon. One was a cop who, at twenty-nine, was much older than everyone else. He said he couldn't put up with the bullshit any longer and wrote a letter home to his mommy who knew somebody in the government and they let him out. The other was a quiet kid, the kind of person you'd expect to see one day on the news after he'd cut bodies into bits and kept them in the fridge. He wanted out so badly that, one night, he sliced open his own back with a razor blade. The following morning, the DI called me over and showed me his wounds. I was horrified. He had completely carved himself up.

He told the DIs that we had done it to punish him for messing up and he was taken away. We spent the next twenty-four hours getting our butts killed for hours on end. It was truly a horrible day and, although we hadn't touched him, it was possible that some of the other recruits in the platoon may have. We were all questioned individually, one after the other, and a big deal was made of it. We had high-ranking officers come by to conduct the interrogations and each of us had to make a written statement.

The following morning, our senior DI announced that the 'piece of shit', as he called him, had confessed to carving himself up. It was a tough blow that one of our own should betray the rest of us like that. The DI added that the recruit had done it to get out of boot camp but that the Marines had other plans for him. First, he was going to be charged with making false accusations against us and, second, he would be psychologically evaluated and held indefinitely due to his mental condition. The matter ended there – we got on with our training and forgot all about him.

As we neared the end of our three months in boot camp, the DIs started to lay off a bit, although we were never allowed to fully relax. I realised that I was going to be there for St Patrick's Day and I hoped it would pass without anyone noticing. On the morning, though, two of the DIs approached me from behind and one whispered in my ear, 'Hey, Dale, guess what day it is today.'

I tried to pretend like I didn't know what he was talking about and replied, 'Sir, this recruit believes that it is Sunday, Sir.'

He thought that was funny and said, 'Nice try, Dale.'

Then the other one leaned in. 'Dale, it's St Patrick's Day, and the luck of the Irish just ran out for you. Stand by, Dale, we are going to help you celebrate your Irish holiday.'

Then they walked away, leaving me sweating. I didn't know what they had in store, although I was pretty sure it didn't involve a few beers and a little parade. I spent the rest of that day worrying about it so much that I couldn't think of anything else. Later, the same two DIs took me downstairs and had me march around with a mop at right shoulder arms. I did as I was ordered and marched around in a square until an officer stopped and asked me what I was doing. I told him, 'Sir, this recruit is having his own St Patrick's Day parade, Sir.' He thought that was pretty damn funny. When the DIs were done with me, one of them told me to tell my family that the Marine Corps were really nice folks who had given me my own little parade and dressed me in green clothes for the day. Whenever I think about it, I smile because I know that I will always remember it like no other St Patrick's.

Towards the end of boot camp, we faced one of the last obstacles to becoming fully fledged Marines. We were brought back up to Camp Pendleton to take part in the infamous Crucible – a fifty-four-hour endurance challenge that defines the final transformation from civilian to Marine. In the Crucible, you got two-and-a-half ready-to-eat meals (MREs) that you needed to ration. These meals were a challenge in themselves and were the military equivalent of food on the move, although calling it food was a slight exaggeration. They contained enough material for a single meal. It was highly nutritious and packed full of calories, but there were so many preservatives that there were no expiration dates on the packs and it showed in the taste.

In the Crucible, we were put through a series of tough physical activities that included road marches, night infiltration moves and obstacle courses. We humped about forty miles in those fifty-four hours and the final stretch was a forced march up a steep hill. It was a killing exercise but we all had to complete it. Some of the recruits who were struggling up the hill had to be dragged along the last few metres by the rest of us. Nobody failed, which was a major achievement. We had passed the test and were about to become US Marines.

Not long after that, boot camp came to an end. I was relieved to have survived, and I think the DIs were impressed that I was still there – standing to attention in my Marine-issued skivvies, with my platoon-recruit number painted on the crotch – alongside all the others.

The day before we graduated, there was a ceremony during which we were awarded the title of United States Marine. I was so proud of myself for enduring three of the toughest months of my life. The senior DI, Staff Sergeant Ortega, awarded me the EGA, the famed Eagle, Globe and Anchor symbol of the US Marine Corps, putting it into my left hand while shaking my right. Grinning, he said, 'Congratulations, Marine.' I had made it.

The following day, the entire company of two hundred new Marines stood to attention on the parade ground in the green-jacketed uniforms that we call our Alphas. We marched to the sound of the Marine Corps Band past the reviewing stands, where our families and loved ones stood cheering. My parents and sister, along with Tony, her husband, and their kids, were all there for the ceremony and, as soon as it was over, I ran over to hug them.

My nephew, Conor, who was only three at the time, wanted to be a Marine like his Uncle Graham, and he was standing there too, wearing his little camouflage uniform. When a platoon of recruits marched past, Conor ran over to the DI, saluted and shouted 'Sir, yes, Sir,' much to the DI's amusement. When the ceremony had finished, I quickly changed into a tracksuit in the back of my sister's SUV and smoked a John Player Blue cigarette that had been brought all the way from home.

The best thing about that day, apart from my first smoke in three months, was the eight or nine pints of Guinness I downed later that night in the Gas Lamp district in San Diego City with my buddy, Jones. We got drunk and sang long into the night. I remember telling Jones how my local police station back home in Dublin had once refused me permission to own an air rifle, and now here I was going forward to infantry training school to learn how to use high-powered mortars and heavy machine guns.

Chapter 6

On my time off before infantry school, I stopped off in Las Vegas with my parents, where we spent a few days staying at a hotel on the strip. I'm not much of a gambler, and when I won nothing after I threw a quarter into a slot machine, I walked away and went to join my parents for a drink.

After saying goodbye to my folks, I was on my way back to Camp Pendleton, where I would learn how to be a mortar man. Infantry school was very different to boot camp. For a start, we were now Marines and with the honour came a few privileges. We were allowed to speak in the first person and so could refer to ourselves as 'I' instead of 'this recruit'. We could buy beer at the PX – the Post Exchange – which was basically a store on base that sold goods without the local sales tax added on. We could even go out most weekends. Me and my new mates got into plenty of trouble along the way, but we always made it back on time to tell the tales of another wild weekend in southern California.

At first, I wasn't too impressed with being assigned to mortars. A mortar is like a modern-day cannon fired at a high angle into the air. I couldn't understand what we were doing wasting our time on these outdated tubes when we, apparently, had endless quantities of laser-operated, billion-dollar weapons systems. I didn't want to be stuck behind the lines firing at invisible targets, I wanted to be a rifleman so that combat would be more up close and personal when it came down to it. But the mortar training grew on me after a while, as it was pretty laid back compared to most other jobs in the infantry. There was a lot of theory involving complicated co-ordinates, deflections and elevations, all of which meant that we got to sit around on our backsides in front of a blackboard most of the time instead of being out training, and that was all right by me.

We would go out to the firing line from day to day, practising gun drills and learning how to fire most of the other weapons used in the infantry. It was pretty cool. We got to throw a few grenades around and that sort of thing, although it wasn't all fun. It wouldn't be the Marines without going on humps and, man, we humped a lot – sometimes up to twenty miles, with all our gear, weapons and packs on our backs.

I spent the next two months learning how to be an infantryman and partying by the beach with my mates whenever we got the chance. I was enjoying myself – more than I had in boot camp at any rate. Although, one weekend, my good friend White, who was from Chicago, and I fell asleep on the sand in Huntington Beach after drinking some beer. We woke up hours later, severely sunburned, and dragged ourselves back to base feeling sorry for ourselves. After the embarrassment of having to rub after-sun lotion onto each other's backs, we had to go on another hump and carry 60 mm mortar systems up a goat trail for a training shoot. As we put on our flak jackets and Kevlars, we held back the tears from the pain and hid our injuries because, in the Marines, sunburn is technically a self-inflicted wound. If we had confessed, we would have been taken to medical and, after that, we would have to start infantry school all over again. Both of us were reservists and were eager to get the hell home. We gritted our teeth and somehow got through the exercise under the hot summer sun.

With infantry training complete, it was time to go home to Austin and pick up where I left off. We had a last graduation ceremony and said our final farewells. Those of us who were reservists were issued tickets for a flight home and we happily boarded the coaches that would take us to the airport. We waved at some of the other guys who were going on active duty. They had to stay behind on base, as their assignment was with a battalion just down the road, whereas two hours later, I was drinking a cool Heineken in LAX airport, waiting to go home.

I returned to Texas in mid-June 2002 and was assigned to a reserve unit based at Camp Mabry, near Austin. Although our forces were still taking down the Taliban in Afghanistan, there was no sign of our unit going over, so, for the time being, we were like part-time soldiers. We were ordered to show up for drill training and then we hung around waiting for orders and getting on with life.

In the meantime, I was living in an apartment and badly in need of a decent job. The reserve pay wasn't enough to cover even half my monthly car repayments. Unfortunately for me, while I had been away, the arse had pretty much fallen out of the dot-com industry in the wake of the 9/11 attacks, and I suddenly found myself out of work.

I tried in vain to get my IBM contract back, but they weren't interested. I was simply told that it wasn't going to happen. I started looking for another computer position, but I couldn't even get so much as an interview. I quickly found out that I was not the only computer freak applying for any job in town. I started talking to clerks at checkout counters and waiters in restaurants who had all previously been computer programmers and IT managers. I knew I was going to have to switch gears and be willing to get any kind of job while I figured out how I was going to support myself. It depressed me that I had just gone off and volunteered to play my part in defending America and now here I was, out of work and pretty much broke.

I met a guy in a pub who told me there was a federal law in the States that said you were entitled to get your job back when you returned from military service. I enquired about it one day but the person from the government I talked to on the phone told me I was ineligible as I had only been a contract employee while I had been with IBM.

I still had to report to my Marine Reserve Station and show up for drills every month. Drills consisted of a weekend away in the field engaged in various aspects of military training. But for me, it really meant being the new guy – and I hated being the new guy.

At boot camp, everyone had been in the same boat but in the reserves, there was a hierarchy that I didn't care for too much. Most of the guys had been there for a while and knew each other quite well. As a new Private First Class, I was pretty much back on the lowest rung of the ladder. Despite all their best efforts at boot camp, I don't think the military machine had changed me all that much and I found it difficult to adapt to my new role. Maybe I was too old for all that psychological reconditioning, but, in any case, I still felt like the same old me with the same old hard-headed attitudes.

I did my job as best I could and kept myself to myself while I concentrated on getting back on my feet, which was proving much harder than anything the Marines had thrown at me. Nothing much was showing up on the employment front. I even asked the Marines if I could go on active duty so I could earn more pay, but they basically told me to fuck off and sort out my own shit. It was humiliating, especially when I found myself having to occasionally steal field rations from the base on drill weekends just to feed myself. The fact that they wouldn't even look out for one of their own soured my relationship with the Corps at the time.

Eventually, I got taken on as a short-term contractor moving computer equipment around – it covered the bills and not much more, but at least it was a regular income.

But before I knew it, I hit a low point. I pretty much resigned myself to getting on with the daily grind of waking up and working in a job that was paying about one-quarter of what I had been used to. I was starting to accept that perhaps the good life wasn't all that it was cracked up to be. I pressed on and got up every morning and went to my job – clocked in and clocked out – and another day was gone. I had been through some ups and downs in the past, but I was really brought down to earth at this point. A month after I got home from graduating from the Marines, I was living in a shabby apartment that I had to share and, instead of eating steak and fries, I survived by becoming an expert ramen noodle chef.

I got by, but I really wanted a purpose in life other than paying bills and being broke all the time. I could have done that back home in Ireland.

Chapter 7

By the summer of 2002, US troops were still in Afghanistan. By this stage, the country was pretty much under our control and the Taliban was on the run. But the new buzzword on the horizon was Iraq. I have to admit that I knew very little about Iraq. What I did know was that they had fought a long war with Iran and had even been allies, to some extent, of America until they invaded Kuwait in 1990.

Now the news was full of intelligence reports about how Saddam Hussein was more or less in bed with Al-Qaeda. There was all sorts of talk in the press about mobile chemical-weapon plants being found and allegations of weapons of mass destruction. I bought into all those claims, hook, line and sinker. After all, this was the same guy who had invaded Kuwait and used chemical weapons on his own people. There was a real fear that Saddam was intent on attacking the United States. I was so angry at the time that I would have gladly shot him myself. I had nothing else going on in my life. If someone had ordered me to do it, I was more than willing, and on a Private First Class' pay cheque too.

In August 2002, I started working part-time for a private ambulance company, transporting patients around the city, which helped to rebuild my self-esteem. It was a really good feeling going to work each morning knowing that I could brighten someone's day just by talking to them for a few minutes and offering them comfort.

I also met a girl who swept me off my feet, and I fell in love again. Despite my best intentions, I would eventually screw up the relationship pretty good but, for the time being, things were looking up. Then one day, totally out of the blue, IBM called and said they wanted to offer me another contract. Big Blue wanted to be my friend again and soon I was sitting back at the very same desk with the exact same job as I'd had before I joined the military, but working for significantly less money.

Things continued to improve over the next few months. I stayed working part-time as a volunteer with the fire department and, eventually, found myself back in a comfortable place in life, but with the added advantage of having learned a lot through my experiences. I had got my job back, I could eat something that wasn't on the dollar menu at McDonald's and I didn't have to worry about having enough money to see a doctor.

The US invaded Iraq in March 2003 and the powers that be issued orders for reserve units like mine to be mobilised. We were now on high alert and, at drill, we were warned to be ready for immediate deployment. I had a boyish sense of excitement as I watched the daily live footage from the first days of the invasion. To me, it looked like a television show with embedded reporters sitting in the back seat of Humvees racing across the empty desert filming the Americans as they blasted the small pockets of resistance away like in a Nintendo game. We seemed to push aside the Iraqi army without much difficulty, and I worried it would be all over before I even got there.

I did have one unsettling feeling in the pit of my stomach, though. Although we had swept through the country, I figured there must be an element of the people who would never accept an occupation by the imperial Yankees. Even then, I felt that if we were deployed, we could find ourselves in a Northern Ireland-type situation. If I learned one thing from Irish history, or even the Vietnam War, it was that you couldn't defeat an entire people who were determined to resist an occupation by a foreign power. It doesn't matter how big your army is or how much great gear you have, simple people with simple tools can ruin your day completely.

Soon after the end of major military operations was declared, an insurgency broke out that caught the allied forces off guard. They were a conventional military force prepared for a conventional war. Stories started filling the airwaves every day with news of improvised explosive devices (IEDs) and suicide bombers. How would we fight such a threat? The nagging doubts subsided as the months passed and we waited for orders which never came. Then, one day in April 2004, I opened an email. It was about nine in the morning and I was sitting at my desk, a little tired from working late the night before. I was going through my inbox to see if there was anything important there. I glanced down through the list of unopened mails, ignoring all the usual spam, and opened the first one that caught my eye. It was entitled 'Deployment'. I figured that it might have something to do with a new software code but when I opened it, I noticed that it was from my staff sergeant in the Marine Reserve Unit I was attached to. As my eyes scanned quickly down the page, it became apparent that I was being sent to Iraq.

I had just been told that I was going to war – by email. How absurd, I thought, as I turned my eyes away and tried to let it sink in.

Try as I might, I couldn't concentrate on anything for the next few hours. I left work early and took off in the direction of home but ended up going straight down to Razzoo's. For some reason, that bar seemed to have a magnetic power that made my car drive in that direction when I had things on my mind. It wasn't until I was sitting down on my stool that I realised there would be no pints for another year. That was a right shock to the system, so I started pounding them down as quickly as I could, as if each one was my last.

Chapter 8

I had two months to get everything together, then I would be going on active service duty with the Marines for twelve months. All I knew was that there would be more training to prepare us for deployment, but I had no other details. I had no idea about when I would be going or what I would be doing when I got there.

I was on my way to Iraq, and I had very little time to take care of things before I went. Above all else, I needed to fly home to say goodbye to my family – I couldn't imagine not seeing them before I left. Once again, I found myself relying on my sister to gently let my folks know that I was being sent off to war and, once more, it worked out as planned. My poor mother took it hard, and I felt so bad for her. For her sake, I kept up the lie that I would be sitting in one of those rear bases working on a computer system in a bunker. But, with a mother's instinct, she knew better. I'm sure that as soon as I was off the phone, she was down in the local church lighting enough candles to the Sacred Heart to burn another huge hole in the ozone layer. A week before I was to report for active duty and be shipped out for more training, I boarded a plane back to Dublin.

It felt strange sitting at the bar in my old local, the Donaghmede Inn, telling my oldest mate from school that I was going to Iraq to fight with the Marines. The bloke looked at me like I had just told him the Pope was Protestant. Most people at home were shocked when I told them, and nobody wanted me to go. There was very little support for the war in Ireland and pretty much everybody tried to convince me that I should tell the Marines to go fuck themselves and stay in Dublin. I suppose that if I had been in their shoes I'd have said the same thing, but the thought never entered my head. I was a Marine. I couldn't let my friends down. I had made one of those deals – you watch my back and I'll watch yours – and I couldn't back out now.

I spent the week at home drinking pints and endless cups of tea around my mother's kitchen table, trying unsuccessfully to convince everybody that I wasn't insane. My brothers thought I was mad, but they knew that I was going to go no matter what, and so we just enjoyed the time we had left, and drank our fair share of beer. It was an enjoyable few days, though I couldn't relax as my mind was working overtime, trying to focus on the task to come. Then I woke up one morning and realised it was time to get back on the plane.

On the way to the airport, my mother was very quiet. I tried to make idle chat, but she didn't say much. I understood why. Then, all of a sudden, I was standing at the security screening point in the departure lounge in Dublin airport. I hugged and kissed my mother, not knowing if I would ever see her again. I looked the old man in the eye and got his nervous nod of approval. I said my goodbyes and walked away, telling myself not to look back.

Chapter 9

I arrived back in Texas on 13 May 2004 and the very next day, we bussed out to Fort Polk, Louisiana, where we spent two weeks on urban-assault training in the humidity of the Deep South. We learned the skills that we needed to give us the best chance of surviving while out on patrol in dangerous built-up environments. Cautiously, we moved down mock-up streets and were taught how to enter buildings in small teams and clear them of bad guys. We practised kicking open doors and windows, moving up staircases, clearing rooms and taking people down while shouting commands to each other the whole time. It was a very tough two weeks. We spent sixteen-to-eighteen-hour days under the hot and humid Louisiana sun continuously training, teaching, learning and sweating. I gave medical classes to my squad, as I was one of only two in the platoon with any hands-on trauma experience.

With less than a week gone, I was already as tired as shit. The days were so long that we could only get through them by counting down the hours to our next meal. And this was only the beginning. I had no idea of how long the journey ahead was going to be.

Pretty much all we talked about was Iraq. We really had no idea what was going on in the Middle East. We were told all kinds of tall tales about the situation over there but, even at that late stage, we didn't really know what we would be doing or when we were going to be deployed. We kept an open mind and decided to only believe what we saw with our own eyes.

We got through the two weeks at Fort Polk and returned to Austin, where we waited for three days for our transfer to California to continue pre-deployment training. We were now officially on active-service duty and had received our orders to deploy to Iraq for seven months in support of Operation Iraqi Freedom. I sat in the pub before we shipped out to California, slowly drinking a Bud, staring at the orders in my hand and wondering how on earth I had managed to get myself into this. I had always thought that I was ready to fight but, now that it was definitely going to happen, the reality freaked me out a bit. It was surreal. This wasn't some movie on television that I could switch off. The realisation that I was going triggered three days of non-stop partying. I'd tell you more about those few days if I could remember anything about them.

Arriving at the airport for our flight to California, we bypassed the whole security check-in procedure and got straight onto the bird – my first time sitting on an aeroplane with an assault rifle in my hand. We were on our way to Twentynine Palms in southern San Bernardino County, home to the Marine Air Ground Task Force Training Command, the largest Marine base in the world. It was located in the middle of a huge desert that stretched as far as the eye could see and it was hotter than hell – in other words, the perfect environment in which to train before we got to the Middle East. We spent two more months in training, with most of the instruction revolving around mortars, and were sent to another installation in California where we got to play in Combat Town, a derelict military housing complex complete with Marines playing the parts of insurgents and civilians.

The question that dominated our thoughts, though, was what we would be doing when we got to Iraq. With our exact roles still up in the air, we speculated wildly about what our duties would be. Our training was done in such a way that it covered the basics but gave us little or no clue about what we were preparing for. We would be out firing mortars on the range one day, while the next we were practising regular rifleman tactics. The plan changed constantly. As the training progressed and we improved our urban combat skills and mounted infantry tactics, it became more obvious that we would never be used as a mortar team. I was issued with an M-240 Golf, a medium-sized machine gun that is capable of firing up to nine hundred and fifty 7.62 mm rounds a minute. It was an awesome weapon, and I quickly formed a beautiful new relationship with the weapon I nicknamed Bitch.

We took class after class on every aspect of combat, some of which was important, the rest I thought useless. We were also made to sit through ridiculous jungle-survival videos even though we were on our way to the desert. The only useful bit of information we picked up was that those ropes you see in the Tarzan films could be a good source of water. I also attended a two-day Arabic language class but by the end of it could only ask a few simple questions, and I knew I'd be fucked if anyone actually answered in Arabic. Apart from that, I knew little about Arabic culture. We were told very little about the insurgents we would be fighting other than that they were generally from outside Iraq and that we'd be able to tell them apart. We also learned how to search vehicles, people and houses in a manner sensitive to the Islamic religion in an effort to avoid offending anyone, such as not putting the Koran on the ground or talking to Iraqi women.

After two months at Twentynine Palms, we were given almost an entire week off before going to war. This was my last chance to let off a bit of steam, so I flew back to Texas and made the most of it. The pints of Guinness flowed in Razzoo's all that week, I can tell you, and I managed to get into a minor physical argument with another Marine. It wasn't a big deal, just one of those rows that young men get into all the time, but the Marines didn't see it that way when I got back. The other guy had told them all about it and in his version, of course, I was the bad guy. They treated me like I was a misbehaved schoolboy and I had to stand in the corner while I got a stern lecture from my captain. He said the fact that I was Irish was no excuse for getting drunk and he banned me from drinking alcohol for the last few days before we left for Iraq. He warned me that he would see about having me dealt with after we came back. I was confined to barracks while all the others were out getting pissed on their last night out, but it gave me a chance to make my last preparations as deployment day loomed.

The Marines had a programme that enabled them to contact my family and offer them support if anything happened to me, but I warned them that if I came home in a box, they had better not show up at my funeral or my ma would smack them around with her rolling pin. I did write up a list of special instructions, though, in case I got killed. I put a few bob aside for the lads at home to have a beer or two on me, and I left another little bit for the boys from my unit when they got back.

Apart from the fact that I had just signed what was effectively my last will and testament, the thought that something might actually happen to me didn't really bother me as much as I thought it would. I had accepted my fate. I spent the last few hours in the squad room calmly counting down the hours to deployment. I was ready to go.

Part 2

IRAQ

Chapter 10

On 25 August 2004, we boarded the plane in California for our long journey to the Middle East. We were due to land at Frankfurt airport for a brief layover on our way to Kuwait and, during the flight over the Atlantic, I told some of the lads that I was glad we weren't passing through Shannon. When one of them asked why, I told him it was because I'd be tempted to jump over a fence, get to Dublin and hide in my ma's house. They laughed and said they'd have gone with me. I bet my ma would have taken them in too, if we had.

Behind the laughter, we were anxious. Vick and Peter, two guys who I had become close buddies with, sat beside me on the plane. Vick, who was from a small country town outside Austin, was the typical all-American boy who played football and worked in construction. We'd spent a lot of time hanging out and drinking pints since we first met in the Corps, and I'd even converted him into a Guinness man. Although he was only twenty-four, Vick had a son going to school and was already missing him. The way he talked, he was more worried about his little boy than he was for himself. Peter was a twenty-five-year-old Californian surfer who called everyone 'dude'. He was like me – didn't have a woman in his life, spent more money on booze than food and thought he'd live for ever. When we were leaving Austin and everybody was hugging and kissing their wives and girlfriends, he and I were smoking cigarettes, laughing about the fact that at least there would be no young girl crying for her loss if we got blown up.

The first thing I noticed when we finally stepped off the plane in Kuwait City was the intense heat. It blasted me in the face as if I'd opened an oven door. It was so intense that it caught my breath and, for a moment, it felt as if there was no oxygen in the air, only dry, dead heat. And then there was that strange, exotic smell I can't really describe, but you always get it when you first land in a different part of the world. I looked around at the surreal landscape surrounding me. It was like a huge, endless beach that stretched to the horizon in every direction. I had never been to an Arabic country before. I stared at the locals and eyeballed them warily. To me, they all looked like terrorists.

The relatively fresh set of clean cammies we had been issued before we left the US were soaked in sweat in an instant when we started to unload our gear from the hold of the aircraft. Then we were marched over to a waiting bus and told to sit down and shut up. There was no air conditioning and we sat there on the tarmac, meliting, for what seemed like ages. The heat really was unbelievable. I had never felt anything like it before in my life. Not even when we were training in California or Louisiana had it been this bad. It was actually difficult to breathe and I felt a rising sense of mild panic with every shallow breath I took. I tried to reassure myself that I was hardly the first visitor to this alien place. If others had managed, then surely I wasn't going to pass out and suffocate. All this wasn't helped by the fact that I was fucking gagging for a smoke. It had been hours since my last cigarette and my head was wrecked, but the thought of lighting up in the heat made me gasp.

Finally, the engine started, and Staff Sergeant Huerra came over and handed me a single 5.56 mm magazine. He told me to load up my M-16 as I would be providing security with him. It would be our job to protect the others in case we got hit. He warned me to stay awake and keep my eyes open, which was funny considering I was already on high alert and edgy. Everyone else on the bus had their rifles too, but only the staff sergeant and myself had loaded weapons. All the other boxes of ammunition that had been issued to us had been stowed away in the bellies of the buses. I had absolutely no idea why. Even though we were still only in Kuwait, as far as I was concerned, we were in a fucking war zone. Four buses full of Marines with only two armed in each? What would happen if we were attacked on the open highway? It struck me as crazy. Officially, we were in a friendly country, but it didn't feel very friendly to me, even though we were being escorted by the Kuwaiti Police.

I sat bolt upright behind the driver, ready in case I had to jump off quickly and shoot someone. I cradled my rifle in my sweaty hands while nervously scanning every car and terrain feature that came into view. I hardly blinked during the one-and-a-half-hour journey to our new temporary home, a massive army base called Camp Victory.

It was already dark by the time we crossed through into relative safety behind the wire. There was a murmur of voices as everyone on the bus started waking up. One of the lads said out loud, 'Hey, there's a Hardee's,' pointing out a popular American burger joint, and I was about to join in with 'And there's a Subway too' when Captain Fantastic, our platoon commander, jumped up from his seat. 'You better lock that fucking shit up! We are in a fucking war zone and you better start acting like it!'

As he was shouting at us, we drove past a volleyball court where about twenty army soldiers were playing in the sand under flood-lights, sporting shorts and flip-flops. No weapons in sight, just all these big smiley faces looking like they were enjoying themselves. We stifled our laughter, enjoying the release of tension.

Captain Fantastic, as we called him behind his back, liked to get very vocal and it got to the point where it no longer fazed you. He was a cop and a SWAT officer, and he took things very seriously. Back in pre-deployment training, he had us perform magazine changes on our weapons for hours on end and he once threatened to bust me down to private for not addressing my sergeant properly. I was thankful for his training, though, and was happy to have him lead us to Iraq. The last thing we needed out here was a Mary Poppins-type mother figure.

We got off the bus and, before anything else, were marched into a huge tent and given a bullshit welcome-to-the-war-zone brief. There were a few hundred of us in there with the same stupid look on all our faces that basically said, 'I would like to go home now.' The officers stood before us and laid down the rules of engagement. It was important stuff about what we were and were not to do, but I hardly listened to a word. I was too tired. Send me to Iraq now or let me sleep, was all I was thinking. On top of it all, I still needed that nicotine fix.

Finally, we were allocated a tent, which was more like a huge circus marquee in the middle of this city of canvas. We were just settling in when, in true Marine Corps style, we were told to move as we had been assigned to the wrong tent. It's still something that never ceases to amaze me about the Corps – how they get simple things like this wrong every day and are still able to carry out high-tech tactical operations. But by that stage, I was beyond caring. Wearily, we trudged over to our new quarters, where I dumped my gear on my rack so that I could go out for that smoke. Just as I was about to light up in the smoking pit, Sergeant Huerra shouted from the tent, 'Dale, firewatch, you're up first.'

'Fucking hell,' I groaned, picking up my gear.

Outside, the desert was pitch black. Apart from the far-off rumble of vehicles, the night was strangely quiet. There were probably more than ten thousand Marines and soldiers asleep around me for miles in every direction, but I felt as alone as if I was walking along the cliffs in Howth back home. I slung my weapon over my shoulder and kicked the sand and stones in my path, trying to stay awake and thinking about what it would be like to be heading for a few pints in the Donaghmede Inn on a Friday night with my brothers.

There was a slight whiff of kerosene in the air. The tents where the Marines slept were soaked in the stuff. I think it's to keep mosquitoes away or to waterproof them, but it struck me that it also made them a fucking death trap. It wouldn't take much for some genius to burn the whole camp to the ground. I double-checked my rifle and made sure my bayonet was still firmly strapped to my holster belt.

I did my hour of firewatch before passing it on to the next guy on the list. Going back into the tent, I stumbled over everybody's gear in the dark, trying to find my rack, where I finally got some sleep.

We were out of our tents the following morning as soon as the sun came up. Even though there was an air-conditioning system, the heat under the canvas was unbearable and, as we couldn't sleep, we went looking for morning chow instead. We found the chow hall, and I have to say, after my initial negative impressions of the place, I was really impressed with the whole setup. The food was actually OK. I was thinking to myself that if we were going to be eating like this for the next seven months, then I was going to be pretty happy with that end of things. I should have realised that it was an army base, not a Marine one, and the army always has better facilities and food than the Marines but, for the moment, I was too busy stuffing my face with eggs and bacon to notice.

We had received our instructions to stand by for insertion into Iraq and, later that day, we were given the order to go. We stowed away our gear and checked and double-checked our weapons. This was it. Then the appointed hour arrived, and nothing happened. We were stood down and told to wait. An hour later, we were given another order to move out and then that too was pushed back. Eventually, despite the build-up of tension, we stopped listening to the announcements and just accepted the fact that we were going when we were going. We couldn't know what the future would hold for us, so, instead of worrying about it, we took full advantage of our downtime to get as much sleep and good food as we could.

We ended up waiting three days in that unholy heat. By 07:30 each morning, the sun was already baking the white sand. We couldn't go outside without shades because the reflection from the light was blinding. I spent the hours lolling about in the shade, daydreaming about cool, creamy pints of stout. I promised myself that if I lived through this, I would drink a million of them. I thought about my mother a lot and all the other people who cared about me. I called home once or twice and tried to get my mother to relax, but all I could really do was promise to write and call as often as possible.

At least we were now at the beginning of our seven-month deployment and I could get stuck in and get on with the job. The anticipation of pre-deployment was over. As much as I had looked forward to going, I think that now I was actually there, I felt a natural tendency that soldiers have to count down the days until they can taste real life again. Each day that passed from there on in was another one that would bring me closer to home. That's what I told myself – and everyone at home – to sugar coat the reality and put our minds at ease.

On 26 August, I sent an email home that downplayed my fears.

26 August 2004

Morning all, Graham here.

Lots and lots of sand, as far as the eye can see, and so on and so forth …

I am in Kuwait, near the border, waiting on a ride to Iraq. I thought it was only commercial airlines that messed up flight times, but it seems that the military fares no better. (And don't even try asking to be upgraded to first class!)

Anyway, I'll be in Iraq in the next few hours and if our base there is anything like the one I am on right now, it's gonna be great!

The army has it so nice, I cannot begin to describe the luxuries that these guys have. If the army was one country and the Marines another, they would be America and we would be Cameroon or the Ivory Coast!

Having fun so far. Now I have a machine gun, a rifle, a handgun, two bayonets, three personal knives and I shaved all the rest of me hair off. Talk about a lost child!

I suppose the game really begins today when we get to Iraq. Should I be afraid? Some of these fellas we'll be up against probably can't even read or write, so I don't think they'll be much better at shooting! I'm only joking, but the Marines have trained us well and I am as ready as I possibly can be. Without a constant stream of beer in my life to calm me down, watch just how angry I can become …

Anyway, it seems like an easy deal compared to the poor feckers in wars of days gone by. At least I don't have to land on a well-fortified French beach under the onslaught of German machine guns.

Not undermining this operation all the same – I mean, some of us will get hurt – but I have yet to hear of another war where the soldiers were able to come back to base in the evening and eat a bloody ice cream.

So that's it, just like a postcard: having a ball, weather is great, wish I was not here, and see you next year.

Luv

Graham

Chapter 11

It was hard to believe that, after all the messing around, we were finally on our way. We loaded all our shit back onto the buses and were driven towards an airfield, the name of which was written in Arabic and meant nothing to me.

When we got there, we unloaded everything and marched over to one of the empty terminal buildings, where we were told to wait. It was more like a big aircraft hangar, but at least it had air conditioning, so we were pretty happy with ourselves. Hundreds of heavily armed Marines slouched around the walls with their gear at their feet. Other military personnel and civilian contractors were coming and going through the base and my platoon got talking to some air-force blokes who were also on their way in. We gathered together and talked about the mission. We were all so excited that but for the fact that we were wearing uniforms and toting rifles, flak jackets and Kevlar helmets, we could have been on a cheap package holiday to Spain.

We finally boarded our C-130 transport plane, which is as far away from your typical passenger aircraft as you can get, a few hours later.

A C-130 is basically a shipping container with wings and a row of propellers to drive it along. Inside, there were wires and cables all over the place; sitting in the back of it reminded me of the inside of a television set. There were no windows and the seats along the sides were just long benches that looked like they'd been stolen from the dressing rooms of a local football team. We crammed ourselves onto the seats as the engine pitch rose to a roar. Suddenly, there was a burst of momentum and we were all pushed together. The C-130 pitched nose up into the air at a sharp angle as a precaution against hostile fire. I looked around in the gloom but could barely make out the faces of my platoon around me. It was so fucking loud that I couldn't hear anyone talk, which was no bad thing as I was done listening to stories about American football. Despite the scream of the propellers, I was asleep in a flash and when I woke up, the wheels were screeching on the tarmac of Al Asad air base.

We scrambled off into the dust cloud thrown up by the propellers and, once again, the severe heat and the smell in the air hit me. I couldn't help but wonder how the fuck we were expected to do anything other than die in this climate. Apart from the essential packet of smokes, we were weighed down by flak jackets with armoured plates and were carrying rifles, bayonets and seven magazines of ammunition. We were led to another building at the edge of the airfield where the officers started playing their counting game, going over the Marines and the equipment again and again, making sure everyone was there.

After we had been counted several times, we were given a mini welcome-to-Iraq speech, and then it was on to yet another bus to our temporary living area. Once we got there, we offloaded all our shit and stood around under the sweltering sun feeling very new and very green. We managed to get some food into us quickly, which helped hit the spot, before we were moved to yet another tent. We were getting smart, though, and this time nobody opened a single bag until we knew we were staying put. Finally, we were told to rest and we spent the rest of our first day in Iraq crashed out on our racks catching up on some sleep.

The next day, we got up early and strolled around to check out our new surroundings. We were on Al Asad air base, in the Al Anbar province of western Iraq. This was the Sunni Triangle, an area inhabited mostly by Sunni Muslim Arabs who had been strong supporters of Saddam Hussein. In fact, he had been captured in a raid on the village of ad-Dawr about fifteen kilometres south of Tikrit in December 2003. Since the invasion, it had become a hotbed for the armed insurgency against coalition rule.

Al Asad was located almost in the middle of the triangle, nearly two hundred kilometres west of Baghdad and twelve kilometres southwest of the River Euphrates – apparently, Al Asad means 'the lion' in Arabic. I had been able to research it before we got there. It had been an Iraqi air-force base before the Australian SAS captured it during the invasion, and there were still wrecked Iraqi Mig and Mirage jets sitting around where they had either been damaged during bombing raids or had been abandoned behind built-up defensive positions, known as berms. This would be our home for the next few months, and it didn't take long for us to figure out that our main enemy here was going to be boredom.

The infantry units were housed and fed in a remote corner called 'the Ranch', far away from anything of any interest. The few amenities there were included a PX – the on-base store – and a recreation facility that showed movies and had a poxie gym that was full of boneheads who just wanted to get buffed up.

The food at the Ranch left a lot to be desired compared to the almost four-star conditions over at Mainside, the main camp where the Pogues lived – they were the Marines who worked in the rear and provided the typical support functions on a base. They had the crisp uniforms and were well versed on military mannerisms and customs and were universally derided by the combat units, who were convinced that all they ever did was eat and work out.

Accommodation at the Ranch was basic but sufficient. Some of the original structures built by the Iraqis were still in place, but they were used mainly by administration and command elements. The rest of the housing consisted of small trailer-type containers that were basically just big tin cans that the US had shipped in.

During transition periods, overflow tents were used and these were where we would be staying for the time being. The guys we were replacing lived in two-man rooms in the tin cans. They looked quite comfortable compared to our tents, which housed sixty bodies and one hundred and twenty smelly feet.

For the first few days, we had virtually nothing to do except go out on the odd working party to move equipment or anything else that needed to be done, but it amounted to fuck-all to be honest. We slept, we ate and we sweated, and this quickly became our routine as we settled into our new home in the desert.

We did have phone and internet access, which was a blessing, but because of the changeover in command, there were now almost five times the normal number of Marines on deck. Sometimes you had to wait eight hours for your turn to use the phone. As there was nothing else to do, I would sign up on the list, go back to bed to get a few hours' sleep, then check back on the queue or get something to eat until my slot came up.

30 August 2004

Good morning to one and all!

Hey, this country Iraq is great … they have the most square footage of sandy beaches I have ever seen!

If you like creepy crawlies then this is the place for you. Sunshine? [laugh] Iraq has more sunshine than California and compare those real estate rates … for the price of a four-bedroom house in Oceanside, you can buy a whole county or region or whatever the fuck it's called out here. Then you could elect yourself king and lay down the kind of stupid laws they have here. I dunno whose idea it was to sit down and decide 'Hey lads, from now on, no more beer', but it was a fucking bad decision! Anyway, I doubt Six Flags or Disney World would go down well over here. Not much demand, you see. Maybe they could get away with organising a sand-castle competition or something, but other than that, it does not look like the place has much potential for theme parks.

I cannot go into too much detail about where I am or what I am doing for obvious reasons. I have to be briefed, I guess, on the things I can and cannot say, but I can see a lot of fighter jets flying overhead, which makes sense because we are right next to a runway on an air base. Needless to say, there are no direct flights back home or anywhere else.

So, that's it from me, I'll talk to you next time – again, don't worry. I'm having lots of fun, the weather is beautiful, wish you were here, will be home soon. Please pick me up at the airport when I get back and for God's sake have a beer in the fridge upon my return.

Peace!

Graham

Chapter 12

Al Asad was a major transport hub used by the hundreds of supply trucks that trundled through the region, day and night. These massive lumbering columns would pass by the base and make their way to destinations all over Iraq. There were also huge shipments of fuel coming along the dangerous routes from the border areas, providing a rich target for insurgents. It would be our job to provide security on the roads to make them safer for the convoys. We would be patrolling in HMMWVs, the military equivalent of a pick-up truck. They were big, diesel-fuelled, four-wheeled vehicles, the workhorse of the American armed forces. The abbreviation stands for high-mobility multipurpose wheeled vehicles, but they're more commonly known as Humvees.

We were taking over from an active-duty unit that was finishing its tour and, I can tell you, they were one bunch of happy campers to be on their way home. A few of us started hanging out where these guys did their radio watch to avoid being roped into doing some shitty work by an overeager NCO. The radio post was a simple cammo net hoisted over one of their Humvees. We'd sit there in the shade listening to the lads as they ran through the drill, telling us how it all worked. The base itself was pretty safe, they said, but outside the wire was another matter. Each of the roads in the area was given a code name. Some of them were designated 'military only' and were off limits to civilians in an effort to cut down on the number of attacks. Despite this, they warned us that the towns and routes near Al Asad were just as dangerous, if not more so, than anywhere else in Iraq. They were basically occupied by the insurgents, or the Hajji, as they called them, and the US had zero presence there. We still had to patrol them, though, and this meant whizzing in and out every now and again, hoping the whole time you didn't get hit.

In spite of everything they were telling us, I thought that it didn't sound like too bad a gig. At least we would be able to come back after patrols, get something to eat and sleep in a bed. After sitting around the base with nothing to do, I was eager to get my hands dirty so I could kill my boredom.

I noticed that the guys we were relieving were much younger than us. Most of them had joined up straight from high school and were out there on active duty even though they were still not old enough, legally, to drink a pint. Reservists like me had joined for different reasons and were generally a little bit older. We had a lot of college students and professional people in our ranks and some were already married and had kids themselves. The guys we were replacing were amazed by this. They couldn't believe that I was almost twenty-six and that we all had careers at home. I couldn't help thinking that some of them were younger than my little brother.

We'd hang around with them all day, giving out shit about the

Marine Corps, boasting about great sexual experiences that never actually happened, talking about drinking pints and God only knows what else. I knew a million jokes and shared them out. We talked until we were bored looking at each other and then we sat silently and drew stuff in the sand and smoked cigarettes.

Chapter 13

1 September 2004

Subject: War movies

You know when you watch a really good war movie and it has a cool soundtrack that plays alongside the dramatic action scenes? Like the 'Ride of the Valkyries' from Apocalypse Now? *Well, that's all blarney, I'll have you know. While I was waiting to get on the plane to Iraq, the song that was stuck in my head was a Michael Jackson number, for feck's sake. You know that 'You Are Not Alone' crap?*

So, that just ruined it for me. I had always dreamed that the day I finally went off to war I would be pumped up and ready for action. I didn't think it would be spent trying to get a Michael bloody Jackson song out of my head and wondering if I had forgotten the teabags.

And another thing. Soldiers don't talk like heroes or come out with cool or dramatic or flag-waving statements like in Hollywood. It's actually really more like, 'What the f**k was

*that?' 'F**k that,' 'F**k you,' 'No, f**k you.' It's all very
different to the movies, I can tell ya!*

*Still having fun though. Practised firing my 9 mm yesterday,
the first time I have ever used a pistol. Apart from that, there
have been no major developments over the past few days. I'm
just getting settled in really, but I am kept busy and am not
always just hanging around writing emails, just in case that's
how you think I spend all my time, OK?*

Anyway got to go, take care,
Graham

We had been at Al Asad a week when our platoon leaders started
going out on patrol with the squads we were replacing to familiarise
themselves with the area and to get all the pointers and other good
advice that we badly needed.

They'd come back in the evening and brief us on how the whole
thing worked. Basically, there were three squads in every platoon and
four Humvees to each squad. One squad mounted patrols for a week
while another stood by as a Quick Reaction Force (QRF), ready to
respond to any enemy threat or incident throughout the region. Put
simply, if the shit went down, these guys were called in as back-up.
Then there was the third squad that escorted the Explosives
Ordinance Disposal (EOD) teams whenever they were called out to
suspect devices found in the field.

The three squads rotated every week, taking turns in all three roles.
The week spent running patrols was apparently the hardest, as you
were on the go all day, every day and sometimes throughout the night
too. There was less to do on the QRF, but you had to be ready to
respond to a call-out and have your vehicles heading out the gate in

less than three minutes. You had to maintain vigilance on that team and that meant running a two-man radio watch 24/7 to monitor the radio. The EOD escort job was supposed to be the easiest. They got to sit around until they were called out, and even then they weren't expected to be as quick as the QRF. This was the theory anyway but as we would soon find out, the reality was that it all could become pretty fluid and you could be doing any of the three jobs from one day to the next.

After a few days, the vehicle commanders also started going out on patrol. They promised the rest of us pawns that we would get our chance soon. We couldn't wait to get going, but when the official handover finally took place and each squad got their first close look at their four Humvees, we were shocked. Every single vehicle looked like it had been pulled out of a wrecking yard. They were all different colours and the equipment was equally mismatched and had seen better days. For the most part, the lads had to use bungee cords to hold down the ammo cans for the machine guns because there was nothing else available. More worryingly, most of them had no armour and there was no protection for the gunner up in the turret. I couldn't believe we were expected to risk our lives in these wrecks. We were supposed to be the most powerful military force in the world, yet there I was, standing in front of a piece of shit with a handful of bungee cords in my hand.

Only the lead Humvee in each squad had any added armour and that was only because it faced the greatest risk of going over a landmine – not a very comforting thought for my best mate Vick, who was to be the machine-gunner in the lead truck in our squad. I don't want to go into the reasons why the rest had no armour, but let's just say it was probably cheaper to give a flag to your mother when you died.

One of the Humvees was designated for carrying troops, casualties or prisoners or all three and this is where the Navy Corpsman, the medic, was stationed. It had a 'highback' design – instead of a turret on the roof, it had an open bed behind the cab like a pick-up truck where our dismounts sat. These were Marines who would patrol on foot whenever we stopped while my vehicle, Black 4, the gun truck, would provide rear security.

I, at least, felt some relief in that I was assigned to be the machine-gunner in Sergeant Harry's vehicle. He was a pretty down-to-earth and smart guy and I had a lot of respect for him The rest of the crew was pretty cool too. There was Romero and Mendez, who were both lance corporals like me. Romero, the driver, was a Latino from a small town in west Texas. He was an energetic, funny guy who loved cracking jokes and getting into mischief. He used to be a prison guard and he told the kind of stories about jail that would make any budding criminal turn his back on a life of crime. Mendez was a native Spanish speaker who had a heavy Latino accent. I'm not sure, but I think he was born in Mexico. He was very calm, and I never saw him lose his cool the whole time we were in Iraq. He was a good, all-round guy, one you would want by your side if the shit ever hit the fan.

Together with Sergeant Harry, the four of us would become known as 'La Guente' (pronounced 'la huente'). It's Mexican/Spanish for 'the people', and we would earn quite a reputation among the other Marines in our unit as a tough fire team that was not to be messed with. We were all good, God-fearing Catholic men from tough neighbourhoods who would soon earn the respect of the other guys.

Our squad leader, who was in charge of all four Humvees in our squad, was Sergeant Huerra. He was a quiet, well-mannered Peruvian who seldom lost his temper, but on the rare occasion when he did, you knew you were way out of line and deserved everything that was coming. He could switch instantly from being a tough Marine sergeant to a well-read intellectual who could talk about things like physics and theology. He trusted his Marines. He didn't need to know how we got things done, he just cared that they were done. And he enjoyed drinking from the trays of Coca-Cola that frequently, and magically, appeared in the back of our vehicles as much as the next man.

As we were scheduled to run our first patrol the very next day, Sergeant Harry went off for a briefing at command while the rest of us tried our best to get the battered vehicles into shape. We were still only halfway through stowing our equipment and tightening up loose mirrors and doors when the radio suddenly crackled into life and we heard our new call sign for the first time.

'Thunder – Thunder – this is Lonestar, over. Thunder up, repeat, Thunder up.' We stood there in disbelief. 'Thunder up' was the signal to go, but we were still getting our shit together. The heavy crew-served weapons that were usually mounted on the vehicles were in the armoury waiting to be drawn down as part of the handover. We just ran in and grabbed everything we could carry. Quickly, we agreed to sort it out later with the corporal in charge. He understood our predicament and let us take whatever we needed.

I armed myself with an M-240 Golf machine gun and fourteen hundred rounds of ammo, night-vision goggles and an inter-squad radio that came with a headset. Shit, I thought, we hadn't even been outside the wire yet and already we were going into some unknown emergency situation. Somehow, we pulled everything together and by the time Sergeant Huerra got the mission brief ten minutes later, we were mounted up and ready to go, which wasn't bad, given the circumstances. Sergeant Harry was still away at the other briefing, so Corporal Dan was appointed commander of our vehicle for the mission.

Romero took the wheel while Mendez got in the back seat. I clambered up into the turret and readied my machine gun. Riding backwards in the turret, I nervously scanned from left to right as we sped out past the safety of the wire and into the darkening desert. I must admit that although I wasn't obviously afraid, I was a little edgy.

I was also pissed off at how we had been thrown in at the deep end and at the fact that we had no idea what we were doing. I had never actually been in the turret of a gun truck before and I didn't have a clue what was going on. I didn't know where we were heading or what the enemy threat level was. I felt completely vulnerable, stuck up in the turret with absolutely no armour to protect me. We bumped along a narrow road that had been designated Route Neptune on our maps.

With our headlights turned off, we used night-vision goggles to see in the dark. I was frantically turning my head from side to side, thinking the whole time that I could get blown up in a New York minute. The place we were driving through was absolutely barren. There were no houses, buildings, roads, trees or any sign of life. Now and again, I looked over my shoulder and caught a glimpse of the vague outlines of the three Humvees speeding along ahead of us. Through my night-vision goggles, I could make out the illumination of distant lights on the horizon that could have been a town. Apart from that, I couldn't see a thing other than the stars in the night sky. We bounced down the road in the dark and, with every pothole we hit, I clenched my backside that little bit tighter, bracing myself for the impact of a landmine. We'd all heard the stories of twisted bodies and carnage after Marines hit mines on the very same road that we were now on. Talk about a sudden reality check. Eventually, we arrived at the scene of an explosion. A seven-ton truck had gone over a mine with its front tyre and the resulting blast had torn the engine to pieces.

There had been some casualties, but they had already been medivaced out by the time we got there. I found out later that I knew the guy who had been driving the truck, and he had been badly injured. It turned out that the poor bastard had been hit on his very first time out. A security perimeter had been set up while a tow truck was ordered up to take the damaged vehicle back to base. We pulled into defensive positions off the road where we remained on constant alert for the next two hours. The night-vision goggles were straining my eyes. Everything was luminous green, and it was hard to make out any detail in the dark. I was sitting in my turret trying to get used to them when, in the distance, I spotted a large number of lights.

'Hey, Mendez,' I yelled, 'what the fuck is that coming down the road?'

But he didn't even have any night-vision goggles and shouted back, 'Fucked if I know, man. I can't see shit.'

I called my patrol leader on the radio and asked him what he thought the lights could be. He got back to me and told me to hold on while he checked if there were any other friendly elements in the area. By now, I could make out vehicles approaching and they were getting closer the whole time. There appeared to be about fifty of them coming down the road towards us. I didn't know if it was the US military or the entire population of a nearby hostile town coming out to kill us. I stood there with my finger tightening on the trigger guard of my machine gun, waiting for orders from the patrol leader. Then the radio crackled, and we got word back that it was one of our own resupply convoys.

The damaged truck was eventually brought under tow and we escorted the recovery team to safety at Al Asad. The rest of the night passed without incident but, on the way back, I thought about the confusion that could have ended in tragedy. Our first time out had been an unnerving experience and a quick lesson that we weren't caught up in a conventional front line war here. We would be fighting an enemy we would probably never see, chasing shadows and living by chance, hoping that we wouldn't get hit by an invisible roadside bomb, a landmine or a suicide bomber.

Once we were back behind the safety of the wire, I said a quick prayer and thanked God that we were all right. Although we were drained after our night of tension, we went straight over to the armoury to sort out our weapons and make damn sure we would be ready the next time.

Chapter 14

The day after we brought the tow truck in, we were called out to escort the EOD team to a suspect device that had been found in the same area.

We headed out the gate in a different direction, bypassing the military-only road to travel down the Al Asad road to the town of Baghdadi. There, we were to take a right onto a major public road that was called Saturn on our maps.

We were now on roads with civilian traffic and we had been ordered to allow them to pass by our convoy. This really freaked me out. Any one of those fuckers could have had a bomb on board and could drive his car straight into us. We had been told, however, that as we were trying to help the Iraqi people and not conquer them, we couldn't keep them back from our patrols. Yeah, great. Sounds all right if you're a politician sitting behind a desk in Washington, but driving through an Iraqi town propped up in a turret was another fucking thing. So, cars kept coming along and overtaking us while we were exposed to a needless danger.

We reached Baghdadi and for the first time since I'd arrived in Iraq, I saw some of the local people in their natural environment. The dusty little town was like something out of a biblical story. The men were sitting around on the doorsteps in their traditional long robes – I don't know what they were called but we referred to them as man dresses – smoking cigarettes. Bare-footed children, who, moments before, had been playing stopped and stared right through us as we passed. There were goats and dogs all over the place. The smell and atmosphere was overwhelming. If you ignored the satellite dishes on some of the houses, it was like we had stepped back in time. We drove past mosques, homes that were little more than small concrete shacks with no windows, tiny little shops and groves of palm trees.

We trundled on through the town carefully, watching every door and window until we got out into the countryside. Eventually, we arrived at the scene where the suspicious object was lying off to the side of the road. We set up our security perimeter while the EOD guys dismounted to take a look at what they were dealing with. Cautiously, the EOD leader made sure there were no booby traps, then he gingerly picked up the suspect device. Everyone held their breath. It was an empty diesel can. As they were putting it in the back of the vehicle, we did an equipment check and Romero noticed that one of our own diesel cans was missing. We looked at each other guiltily, as if we had been caught stealing from the cookie jar. It had obviously fallen off the night before when we were bouncing around there in the darkness. It should have been tied down properly, and I had been too busy being tossed around in the turret to notice. We agreed to keep it to ourselves. We returned to base without saying a word to anyone and replaced it before anyone noticed.

29 September 2004

Subject: Another fun-filled, action-packed day – rent the movie!

I hope all you folks at home like paying taxes, because it looks like we are going to be here for a very long time. If we could even have a beer, it wouldn't be so bad, but I'm drinking grapefruit juice in the chow hall trying to convince myself it's mixed with vodka. I think I'm getting there slowly but surely. The power of the mind!

Looking forward to Christmas this year, as I won't have to buy any presents, not that I ever do, but at least I'll have a good excuse this time and won't feel too guilty …

If anyone knows someone in the supply office who is responsible for sending over our food, could you please pass the word to them that we have no fucking use for Diet Coke. There is no one out here but blokes who are already underfed and underweight. We do not need Diet Coke. Send some real stuff.

Well, that's all the fun for one day … have to go back now and get ready for a long patrol. Hope some idiot takes a pot shot at me instead of leaving a sneaky bomb while I'm not around so we can have a proper fight. But that's their game. Who'd go up against the Marines with a few buddies armed with AK-47s and think they'll live? Not a fucking chance.

Anyway, have fun and keep paying those taxes …

Love

Graham

A day later, we stopped two guys coming in through the wire who were going to have fun explaining to the powers that be why they had an anti-tank mine in the trunk of their car. Both of them were Iraqi civilian contractors who worked in the chow hall. We actually had a lot of locals working on base, which was pretty controversial among the Marines, as nobody trusted them much, and this incident just added to our suspicions.

We'd received a tip-off about these two particular guys earlier that morning and were sent to arrest them when they came in the gate. We waited in our vehicles just inside the civilian entrance and pounced on them when they got there.

Sure enough, it was just their misfortune to be caught as they were trying to sneak in a mine to fuck someone up. We were furious. I wanted to kick their heads in myself, but as I'm a nice person – or rather, because I wouldn't get away with it – I resisted the urge. Instead, we escorted them to the detention facility on base and handed them over to the authorities. We had the EOD robot search the vehicle and remove the mine.

Apart from that little bit of excitement, the next few weeks saw us run a few missions that pretty much followed the same basic routine. Sometimes we were sent to resupply remote outposts with equipment or fresh Marines. Now and again, there was the odd alert, and we would rush out to deal with a potential threat, but nothing of any consequence ever happened. We had a lot of downtime and we took the opportunity to make ourselves more comfortable.

We had moved out of the tents and were now living in one of the cans. Myself and Vick were room-mates and we chipped in and bought a second-hand television along with a stereo and a microwave. Yep, when Americans put a base together, they do it in style. You could buy anything you wanted in the PX. I even got a DVD player and pretty soon we had set ourselves up in our cool little pad. Peter, my other buddy, was right next door and he roomed with a guy called Silva, but they seemed to spend more time in our can than their own. We weren't used to having so much privacy as we had all spent a lot of time together in a communal squad bay during the work-up to deployment.

We also did a bit of work on our vehicles. They were badly in need of an overhaul. We customised them to our personal liking, using straps and any other material we could find to sort out our equipment the way we wanted it.

From the recent bout of almost constant patrolling, we got to know the area outside the wire quite well. Gradually, we eased into our surroundings without dropping guard for a moment. We started to develop more confidence in our capabilities. Before each patrol, we would sit down and go over our routes, objectives, radio frequency and immediate reaction plans. It was good practice and, after a while, it became redundant, as we had done it so many times. It was engrained in our heads – but that's never a bad thing.

Chapter 15

On 5 October 2004, I woke up at 08:00, which was too late for morning chow but too early for anything else. Not that I had much else to do that day anyway. My room-mate Vick was still asleep, so I decided not to be a prick and wake him up by playing a DVD. Instead, I went and had a shower and put on some clean cammies. This was a real luxury, as I only had two pairs and could only wash one pair once a week at most. It was a nice little treat to have a fresh set of clothes on for a change and I was enjoying the feeling as I sat outside writing a letter to one of my friends.

Just then, one of the guys ran around the corner shouting, 'QRF UP! QRF UP!' Here we go. I sprang to my feet and rushed around helping him to wake everyone else up. Within a minute, we were running towards our vehicles, some half-dressed and the rest half-asleep. We mounted up and I jumped into my turret wearing my flak jacket, Kevlar helmet, radio and all the rest of my gear. By the time Sergeant Huerra came running out of the Command Operations Centre (COC) and leapt into the lead vehicle, I had already gone through several Marlboros.

Before we left the gate, we linked up with a team we were to escort to a weapons cache that had been discovered in a pre-dawn raid. We headed out the gate with a seven-ton military truck crammed full of low-budget grunts just like myself following behind. I guessed they were going to be doing most of the donkey work.

We picked up speed and were soon barrelling down the desert roads, kicking up a cloud of dust in our wake. Despite the fact that it was early October, it was already baking under the early-morning sun. The steel of the turret was hot to the touch and the dry desert air blowing against my face offered little relief. Everything irritated me – my helmet, glasses, goggles and radio all sat uncomfortably on my head.

I was trying to concentrate on the task ahead and keep a sharp lookout for any danger. One of the first things you noticed driving along Iraqi roads was that there wasn't much of an anti-litter policy in place. The roadsides were cluttered with rubbish and dead, rotting animals. This was a big problem for us. The insurgents used the refuse to hide IEDs, and we had to be very careful and pay attention to every object we approached. The frustrating thing about it was that our own troops threw their rubbish around as well, especially water bottles, which looked similar to artillery rounds when viewed through night-vision goggles. I hated the fucking irony that we weren't helping the situation.

Over the past few days, the level of suicide bombings had increased. On an almost daily basis, the radio would crackle and we would hear of yet another attack on a unit based nearby. Thankfully, somebody up above finally made the smart decision to allow us to order oncoming traffic off the road. The new rules also dictated that civilian vehicles were not allowed to follow within a hundred metres of our convoys.

The top brass issued new instructions to what was called the Escalation of Force Plan to deal with the threat. It started out with a verbal and arm signal to approaching vehicles to move aside and let us pass or stay back if they were too close to the rear. If that failed, we were to fire a signal flare – not directly at the vehicle, mind you, but in its general direction. If the driver still did not heed the warning and persisted in coming at us, we could fire a low, warning shot into the ground in front of him. Only with all other options exhausted were we permitted to shoot out the engine block and then, and only then, follow it up with rounds aimed at the passenger compartment of the vehicle. On paper, it sounds nice and fair, but I didn't think it was going to work well in practice. We were going to come across lots of moving vehicles, some of them approaching us at high speed and with confused and frightened drivers at the wheel, with numerous steps to complete and not a lot of time to carry them out. Another problem was that this was a sudden change of policy and the civilians were going to find out about it the hard way. One thing I knew for sure was that we were going to need a hell of a lot of signal flares.

Later that morning, we reached the site where the raid had taken place. It was in a small rural community surrounded by lush fields irrigated by the nearby River Euphrates. There were palm trees everywhere and the houses were really Spartan. Air conditioning? Fuck, some of these guys didn't even have windows, but the green crops and palm trees made a nice change from the endless dull colour of the desert. Chickens roamed freely out on the roads and, once again, I got the feeling that I had travelled back in time to the days of Jesus Christ. I saw some scrawny goats in a pen and a few small children peered at us from the doorways of the surrounding houses. Apart from the sound of farm animals and singing birds, it was eerily quiet. We settled in and beefed up the security that was already there. We had an Iraqi translator with us and I watched him as he pulled something from the branch of a tree outside the house where the weapons had been found. He walked over to me and offered me a bunch of dates. No shit, I thought, that's where those things come from? I tell you, they were the best dates I'd ever eaten in my life.

The hours passed and the sun rose higher into the clear blue sky. It was turning into yet another long, hot day. I was slowly sweating away whatever water was left in my body. Gradually, I drifted off into my own little world and, even though my eyes were wide open, I was miles away, thinking about home and fantasising about how the rain would suddenly pour down on a summer's day, drenching everything in a second and filling the air with that fresh, clean smell. Then I heard it, so quietly at first that I thought I was imagining it. The silence had been gently broken by the tranquil sound of the Muslim call for afternoon prayer that was coming from a mosque hidden beyond the tree line.

It was the first time in my life that I'd heard it that close and it sounded beautiful. It really captured the mood for me as my eyes took in the scenery by the riverbanks. It was a perfect moment – until I realised I had run out of smokes. I almost kicked myself for being so stupid. Running out of bullets was one thing, but not having enough cigarettes was tragic. As no one else in my vehicle smoked, I was going to have to wait until we were back in the rear before I could have one.

That irritated me and I started to get impatient. What the fuck were we doing out here? Weapons cache? Big fucking deal. I couldn't give two flying fucks. I was pissed off that I'd put on my clean cammies that day and now I was drenched in sweat. I must have drunk about six litres of water but hadn't pissed even once. Could you please hurry it up guys so we can get the fuck out of here?, I urged them in my mind.

The Marines we had escorted out there had piled all the weapons they'd found into the back of a seven-ton. There were all kinds of junk in there. Over fifty 155 mm rounds, just as many 122 mm shells, hundreds of AK-47s, Kalashnikovs, rocket-propelled grenades (RPGs), anti-tank mines and loads of other stuff they couldn't even identify. The owners of the house had already been taken away for questioning by the time we'd arrived, but they had enough there to start a small war.

When the search team was finally happy they had found everything, we escorted them out of the neighbourhood and back onto the desert road. They wanted to stop somewhere to blow up all the ordinance, so we took them off to the boonies and set up a very wide security perimeter. They prepared the charge as we broke down our temporary defences and headed off down the road and then they gave us the five-minute warning. When it did go off, the explosion was so powerful that the ground shook underneath us almost a mile away, and it created a mushroom cloud that looked like the aftermath of a nuclear-bomb strike as it stretched out into the sky.

With that taken care of, it was back to the Ranch to prep for the next mission. We refuelled the vehicles and cleaned our weapons, then I had that smoke and another shower. Later that evening, I ate some warm chow and decided that things weren't so bad after all.

5 October 2004
This keybard is messed up and I am having prblems typing an 'o'. I think that I am missing quite a few and I have n time fr spelling s bear with me.

Last night, I dreamed that I came home t a big parade and there were cheering peple and girls thrwing themselves at me singing, 'We love you, Graham.' I was just trying to g for a quiet pint and was hitting them ver the head with a flagple t get them ut off my way … then I wke up. I've decided t put the dream in my jurnal that I have started writing. I already have a few pages s far but I have classified it purely as fiction for nw in case the mental health flk get their hands n it and want t sit me dwn t have a little 'chat'.

The nly ther news I can really talk about right nw has nthing t do with the actual activities that I was sent here to d. I can happily reprt that I just bught seasn ne f Suth Park but cannt tell yu anything mre abut finding weapns caches r anything like that.

What else is new? Hmmm, I saw a dnkey, sme chickens and a cat tday. I als met sme f the lcal children. Pr little feckers. I lve meeting and greeting the kids in the villages and twns but I never feel quite right talking t them, standing there armed t the teeth. They are all fascinated by ur weapns and keep wanting t tuch the barrels of the guns with their tiny little hands, which, of curse, we couldn't permit. We are supposed t be ut here helping them, but smetimes it feels like we are gradually corrupting their childhd as they see us with ur weapns utside their houses frm day t day.

I hpe to have my vide camera son s I can capture some f my experiences fr the future, but it is in a care package that has nt arrived yet. I am als waiting for Indian ndles that my mate is sending me. riginally they had been shipped t his mther in England frm India. Then they were flwn t Texas, and frm there they will be sent t Iraq where we'll eat them. They will be sme well travelled nodles by the time I get them.

Well that's all for now.

Lve

Graham

Chapter 16

After a 22:00 radio watch on 6 October, I went and checked my email. Having access to the internet was an absolute lifesaver. It was our only way of keeping in communication with the outside world, and it was with a fevered rush of anticipation that I signed in and clicked on my inbox to see what was waiting for me. I didn't have one new message, apart from two bits of spam – one promised to increase my penis size and make me a better lover and the other offered a special discount on various household items. Spam is always annoying but because we were stuck out in Iraq and email had become our lifeline, these pointless messages irritated me way beyond what they would have at home. What the fuck use did I have for Viagra or a bedside lamp in the desert with ten thousand Marines? Despite the disappointment, I woke up the following morning and just for the laugh decided to check my email again, in case there was anything new or exciting. All I got this time was another prick trying to sell me sexual stimulants.

Later, there was a mail call, which was always a source of great excitement. One of the lads got a curious package and we all eagerly gathered around as he opened it. Out fell an assortment of gay porn, lubricants and something called a Pocket Pussy that somebody had sent him for a laugh. He proudly displayed his loot and then we took turns putting the gay magazines under other Marines' pillows, where they would be found. One of the guys was asleep and we put the Pocket Pussy in his hands. When he woke up, he got the fright of his life and we laughed our asses off about it all day. As to the effectiveness of the Pocket Pussy, well, a Marine, who shall remain nameless, would only say that 'it felt weird' and he threw it away as soon as his new rubber girlfriend had lost her virginity.

I had waited with the others for my name to be called during mail call, but I didn't get a single letter and that pissed me off. Instead, I reread the few letters I had already received from home and discovered a common theme. Nothing was happening in the world, everything was grand and everyone was happy and proud of me, and so on, and so on. It kind of felt like the Waltons were writing to me. I got bored reading the same stuff over and over again, so I decided to sit down somewhere quietly and write a few letters to anyone and everyone. There was plenty to write about.

The one thing about Iraq was that there was ample opportunity to think about your life. During downtime, there was nothing else to do. I thought about my ex in America a lot and felt bad for not being the best boyfriend in the world when I'd had the chance to be. I had been pretty beat up after I had finished with her, which was a while before I left for Iraq, but at least back home I could hang out with my good friend Mr Budweiser and tell him all about it.

I guess I had a lot of things going on in my personal life at the time I was with her, which, when I thought about it, started spiralling downwards after I got home from my initial training. I was pissed off when I came back, as I had no job and no money, and I was angry at the world for being the way it was. I let it get to me and I ended up pushing my girlfriend away. Now, with more than enough time to dwell on the ifs and the buts, I felt really stupid and selfish. I wrote her a letter to say sorry once again and told her I always wanted to be her friend, if nothing else. Then I tried to get some sleep.

Later in the evening, I was woken up for room inspection, which I wasn't too happy about. Staff Sergeant Ortega stalked around our little hovel and stared at all the empty non-alcoholic beer bottles that had gathered on top of our television set. Noticing his frown, I informed him that I found the beer bottles made great ornaments in the absence of anything else to decorate the room with. After a short pause, I added, 'Staff Sergeant.' He nodded in silence, probably thinking to himself that I was going mad in the head.

6 October 2004

Subject: STUFF – from the misinformation ministry

How are y'all?

Today, nothing happened, absolutely nothing. The most exciting part of my day was watching the bin men picking up the trash. I think I have the entire procedure down now and if there is no need for machine-gunners when I get back home, I could have a back-up career. Just a thought anyways.

What's adding to the boredom is the fact that I didn't get any mail again. I'm so bored that I'm developing theories about crop circles and the Loch Ness Monster. At the moment, I'm trying to find a correlation between the two.

I did, however, get a chance to clean my weapons again and

I recounted my bullets. I've been here over a month now and I still have the same number I started out with, which makes sense since I haven't had the opportunity to fire any.

I was going to sharpen my knife, but who am I kidding? If it comes down to depending on a bloody knife to save my life, well, I think the enemy probably deserves the privilege of taking me out, considering he would have made it through everything else that we could throw at him, such as machine guns, rifles, side arms, an endless supply of bullets and rockets as well as close air support and QRF. I wouldn't want to try to explain how we couldn't stop a bloke with less than fifteen minutes of military experience under his belt with all the toys we possess. So I've dropped the combat knife back into its sleeve attached to my belt, hoping at the same time that this paragraph doesn't come back to haunt me!

I did have another radio watch today for four hours. How ridiculous that must sound to civilians ... 'We're in the military.' 'Oh, yeah? Waddya do?' 'We watch radios!' It was really boring, but I couldn't just go off and do something else, as I had to stand by in case we called out for 'Stuff'.

Just in case any of you are wondering, 'Stuff' is anything that I cannot talk about here. Because I can't go into any details right now, I will merely call it 'Stuff' until I learn more about what I can and cannot tell you.

So, that's all that happened today ... oh yeah, I ate a weird conceptual meal this afternoon that they tried to pass off as dinner! We were thinking about getting it sent to a lab for a more thorough investigation to find out what it actually was.

Tomorrow, thank God, has more things in store, but I cannot tell you anything about them right now in case some Iraqi fella learns all about our crazy 'Stuff'. Well, at least I won't have to sit around all day feeling as useful as an ashtray on a motorbike.

Take care

Graham

On 7 October, we were woken up at 06:30 for a QRF mission. We didn't have time for morning chow, which is understandable – wars aren't fought around mealtimes, it would seem.

Mission: to provide security for the Navy Seabees, the combat engineers, who were going out to Route Neptune to fix a section of road that crosses over some water. The crossing was vital to the resupply convoys that travelled through the region, but the continuous military traffic had taken its toll, and it needed constant care and attention.

As always, it was already hot out there despite the early hour. The thought of spending another day under the desert sun distracted me from my fears of taking fire or hitting a landmine. Some days, the prospect of getting injured didn't cross my mind; other times, it was all I could think about. I tried to adopt an attitude that if it was going to happen, it was going to happen. If it did, then I hoped I would be killed outright and not just injured, left behind to a life of pain and misery with missing limbs or organs. I suppose it doesn't sound like a great deal, but nobody ever said I needed to be happy about doing this in the first place. Instead, I tried to concentrate on doing my job as best I could while the puddle of sweat around my boots got bigger.

We arrived at the objective and positioned our four vehicles in a 360-degree security perimeter while the Seabees immediately set about their work. Nobody wanted to spend one minute more than they had to out there. The ground itself was pretty flat and you could see for a few kilometres in every direction. To our east, though, was a small rise to a plateau which presented an excellent area from which to attack us with mortars. It was only a click or so away, but we didn't have a great visual on most of the ground on top and we all eyed it nervously. The pool itself was large, about five to six acres in size, and was an oasis for animals of all kinds, judging by the many tracks but, for the moment, there was no sign of life.

Sergeant Harry called for someone to join him on foot patrol to scout the area. I felt like a change of scenery, so I asked Mendez if he would switch with me while I went out with the sergeant to explore the vicinity. He was cool with that and myself and the sergeant set off around the west side of the oasis, rifles at the ready. We found that although the dirt was baked dry on the surface, underneath it was soft and wet. I could make out the tracks made by wild dogs, goats and large birds. We also noticed that some of the reeds were pretty brittle and it would have been obvious if anybody had walked through them. As we moved around the pool, we could see the place hadn't been visited by any human since at least before the time of the last rainfall, which was probably about five months or so previously.

With the area immediately around the water clear, we set off a little further towards an adjacent wadi about half a click away, looking for anything out of place. We were walking along, scanning the ground, when Sergeant Harry stopped. He pointed out something that looked suspicious under a bush about twenty feet away. We ventured over and discovered the upper receiver to a German H&K 7.62 mm rifle. It was pretty beat up and looked like it had being lying there for a long time. There were some Arabic characters on the weapon that I took to be the serial number, so we figured that it was some kind of knock-off version.

I continued searching while Sergeant Harry called in our find over the inter-squad radio and I found the butt stock from the same rifle lying under a bush another twenty feet away. We were convinced that the remaining components were nearby and, sure enough, we recovered the lower receiver of the same weapon. We widened our search for the bolt assembly but couldn't find it.

We put the various bits and pieces together and posed for photos with our little discovery. They were in a pretty useless condition, but we took them back with us all the same. Sergeant Harry decided to leave a little present for the owner in case he ever came back to recover his stash – he squatted down and took a shit in the spot where he had found the first piece. I covered him while he did his business, thinking the whole time how it would suck to get shot taking a dump.

After striking our little blow for freedom, we moved on around the far side of the water. We were now a good bit away from the rest of the squad, so every five to ten minutes, we did a radio check to maintain contact. If we couldn't communicate with our vehicles, we moved back closer to re-establish a link. We treated communications very seriously and constantly relayed our position back to the squad to ensure that nobody mistook us for the bad guys. We patrolled around for a few more hours before returning to the vehicles. We switched around to let Romero and Mendez go walkabout. I needed to hydrate and get some food into me. We had missed morning chow, but I was relieved we had managed to get ice. Jesus, the cold water felt good. It was immensely hot in the mid-afternoon and I was so tired from humping around in the dirt that I was happy to sit on my backside again just like any other mounted machine-gunner.

After a few hours, the Seabees passed word that they were wrapping it up and would be ready to move out in fifteen minutes. We started bringing in our dismounts, all thankful to be heading home. I was completely exhausted and hungry, but I enjoyed the trip back with the wind in my face after a long day in the dead heat. Back at base, we got some chow over at Mainside for a change.

For the next two days we were on the QRF, but as no missions came in, we stayed on radio watch. It was a two-man deal, with one guy from our squad sharing duties with another from the EOD escort team when they weren't out on call. As I'm not much of a morning person, Vick agreed to take the early one from 10:00 hours to 12:00 while I took the late one. As it turned out, EOD was called out, so both of us ended up standing the morning watch together.

We had forgotten to charge up my personal DVD player overnight and, shit out of luck, ended up sitting in the vehicle for two hours bored out of our heads with absolutely nothing to talk about. After watch, I ventured over to the chow hall to check out their latest creations. I wasn't in very good humour, so I sat there alone facing the wall, hoping that nobody would recognise me and come over to sit down and chat. I just wasn't in the mood for people. I was already starting to get frustrated there in Iraq and just needed some time to myself to think. Instead, I turned my attention to the fact that the chow was all screwed up again and wondered, for the hundredth time, how the so-called cooks could mess up the simplest of foods.

The highlight of the day was to be a call to a radio station in Austin called KVET 98.1 FM. We were told that at 17:00 hours, we would have an opportunity to say hello to everybody at home over the airwaves. This little difference to our day had taken on major significance and the hall was buzzing with Marines talking about it. But I never got a chance to participate. I had no sooner eaten my chow when one of my mates ran in shouting, 'QRF up!' I sprinted out of the chow hall with a mouth full of food and towards the staging area. Most of the other members of the squad were already mounting up ready to go as I jumped up onto the hood of the Humvee. We waited for Sergeant Huerra to come out of the COC with our orders, which he would give us on the move.

Within another few minutes, we were heading over to the other side of the base to pick up the EOD team at Camp Ripper. Along the way, Sergeant Huerra told us a landmine had been found just outside the wire along with a few 122 mm artillery rounds that were lying about nearby. We were to take the EOD team out to the find and set up a security perimeter while they dealt with the ordinance. No worries there, it was just like any other day. In fact, we were finding so many of these things that 'Quick Reaction Force' was becoming a joke – we had practically become a second permanent bomb-disposal escort team. We had only gone about five hundred metres up the road when we spotted eight Iraqi men carrying canvas bags and armed with AK-47s walking away from the base.

Our vehicle commanders decided to stop them and find out what they were doing. We had a fairly good idea that they were just coming from one of the police or army training academies on base and were probably all right, but we stopped to check them out all the same. We pulled over beside them and set up security. Sergeant Huerra walked over to talk to them while we watched carefully with weapons drawn. It was a bit of a tense stand-off as each group stared the other down, but as long as they didn't unsling their machine guns from their shoulders, everything was going to be OK. If they did, then it was going to turn into a very bad day for them. Sergeant

Huerra radioed back to the front gate and asked what the deal was with these guys. A radio call came back that they were cleared. They had apparently just graduated from the border-guard service and were on their way home for a few days before they were posted up to the Syrian border. They were heading in the direction of the town of Baghdadi a few clicks away and, as they were brothers in arms, we offered them a ride. There were smiles all round when we offered them a lift, but when we informed the COC of the situation, they, in their infinite wisdom and perhaps due to a breakdown in communications – I'm not totally sure how they manage to pull this shit out of their heads, to be honest – told us to arrest them on the spot and bring them back to the detention facility.

At this point, the Iraqi border guardsmen were already sitting comfortably in the back seats of our gun trucks with their rifles in their hands. Arrest them? For fuck's sake, one of them was sitting right by my feet in the vehicle. The smiles dropped from their faces when they realised something was up. They glanced suspiciously at us and start yammering on to each other in Arabic. Nervously, I undid the holster for my 9 mm while Sergeant Huerra tried to talk sense into whoever had radio watch over at the COC. Eventually, they got the picture and told us to ignore the arrest order and proceed as planned. We set off with the Iraqis now glaring suspiciously at us and dropped them off a little closer to the town, but the brief moment of comradeship was gone. They walked away, glancing contemptuously over their shoulders every now and then at the odd Americans. It was a pretty fucked-up situation, offering someone a lift and then threatening to arrest them. As my own ma used to tell me, never take a lift from strange people.

After dropping off the Iraqis, we continued north on Neptune to where the landmine had been found. We set up our security perimeter while the EOD team went in with a robot to deal with the device. My vehicle was pointing off west, out towards the desert wastes where power lines stretched off into the distance.

Underneath the nearest pylon, we could see a tent. It belonged to Restore Iraqi Electricity (RIE), a government agency that was responsible for repairing the national electricity grid. They employed Iraqi men whose job it was to camp out under the wires in remote parts of the country to make sure that terrorists didn't bring them down.

We saw them everywhere we went. Usually, it would be just one skinny guy on his own armed with an AK-47 with a single magazine. Not exactly a deterrent against the insurgents, but at least it was giving a guy something to do. But after a while, we started to get suspicious of them. Too many other units had been hit by landmines or IEDs in areas coincidentally near where these guys hung out. Yet, even though they were out there all the time, they always claimed they knew nothing and saw nothing.

We were convinced that these guys were, if not directly part of the attacks, at least turning a blind eye when the insurgents moved through. Now and again, we'd search their tents for any contraband and we decided to drive over and check out this one. We pulled up and told him to stand outside without his weapon while Mendez went through the few scant possessions in his tent. We asked him if he had seen any insurgents and, of course, he replied, 'No Mujahedin, Mister. America number one!' Yeah, right. I didn't trust this fucker as far as I could throw him. If I had my way, I'd have them all moved off away from the roads. But what else could we do? We returned to our position and started scanning the area. Nothing. The hours passed and I got so bloody bored that I started naming each rock I could see on the ground. I started out with simple names but moved on to made-up, Latin-sounding names the more bored I got.

This was probably the dullest thing I'd ever done in my life and, yet, it was also the most dangerous. It was a bizarre scenario. If you got bored, you grew complacent, and that could get you killed. I fought it off with whatever worked. I thought about my life and sang songs in my head over and over again.

Some time later, the EOD team informed us that they had disarmed the landmine and were loading up all the ordinance they had found. Happy days. Speeding down the road towards base, I noticed some strange shapes forming up in the sky. Looking closely at them, I realised they were clouds, white fluffy clouds. In Iraq! A few minutes later, I felt a drop of water on my face and then another. I couldn't believe it. It started raining lightly and I loved it. It was the first time it had rained since we'd got there. It only lasted a few moments, but it was the symbolism that put a smile on everyone's faces. It was literally a drop of normality and reminded most of us of home, especially me! Sitting around in the pissing rain in Dublin, there was no way I would have thought I'd ever be so delighted to get soaked in a cloudburst. It was the talk of the town back at base and that night we enjoyed a beautiful lightning storm. It breathed fresh life into the place. Everyone was looking forward to the end of the sweltering summer.

Chapter 17

We were woken up some time early on the morning of 10 October. I can't remember exactly what time it was, just that I didn't care. Time was starting to make very little difference to me. I do know that I didn't get any morning chow again and that meant I was going to be starving for the rest of the day, as me and the ready-made meals (MREs) didn't go well together. Within minutes, we were geared up and sitting in our vehicles, ready to roll. All we were waiting on was Sergeant Huerra and, as soon as he popped his head out of the Battalion COC, we'd be on our way.

Just then, Captain Fantastic came storming over. One or two of the lads hadn't put their helmets on and that set him off. He started screaming at us that we were responding to an ambush and that there had been casualties. This was the real thing, he told us, so it was time to unfuck ourselves. Captain Fantastic was a good officer but apart from the two lads who hadn't put on their helmets yet, we had been ready and the unfair bollocking pissed us off. I was ready to go shoot somebody and I hadn't even had a cup of tea yet! Captain Fantastic stormed off back to his hooch to grab his rifle while we sat around waiting on Sergeant Huerra to come out of the COC. Fifteen minutes later, they were finally finished briefing him and he came running out with the orders. Suddenly, we were on a mad dash to rescue whoever was in trouble. I hoped we weren't too late.

We hauled ass to the reported ambush site, mentally preparing ourselves to get stuck in, but when we got there, we found nothing. No friendlies and no bad guys, no shell casings and no bodies. In a panic, we radioed back to the COC and asked them what the fuck was going on. We were sent to another location and, again, the same thing. Nothing! Finally, someone figured out that the element that had taken fire had called in a ten-digit grid reference long after they had made contact. The location they called in was nowhere near where the ambush had actually taken place. The mission was scrapped and we headed back to Al Asad. Apparently, nobody had been hurt on our side but, man, it was a fucked-up situation. Nearly forty-five minutes after a call for help had come in, we had arrived at the wrong place. Then, we had been sent running around chasing our tails. Not only was it a waste of time, it was also a scary lesson. If this was the kind of support we had to rely on in a crisis, then some day we were going to be in serious fucking trouble.

Back on base, I went by the post office to send some packages home, just bits and pieces I had picked up for my nephews and nieces. One thing that always annoyed me was the fact that, as a non-US citizen, I had to pay for my post and packages to be sent to Ireland. I bought some snack food and a few DVDs at the PX and got back in the Humvee, looking forward to a quiet night in. We rolled into the Ranch and were parking our vehicles when orders came through to prepare to move out immediately to a Forward Operating Base (FOB) near the city of Hit. Located on the River Euphrates between the city of Haditha and the provincial capital Ramadi, Hit was a small city, yet had caused the US forces serious problems. Like almost all of the towns in Al Anbar, it was predominantly populated by Sunni Muslims and had been the scene of intermittent fighting between US forces and Iraqi insurgents since the invasion. It was considered extremely hostile. It was also suspected to be on the main route travelled by non-Iraqi insurgents on their way from Syria into central Iraq. Word had it that there were up to two hundred bad guys dug into the city who were ready to play ball. Well, it was about bloody time, I thought as we hurried back to our cans to get our personal gear. I grabbed as much underwear as I could, as I was sure to shit my pants a few times if this was the real deal. Under some administration rule, I was only supposed to have twelve hundred rounds of belt-fed 7.62 mm ammo for my M-240 Golf, but I told the armourer I only had six hundred rounds left so he'd give me some more. I ended up with almost two thousand, which made me that little bit more comfortable.

With not much more information other than the fact there was a sizeable force of insurgents holed up in Hit, we took off for the FOB, which lay just west of the River Euphrates and north of the city.

We travelled along Route Neptune and across Route Mars. From there, it was another two minutes' drive south on the public highway of Saturn before we got to the gates of the FOB. It was a small outpost that housed barely a single company of Marines, a fair few of whom were out in the field at any given time. There were three buildings in one grouping and a single structure standing beside a tiny mosque on the other side of the compound. We were told that this particular base had been formerly used as a barracks by the Iraqi army and had been built by the British in the nineteenth century when they were trying to take over the world. From what I understood, it was now an Iraqi

National Guardsmen recruit training facility, but I didn't see any of them around when we got there. We refuelled while Sergeant Huerra went to the COC to report in and get further instructions. After topping up with diesel, we staged our vehicles and tried to prepare ourselves for whatever was to come. I got up onto the roof of the Humvee, from where I could see the lights of the city, which was only about a mile or two away. But I couldn't hear any activity in the town, and all looked calm.

We got orders to bed down for the night, so we made quarters in an empty squad bay that had seven-foot slabs of concrete for beds. It was moderately comfortable even by our standards, but at that point I couldn't have cared less where I was. I was so tired I just wanted to lay my head down and get as much rest as possible. I had the feeling that sleep wasn't going to be high on our list of priorities for the next few days.

An hour before daybreak, we were woken up and told to mount up on our vehicles. We were warned to make sure everything was prepped and good to go. As we got ready in the dark, we could hear the sounds of heavy gunfire rumbling in the distance. We found out that a platoon from Bravo Company was trapped on the west side of the River Euphrates, where they were taking heavy fire from insurgents east of the city. We checked all of our equipment and double-checked it again. We anxiously waited for our orders to move out. I smoked a cigarette and tried to eat an MRE. The food out of these things normally tasted like shit, but that morning, it was particularly bad for some reason. I spat most of it away in disgust. The night gradually gave way to day, and the gunfire got heavier. 'What the fuck? What are we waiting for?' I said out loud to nobody in particular. Sergeant Huerra was still in the COC getting briefed on our response and, while we waited, we tuned into Bravo Company's radio frequency. As we gathered around the set, we could clearly hear the noise of shooting in the background and Marines frantically calling for air support on another frequency. We had switched over and listened in on the communication between the guys on the ground and the helicopter pilots who were flying in from Al Asad.

The Marines were giving out multiple 'call for fire' orders, directing the Cobras to targets, and soon they were lighting up the enemy's positions. It sounded like a video game, but the reality was far from that. When I looked up from the radio speaker, I could see tracer fire from the insurgents' weapons streaming up towards the over-flying helicopters. The only thing that achieved was to help the pilots identify their positions better.

I got up onto the roof of my Humvee and opened a can of Coke and a packet of crisps. From where I was sitting, it seemed like the air support was suppressing the insurgents pretty well. It sounded like the tide was turning and the Marines were gaining the upper hand, but it was extremely frustrating to be sitting there watching an actual fire fight in progress less than a mile or two away while people were presumably dying. I wondered how we got ourselves into a position in this war where we were outgunned by a bunch of terrorists with light arms and needed choppers to take them out. Were we not the big boys in town with the billion-dollar budget?

I wanted to get in there and help the guys trapped in Hit, and I wasn't the only one. We were all itching for the fight. We found out later there was no way we could have got through to them. Barricades had been erected in the streets throughout the city and we would have been badly cut up had we tried, especially with the limited resources we had on deck. Of course, we didn't know that at the time and we all felt like shite! Marines were pinned down fighting for their lives, and I was up the road watching it all and drinking a can of Coke.

While we were still trying to work out what was going on, it was decided to send my squad out on a dummy patrol to confuse the enemy. The idea was to make it look like we were sending troops into the city so the remaining insurgents would have to redirect manpower to prevent our advance. Apparently, this would cause the fighters to come out in the open, where our air support could engage them.

We mounted up and ran the dummy patrols for a while, driving rapidly towards the town and then making sudden U-turns and speeding away in the opposite direction before doing it again from a different route. By the fourth or fifth time, I think we were more confused than they were. Then we were ordered to set up a vehicle control point (VCP) on Route Mercury, the highway that connected Hit with Karbala to the south. There was a lot of traffic streaming out of the city and we were told to stop and search every vehicle to ensure that there was no one trying to sneak out any arms or injured Mujahedin fighters. There were two roads, both running parallel to each other, and we set up our VCPs on each of them, facing opposite directions.

The rules of the road didn't really apply anywhere in Iraq, but this road was total chaos. Vehicles on both roads were travelling in whatever lane took their fancy and in any direction they chose. We needed to take control of the situation quickly. Our Humvee was set facing the westbound traffic on the high road. About one hundred and fifty metres out, we placed reflective triangles and concertina wire at an angle to force vehicles to move onto the lower road, slowing them down as they approached the checkpoint. We shut down traffic going in the other direction too, although it was light, because nobody was in a hurry to drive towards the combat zone. This enabled us to focus on a single stream of traffic on one road coming from one direction and we quickly got the situation under control.

Out at the wire, Romero and Sergeant Harry were stopping vehicles. Using their basic Arabic, one of them would order the driver to stop the car, turn off the engine and get out while the other provided over-watch and made sure the next vehicle in line stayed back at least thirty metres. Rather than opening the doors and compartments themselves, the Marine would stand back and tell the driver to do it so that he would take the brunt of any blast caused by a booby trap. It wasn't going to really protect you if a bomb went off, but it was safer to make them do it than do it yourself.

Our other two Humvees had taken over-watch positions to our flanks for extra protection. I envied them. It looked like they were having a great old time over there while we sat out in the open, down the road from where a full-on firefight was taking place. It was highly probable that some of the insurgents would try to flee the city and there we were, sitting in the middle of the road, right in their way.

This was the most dangerous part of the operation. We were always careful to follow the correct procedure when carrying out vehicle searches, but there was not a lot you could do if a guy was intent on committing suicide and taking as many people with him as he could. Our only defence was to shoot them dead before they had the chance. And therein lay the entire problem. At what point would we know for sure that somebody was a suicide bomber? We couldn't just open up and kill innocent people but, in the event of an attack, we would have split seconds to make the call. As the cars approached, we constantly scanned the drivers' faces, watching the way they conducted themselves, how they behaved and how they reacted to us for any slight hint of a hostile intent. If they looked nervous or acted out of place, they were going to find themselves with the muzzle of an M-16 pointed at their heads pretty fucking sharpish.

If a vehicle bust through the control point, I was to take it out with my M-240 Golf while trying to avoid hitting the two Marines on the checkpoint. I had already agreed with them that they should jump into the drainage ditch to the right-hand side of the road so I could maintain a safe line of fire if I needed to shoot. It was very tense. I remained in constant radio contact with my search team and the other vehicles providing over-watch. Everything was running smoothly, although we remained on high alert and stayed like that for the next few hours. When it was time to swap places, Mendez and I switched out with Sergeant Harry and Romero and we became the search party. It felt good to be out and about on firm ground rather than propped up in the turret of the Humvee, an obvious target for suicide bombers.

I met a lot of terrified people down at the checkpoint that day. Most of the cars coming through were packed with large families consisting of many, many scared women and children. Although we were on edge, we tried to treat them with respect and dignity. We really had to be as nice as possible to these people, as they were genuinely afraid for their lives, and our presence wasn't helping one bit. I tried waving at the younger kids, who probably weren't fully aware of the situation, and some of them smiled back, but their parents looked at me like I was going to drag them out of the car at any moment and kill each and every one of them.

I felt so bad for them. When one car went through with a load of kids in it, we radioed back to Sergeant Harry on the gun truck and asked him to take out some of the sweets that had been sent to us in care packages from home and hand them out. Our best intentions backfired, though, when he stopped the vehicle a second time, stressing out the poor adults more than making the kids excited.

We were only supposed to man VCPs for short intervals each time to cut down on the chances of being targeted, but we stayed there for another four hours before we got word to resume our dummy patrols. Hoping again to confuse the enemy, we were ordered to drive around in the dark, switching our lights on and off on various sections of the road. The idea was probably to give the insurgents the impression that there were a lot more Marines on the ground than there actually were, but I bet they just sat up there in the city saying, 'Look at those fucking eejits. What the fuck are they up to?'

It had been a long, hot day, and we only got back to the FOB some time after 22:00. We were told to get some sleep, which wasn't a huge problem. In fact, it was the best order of the day.

On 11 October, we were once again awake before dawn and straight back out the gate before we had time to get morning chow. I was fecking starving and, in desperation, I ripped open an MRE looking for something half-decent to eat. I couldn't stomach the muck inside the horrible brown bag, but I managed to do all right with a few crackers and a sachet of peanut butter. We patrolled around the same area as the day before, but I don't remember anything in particular about the next eighteen hours, other than being thrown around the turret as we navigated the rough off-road terrain of the barren desert. We weren't exactly heading in any given direction, we just continued trying to confuse the enemy by bouncing around and around in circles. At one point, we stopped for an hour to set up a listening post–observation post (LPOP) in the middle of nowhere where the vehicles wouldn't be spotted and we could monitor the surrounding area. I got my elbow bandaged up where I had slammed it against my machine gun after we hit a hole at thirty miles per hour. It was bleeding and I also had a black eye for my troubles, but it was nothing to get worked up about. I wasn't going on any dates for the foreseeable future.

The day seemed endless, and I was ready for a good night's sleep and maybe something to eat when we got back. Completely exhausted, we only returned to quarters at around midnight to find out the chow hall had been closed down since the festivities kicked off a few days ago. It looked like it was going to be crackers and peanut butter for the time being.

It seemed like we were only just asleep when we were woken up again, but when I checked my watch, I realised it was more than a feeling. It was 02:00 – we had been in the sack for less than two hours. What the fuck was going on now? I wondered, as I bumbled around with my eyes half-closed, looking for my boots. The orders for the day were just to go out and continue patrolling. We were told that the idea was to tempt the enemy out to fight us in the open. Yeah, right! Wishful thinking there and, sure enough, another ten hours went by like a year. By the time we got back, we were absolutely drained and seriously pissed off.

We were all willing to get into whatever fight was going on, but nobody wanted to be the decoy patrol playing second fiddle behind the band on game day. My mates felt the same way, and there was a lot of grumbling between us when we got back later that night. The only thing keeping me going was the hope that I could soon get some decent sleep. We sat up cleaning our weapons and tried to eat some MREs. To my good fortune, I found a pack of M&Ms in one, which was like winning the lottery. It was definitely the highlight of my day.

Chapter 18

Another day and another pre-dawn mission. As we mounted up, I listened to the sound of the early-morning call for prayer from the many mosques in the nearby city. An endless day of patrolling beckoned, but at least it was one more down and one less I'd have to sit around without a pint.

We were sent out to the site of a reported skirmish where Marines had apparently taken fire but when we got there, we found that it had been nothing more than a few pot shots and nobody was hurt. We cleared the area, naturally finding nothing of interest, and continued on with the patrol.

By now the city of Hit was surrounded by Marines that had been brought in from other areas of operation (AOs). Overall, the situation seemed to be coming under control. Additional units were on deck, moving to deal with the threat in the city and as resistance was whittled down, the helicopters swooped in closer overhead, less concerned about rocket fire. There was some sporadic fighting throughout the town but as we were still waiting for our invites to the party, we pressed on with our tiresome patrolling. Some time during the day, I lost my cigarette lighter and had to use MRE matches to light my smokes, which is no easy task when you're sitting in a turret careering down dusty roads at fifty miles an hour.

The hot day gradually turned once again to night and, as the sun slipped under the horizon, I could feel the cold closing in. The nights were definitely getting colder. I still didn't have a turret strap on my vehicle and my legs were numb from standing up all day. Fuck, it was so cold. We rolled on into the night and some time later stopped to conduct some LPOPs. I stood upright in the turret scanning the horizon for movement. I don't like LPOPs. For the others, it was a chance to relax a little, but for me it meant keeping constant security in a static position. Nobody was going to swap with me and miss the opportunity of getting some rest.

We pressed on after our LPOP, but hadn't gone far when the vehicle started to veer off the road. We were all screaming at Mendez, who was so tired he had fallen asleep at the wheel. We almost went down into the ditch before he came to and snapped himself awake. It wasn't his fault, poor fella, he was just overworked like the rest of us. We switched him out to let him get some sleep in the back of the vehicle for a bit. I don't know what time we finished up, but after a few hours of sleep back at the FOB, we were back out again so soon it was as if we had never even been back to base at all.

On 14 October, we were told to block off all traffic in both directions on Route Saturn at an abandoned checkpoint, just north of the FOB. There were to be no exceptions to the rule – no one was to get past. The problem was that 14 October was also the first day of Ramadan, when people were trying to get home to their families. This particular roadblock was on the only major road connecting the northwest to the rest of the country and there was pretty much no alternative route nearby. Thousands of people would be prevented from going about their business on one of the most important religious dates in the calendar. I wondered whether our officers were aware of the impact their decisions had on the local population when they sat down to make their plans. We were never really told about why the plans were made – we didn't know how long the road would be closed for – we just followed orders.

We had our wire out and my gun truck was on the north end of the roadblock. We had also sent out dismounts to the flanks to secure our position from every angle. Then, we simply waited. Within minutes, dozens of vehicles had started backing up along the road as they tried to get through. Through loud hailers, we instructed the Iraqis, in Arabic, to turn around and go home, but many of them, thinking that it was only a temporary blockade, stayed where they were. Soon, there was a river of cars snaking back about three hundred metres. Many of the drivers were out of their vehicles talking amongst themselves. I was pretty sure they had nothing good to say about our roadblock. Every now and again, one or two of them would approach our positions on foot with their hands up to show they meant no harm. They demanded to speak to whoever was in charge and asked how long we would be there. All we could tell them was no, they couldn't speak to whoever was in charge and, no, we didn't know how long we would remain. They were pissed off and let us know they were angry by their facial expressions, hand gestures and the various comments they made in Arabic – but everyone on that road knew the score. Nobody was going to dare to try and run through the blockade, as they knew they would be taken down. We were able to maintain the roadblock without too much difficulty, but we did spend a lot of time staring through our binoculars at the Iraqis down the road, because you can never be too careful.

Some of them actually ended up sleeping in their cars overnight. At one point during the evening, a young couple brought a child up to the checkpoint, claiming their child was sick and that they needed to see a doctor. They wanted to go to a clinic in the city of Hit, but it was in an area where there was still fighting, so we turned them away. I offered to check the kid out for them myself, but they called up our corpsman and he took a look – though, to be honest, he didn't know anything about paediatrics. I don't know, maybe they were lying and were just using an excuse to get through. We were well aware that there was a half-decent medical clinic in the city from which they had come and there was no fighting there. Either way, there was nothing we could do for them.

In the meantime, we had been getting official reports that yet another battalion had been brought in to help put down the insurgency. We were totally pissed off that we didn't have a direct role in sorting this out. We understood that the everyday duties had to be taken care of, but this was our backyard, after all. The latest updates were that the remaining insurgents had taken over a mosque. They were probably thinking that the Yanks would never fire on its walls due to the potential negative political reaction that it could generate, but that wasn't the case. As sure as shit, they hit it hard from the air and took them down. I had been so worried about turning the population against us just hours before, but I have to admit it cheered me up a little to hear that the mosque full of insurgents had been taken out. It wasn't that I had anything against their religion, it was just that they continued to attack us and then seek refuge in the mosques. But from then on, as far as the insurgents were concerned, there would be no safe hiding place.

We were relieved later that night and pushed out on another patrol, returning hours later to the FOB, exhausted yet again.

After spending two sixteen-hour days manning the roadblock, we were finally on our way back to Al Asad. For a while, it looked like we would be staying put while the engineers moved in and erected massive barricades across the road to strengthen our positions but by the afternoon of the second day, they had taken them down again.

The only remarkable incident on 16 October was when Captain Fantastic arrived on deck and started bawling out some of the Marines in my squad for not wearing their helmet chinstraps while out in the field. I didn't even have my helmet on, but I was sitting in my turret shielded from his view and he didn't notice me. Just then, some Headquarters and Supply Marine standing watch on the roof of one of the buildings in the FOB just down the road accidentally discharged his 5.56 mm squad automatic weapon. The rounds impacted within thirty metres of us and Captain Fantastic. He went absolutely ballistic and stormed off to get on the radio to sort out the poor unfortunate bastard. Despite the fact that it was pretty close, everyone thought it was hilarious. Fucking Pogues, you couldn't bring them anywhere.

By now, the operation in Hit was officially over. The Marines were pulling out and regrouping back at the FOB. This was the tricky bit for us. There were still hundreds of cars backed down along the road. The Iraqis had stopped approaching the wire and had given up trying to get through, but when they saw the tractors moving in to take down the wire, they scampered to their vehicles and the race was on to see who got through first. It was like a scene out of *Wacky Races*. I had to pop a flare in their direction when they started moving towards us, otherwise they would have come through there like a herd of cattle. We couldn't allow them to get any closer until we were completely stood down and out of harm's way. We made them stay back until the engineers finished removing the barricades, then we all moved aside as the Iraqis started their chaotic rush down the road. They were driving on both sides of the road and on the hard shoulders. Traffic had been opened up on both ends of the roadblock and they were moving in opposite directions. When they met, all hell broke loose. There was a cacophony of noise as horns sounded and people started yelling at each other and shaking their raised fists out of the windows. We stood back and let them at it; we weren't fucking traffic cops. Then we packed up and left the madness behind.

Back at the FOB, we were told to stand by and pack up our shit. The mission was over and we were on our way back to Al Asad. At last! In minutes, we had all our gear in the back of the Humvee, ready to go, thank you, sir, and have a nice day. We were on our way to a good, clean shower and some decent food.

16 October 2004
Subject: I need a new job with a desk and a fax machine, I swear!!!
I'm writing this after thirty hours without sleep, so I'm kind of dazed at the moment … caught somewhere between a state of high alert and being as tired as a well-beaten dog.

I spent a long time writing an email earlier when the internet browser crashed due to the poor state of the computer. It's in a bad way, God love it, but after losing everything I had been writing for over half an hour, I was as mad as hell and called it a day! It seemed to sum up the week I've been having – somewhat interesting but, more often than not, bloody frustrating …

After a busy few days, my not-so-merry bunch of not-so-

Englishmen were called to a situation near the town of Hit out in the badlands. Reports were coming in that a bunch of Marines were trapped under heavy automatic fire and we were sent out as the cavalry to rescue them. We jumped in our Humvees and sped across the desert.

We pulled into our defensive positions at a fire base just outside the town and less than two kilometres away from the insurgents, who had some of our boys pinned down near a mosque. We listened to the sounds of the fire fight and we could hear the gunfire in the distance. I could feel a sadistic anger rise up in my gut. All I wanted to do was tear into those Ali-Babas and get rid of them and go home. I think Ali-Baba is actually the Arabic word for 'thief', but it's generally accepted as the name for a bad guy, so that's what we call them, Ali-Babas.

I was sitting there on top of the Humvee listening to the crackle of gunfire in the early morning. The sun was just rising over the hills and it was still chilly. Suddenly, the shooting stopped. There was silence.

We could hear a low rumble in the distance and then feel a vibration through our hands. Somebody had called in air support and that pissed me off even more. I mean, what could a $30 million dollar helicopter do that we couldn't with a machine gun, a few cases of Budweiser and some smokes? I only cost the taxpayer about forty dollars a day to be here.

And now here come the helicopters over the horizon. It's like being in a movie except I know people are going to die. The chopper roars over our heads and it sounds exactly like it would if you were listening to it over a top-of-the-line surround-sound stereo system.

In a flash of rocket fire, they take out the bad guys' positions. Suddenly, we see a tracer rising up towards one of the choppers – BIG FUCKING MISTAKE THERE, BUDDY! He probably only had enough time to say 'Oh sh**' in Arabic before he was cut into bits and pieces.

At last, we got the call over the radio that we were 'up'. I am pumped, thinking it's our turn to go in, only to be told seconds later that we are to stay out and patrol the perimeter. Man, it was the pits. We drove up and down empty roads like idiots while, in the distance, smoke rose from the rooftops as the choppers finished off the last of the insurgent strong points. We set up roadblocks to deny access to the city and searched the vehicles fleeing the action. We were hoping that we would accidentally bump into one of the bad guys who'd got lost. Maybe we would see one running away and catch him by surprise or perhaps we'd even get a wannabe Ali-Baba trying to join in the fun.

But there was nothing but scared families with young children trying to escape with their lives. I felt so bad for them. Frightened fathers were waving white flags from their cars. We pulled them over and they pleaded with us in a babble of Arabic. Some beat-up trucks had twenty to thirty kids in the back, from infants all the way up to twelve years of age. They must have picked up all the kids on their entire street. We let them through and some of them came back, even though they were obviously petrified, to get more kids out of the danger zone.

They were scared out of their minds, the poor guys. I felt terrible that, just because of me, a kid had to see his dad humiliated like that. It was kind of crap ... We tried our best to be friendly, even though we had a job to do. I was waving to the kids and giving them any sweets we had, the whole time trying to appear non-threatening. Some of the older ones were quiet and resigned. I think these people have been through this more times than they care to remember.

Anyway, if you were one of the blokes I had to search the other day, I'm sorry about that, mate, but I had to do what I had to do.

With the area secured for the time being, the following few days consisted of endless patrols, checkpoints, searches and more races across the desert to respond to brief attacks which turned out to be nothing but a two-or-hree-shot deal.

One, maybe two hours of sleep whenever it was possible and nothing but MRE (meals ready to eat) packages to eat. The crackers and cheese spread is all right and I found some M&Ms too – but other than that, they're cat. From now on, I'm on official MRE strike!

So, I got very little sleep, no food, no showers, sunburned a little, mosquito-bitten a lot. I started wondering what everybody else was doing at home, but that made me depressed so I tried not to think about it too much ... When we finally got back to base a few days later, we were greeted with the dreaded sign that lurks near the showers. Today, it reads, 'No showers, water conservation in progress', which means we basically have feck-all water and won't be able to wash the gritty sand from our bodies.

An hour later, I got called out for another mission with the bomb-disposal team to blow up an IED that turned out to be nothing more than a fucking pillow.

Dear Lord, I need a day off. What I would give for a trip to Dublin Zoo to see the monkeys or a bag of chips from Burdock's on Werburgh Street or, even better, a pint of plain in the Summit in Howth ...

So, that was my week. How was yours by the way?
Graham

Chapter 19

For a few weeks in October, I was locked into some strange male version of a menstrual cycle. I had wild mood swings, from periods of complete depression to elation. Eventually, it passed, but I think the whole situation was getting to me.

I was starting to seriously question what I was doing in Iraq. What was happening out there was not what it said in the brochure, the one about how we were rebuilding freedom in a country that had been repressed for so long. It had been some time since they'd declared the end of hostilities but, there we were, still operating as an occupying force in an increasingly hostile nation.

I think some of my Marine buddies were feeling the same way. We'd been lucky so far not to have suffered any serious casualties, but it could only be a matter of time. We heard of other units getting hit hard almost every day and while we didn't receive official casualty reports, we knew Marines were dying. And why? Wasn't the war already won? Didn't we get rid of the evil dictator and set up a democracy for a new, grateful nation? We were just living from one day to the next, hoping against hope that we got out alive. But as each day passed, the pressure mounted and it was getting harder not to dwell on the negatives.

I also started having nightmares. There's one where I'm about to get on the big freedom bird back to the States when I trip, and the pin comes out of one of my grenades just as a resupply fuel truck is about to roll over my head ... I woke up in a cold sweat and wondered about the significance of it all. I wasn't even close to going home. I had only been there two months – there was still another five to go. It felt like the odds were stacking up against me.

We ran a very brief QRF mission later and, as bizarre as it sounds, I can't even remember why we were called out in the first place. We mounted up and I said my usual Hail Mary as we headed out the gate, but I can't remember anything of any consequence after that.

18 October 2004 marked the first day of 'Map Week', when we started conducting mounted patrols. We were warned that the next few days would be tough but that there was only one way of finding out what it would be like – and that was by getting out there and dealing with it.

For a change, we had some guests with us – a team of Force Recon Marines. They were like our version of the army's Special Forces and they were pretty cool guys. While we mounted up, we talked about the various ins and outs of the job at hand and, more importantly, compared the going rates for strippers from state to state back in the US.

We headed out on our patrol just after daylight and, soon, I was engaged in deep conversation with our ride-along passenger, a Recon Staff Sergeant who was fascinated by the IRA for some reason. He told me he had once trained with a Marine from Belfast who promised to return to Northern Ireland some day to give the

English a really hard time. While we went about our business, he asked me about some lyrics to Wolfe Tones' songs and we talked about the Irish fight for freedom and about the war in which we found ourselves.

It was a strange conversation, but he was a good guy all the same and as we chatted, I suddenly had an idea. Maybe I could get attached to their outfit and do something other than patrol empty desert roads every day and night. It sounded like these guys were actually making a difference over there and I wanted a part of it. I asked if they needed a good machine-gunner and could he swing it for me to join them. He said he appreciated the offer but couldn't do anything for me. As a non-citizen, I was banned from applying to train with Recon in the first place, and there was another, smaller matter – I couldn't swim very well. Those lads were tough and part of the training involved some serious swimming. Then he asked if he could swap places and take over in the turret for a while, as he was bored sitting below. I thought he was taking the piss, but, sure as shit, before the day was out, I had a six-foot-six Marine Recon Staff Sergeant standing in my turret while I relaxed in the padded seat below. He looked like he was having a really great time and more power to him. I was happy to kick back and take it easy for a change.

The patrol was pretty uneventful. We made one quick stop at a RIE tent to conduct a surprise visit, but we didn't even find the guy who was supposed to be staying there. I bet he was slacking off work and still claiming his forty-hour pay cheque.

It wasn't a bad day, to be honest, and when I returned from patrol, I was in better spirits. I called my mother to say hello and told her the usual stuff, that I was eating and sleeping well. Then I called my ex and it was so nice and comforting talking to her. I realised talking to her that I wanted to grow old with this girl, even though I knew I'd probably already lost her. She was just a friend now, but she did give me hope and some purpose in life, and I was a stronger man for it. I really loved her, though, and would have given anything to be able to show her that. But, for the moment, there was nothing I could do. I was in Iraq, not there, and that was the reality of the situation.

The following day, I had a pretty easy day on base, attending to a few chores, and had even got a letter from my ex, which cheered me up no end. Later, we were watching *Godfather II* on my little DVD player when we got word that we would be going out later that night. Night patrol. Bollox. I was not looking forward to this. The general consensus was to sleep for as much of the rest of the day as was humanly possible, so we turned the movie off and tried to rest for an hour or so.

As night descended over the desert, we got our orders to move out. We mounted up, making sure to double-check all our equipment, as we would be out until the following morning. Special consideration was given to where particular items were placed on the trucks. As we would be operating under 'light discipline', we needed to know exactly where everything was. We had a prolonged pre-mission briefing, which was similar to the one the day before only, this time, we would be inserting sniper teams at key strategic positions under the cover of darkness. We paid attention about how and where this was going to go down, as we hadn't done it before.

As we passed through the gate and left the relative safety of Al Asad behind, I said my traditional Hail Mary. It wasn't as cold as previous nights for some reason, but it was particularly dark. The moon hadn't yet risen and it was kind of cloudy. Sometimes, on nights like this, the moon wouldn't come up until just before midnight and that made my job very difficult. The night-vision goggles needed some ambient light to project an image to my eyes but, in that level of darkness, I couldn't see much detail in the surrounding terrain, and we were basically operating blindly as a result. There are special infrared headlights available, but our vehicles weren't equipped with them. Instead, we duct-taped some infrared devices that were normally attached to rifles, onto the sides of the mirror mounts on the Humvee and made do with them.

The night pushed on, and it got colder and colder with each passing hour. Out on the road, there was little to look at – the desert was empty and desolate and we had a hell of a time trying to find our way as the landmarks were few and far between. There were vehicle tracks going in all directions, which just added to the confusion.

Now and again, we would stop to check our position via GPS and relay it on higher up. It was so quiet you could hear a wild dog howling in the distance, but that was all. The highlight of the evening was watching the odd meteorite burning up as it entered the earth's atmosphere. Seen through night-vision goggles, they blazed a spectacular trail over the darkness of the desert, truly making the night sky come alive. Then we were off again, moving quickly and making a lot of noise. Even though I was dying for a smoke, I dared not light up, as the flare from the match would clearly reveal our position. The heavy diesel engines could be heard for miles around, so our only defence was to remain invisible and hope that any bomber with an IED out there didn't have night-vision equipment. Without it, he may have been able to hear us, but with our lights out, he wouldn't be able to see us.

Near a city, we went off road and drove towards a palm grove in the distance. The grove was a bizarre creation in that barren part of the desert and as we approached it, I was overwhelmed by its very existence. The loose gathering of trees lay silent, enveloped by a low-lying mist that hovered about two feet off the ground. It was truly spectral and, for a moment, it reminded me of a scene from some Vietnam War movie. At the same time, there could have been bad guys only metres away and I wouldn't have been able to see them. It was spooky, to say the least. I broke out my thermal-imaging camera and scanned the surrounding terrain for body heat, but it came up clear. We drove into the heart of the grove and made a dummy drop for the snipers. They dismounted along with our own guys and conducted a short security sweep. Then they mounted up again and we drove on deeper into the trees. We dropped them off again in the same fashion but, this time, after we made final radio checks, they disappeared off to find a position that overlooked the city. When they were gone, we pushed on a little more and did one more dummy drop with our own dismounts. Once that was complete, we moved off about a click or so and stayed in place until we got word back that the snipers were safely in place. The insert had gone down well, we thought, and we were happy.

We continued on with the mission and I talked to the voices in my head for lack of better company, as it was impossible to communicate with my crewmates over the noise of the engine. I was in my usual position, facing backwards in my turret, keeping rear security and I didn't see the big pothole in the dirt. I wasn't holding on tightly enough and I almost got bounced out of the turret before I landed back inside the vehicle, flat on my ass. I went fucking ballistic and started shouting and screaming, to the amusement of the rest of the crew. I was rattled, but it gave us something to laugh about for the next few hours.

Night gave way to day as the sun started to break over the distant hills. We returned to base cold and hungry. We refuelled and then parked our vehicles back in the staging area and got some hot chow. I was bolloxed tired, but before going to sleep, I set about cleaning my weapons. I sat there thinking that we should get paid for overtime. I said to the other guys that maybe we should form a union that would ensure all wars ran on a forty-hour week with benefits like holiday pay, but they were too tired to laugh.

We had been asleep for no more than two or three hours when we had to assemble by our vehicles for a full equipment check. It turned out some retard had lost his night-vision goggles the night before and the officers wanted all the rest of the gear accounted for. Fucking idiot. He ended up finding his goggles, but since we had already started, the officers decided to continue with their check, going over the vehicles and examining our weapons. It took over three hours and by the time we were done, we only had forty minutes to eat before our mission brief for later that night. I felt like the walking dead.

We got our briefing and mounted up. The mission was the same as the night before. We would be inserting snipers again, but in a different location that was more in the open. The trick was to get it done early so the snipers would be in place before the moon rose. Nothing stands out about the rest of the night – it was another typical patrol. I was just happy to get back without being hit. Every day at our briefs, they pointed out all the mine strikes, IED finds and IED attacks in the area – there was almost one a day now. Chance had everything to do with whether or not we came back.

Fourteen hours later, we got back to the Ranch and I was so stupefied with tiredness that I didn't even bother eating. Instead, I headed straight back to my rack and fell into a fitful sleep.

The last two nights of Map Week – 21 and 22 October – were indistinguishable from one other. It felt like we were stuck in some weird night-time version of *Groundhog Day*. After sleeping all day, we would head out after sunset and patrol all night until the sun came up. Then, like dusty vampires, we'd flee back to our tin coffins to sweat out the daytime. It sucked, but at least it was getting easier as we'd adjusted to the new schedule. And we still hadn't been hit yet, which was always something to be grateful for.

On the second morning, we had been asleep just a few hours when they came around and woke us up again. 'What the fuck do they want now?' I grumbled in a daze as we were summoned to the briefing room. It turned out they had some good news for a change. Our night patrol had been cancelled and we were on our own for the evening. It wasn't like we could go anywhere or do anything, but it was great just to kick back, watch a movie, take a shower and write a few letters – not that anybody was writing back. I called my ex and got her voicemail, then rang home and got through to my dad, who was sitting in the kitchen in Dublin having a few beers. I love talking to my dad after a few pints – we have really funny conversations – and at that moment, I wanted nothing more than to be sitting right there with him drinking a few Heinekens. After talking for a bit, I hung up. Home had never seemed so far away.

The next night was another night mission to insert snipers. By now, there were teams hidden all around the area and we had to be careful to keep track of them all. It wouldn't have been nice to mistake them for the bad guys. I'm sure they shared our concerns for their health too, and they kept us constantly updated on their positions.

The team was in better spirits that night. I was glad that we had got to hang out and relax the night before; we'd badly needed the break. It wasn't like we were engaged in ongoing firefights, but it was equally draining just trying to stay focused while fighting the boredom of the nightly rut we were in.

Before mounting out, I re-cleaned my weapon for the millionth time. I loved that machine gun. I probably stank to high heaven and looked like I was homeless, but I always kept my baby well cleaned and lubed up.

A few hours into the patrol, we heard the sounds of heavy fighting coming from Hit. We weren't that far away and could clearly see the flicker of gunfire on the roofs and buildings near the skyline. A sitrep (situation report) came in that it was a stand-off between the Iraqi National Police and the insurgents and that we were to stand by. We waited for the command to go in but, once again, it never came. I really wanted to go in there and fuck up every little insurgent in sight, but it was not to be. We were totally pissed off. The city had been cleared just a few days earlier and handed back to the local authorities. Now, the insurgents had obviously moved back in but we were doing nothing about it. There were too few police in the town now and they weren't very well trained. Instead, we sat in the dark and listened in silence as they fought and presumably died.

We were back on QRF/EOD duty after switching around our vehicles. The Humvee we'd been assigned had nowhere to store the ammo cans for the machine gun, so we had to strap them on with bungee cords. Can you believe it? Our equipment was falling apart and we still didn't have any armour on three of our four vehicles. I wondered what the people at home would have said if they knew how ghetto we had become. Would they be pissed off if we told them how it really was and how many soldiers and Marines might still be alive if we had what we needed for the job? Would all the moms and pops and sisters and all the rest of them like to know that Marines were being sent out every day, 24/7, to clear roads of mines and IEDs in vehicles with absolutely no armour and which had holes in the floor through which you could see the ground below?

We stood our two-hour watches in the morning and later that night, but we didn't get one call-out, and we weren't complaining.

The following day, for some reason, our QRF/EOD job was reassigned to a Marine unit in light-armoured vehicles (LAVs). From there on in, we would be running all the patrols in our thin-skinned Humvees, which made no sense. The LAVs were far better suited for patrolling, as they had more armour. They even had night-optical equipment built in. But, of course, it didn't matter what we thought. That was the deal and we just had to get on with it.

Big things were afoot in camp. One of the three squads from our platoon was moved out, along with some other units from our company, to Haditha. They were assigned to another area of operations to free up Marines who were on their way to a big assault on Fallujah. I wasn't sure what all this meant for the rest of us, but I suspected that it would involve longer hours, more frequent patrols and whatever else was thrown at us.

Dawn patrol on 27 October and we were woken up at 02:30 for our orders of the day. They gave us the briefing and then realised they had woken us up too early. We were told to go back to our rooms for another hour and a half of sleep, so we went off to try and catch a bit more shut-eye and were woken again at 05:00. We mounted up on our vehicles and were pretty much ready to go when they remembered that there was a compass call from 06:00 to 07:30 and we couldn't leave the wire until then. Compass call was when a fixed-wing aircraft flew over the area with some form of high-tech gizmo that was supposed to set off any hidden IEDs primed for remote detonation. We had heard of this before, but as far as I was concerned, it was a myth. Whenever we were on patrol, we usually pulled off the road during the compass call, but not once had I ever actually seen a plane fly over, even at high altitude. After we had returned to our rooms for another hour and a half's kip, we were finally on our way.

As it was a day patrol, I could smoke to my heart's content. I could see more of the surrounding area as well and didn't have to wear those bloody annoying night-vision goggles. The day panned out like any other – immensely boring and of little consequence. We finished up at about 20:00 and were told that the next mission would be a night one for the following evening. Until then, everything was all right and I could chill out and dream of home.

Even though we were due to go on night patrol, I was woken up at 08:00 to bring a Humvee over to a staff sergeant in Camp Ripper to have an IED jammer installed. I left it with him and headed off to get some chow. I got a ride back to our camp and, a few hours later, I returned to pick up the Humvee with our new toy attached. The staff sergeant was a cool bloke and he told me everything he knew about the jamming device, which, truth be told, wasn't a whole lot. It consisted of an eight-foot antenna attached to a control unit and it was supposed to jam all radio and mobile phone signals in the immediate area so that Mr Insurgent wouldn't be able to set off his IEDs by remote control.

Unlike the mythological compass call, this sounded like it had the potential to make a difference. The sergeant told me it had come from a group of scientists who conducted all kinds of wonderful experiments and invented devices to make our lives easier. The idea was that we would test it out in the field and report back on how it fared. As it was considered classified, we would have to destroy it if we had to abandon the vehicle to prevent it from falling into enemy hands. It was actually pretty basic. It had an on/off switch and that was about it. We played around with it for a while, but we couldn't figure out a way to get it to work. The staff sergeant said he'd try to contact the people who sent it to him to get more instructions. Great. In the meantime, I was now stuck with a two-hundred-pound piece of shit equipment in the back of our vehicle, taking up even more room.

On the way back, myself and Peter went over to Mainside and picked up a carton of smokes and some other bits and pieces. We were supposed to get straight back, but we masked our disobedience by picking up ice at the ice bank and topping up with fuel.

Finally, we were ready for patrol and soon we were out on Neptune again. I was finding it hard to concentrate. I fought the exhaustion as best I could by thinking about the silliest things in the world. I recited mathematics tables in my head over and over and hummed the tunes to as many national anthems as I could remember. But my eyes were starting to roll, so I took off my raincoat to let the cold keep me awake. I had to rethink that strategy, though, when I nearly froze to death.

After a long, cold night, we were on the home stretch and had just passed through the gate when one of our vehicles broke down. We got the tow bar out and managed to get it over to Motor T (motor transportation). We took all the equipment out of it because you'd be mistaken if you thought you could trust anyone with your stuff. There was a saying in the Corps that there had only ever been one thief in the Marines and the rest of us were just trying to get our shit back. An hour or so later, we were eating chow. They also had some teabags, a rare luxury for me, and I enjoyed a nice cup of tea and a biscuit. Despite the shitty night we'd had, at that moment, things didn't seem so bad.

Minutes later, I was sound asleep and counting sheep in my dreams. I was probably up to about fifty-five when I was woken and told to report to Motor T for a class on engine maintenance. It was 11:30 in the morning. We reluctantly strolled over, only to be told to come back after lunch. Man, it must have been nice not to be in the infantry and have the whole day to get your shit together. So we headed off to get something to eat and returned at 13:30 to be officially taught how to check the fluids and make sure we had enough oil and all that other nonsense. This was after nearly three months knocking around the desert – all of a sudden we need a class? The kicker was when we were told that a driver was required to have a minimum of eight hours' sleep before he was permitted to operate a military vehicle. The whole class laughed out loud at that. What about the fourteen hours in the saddle we'd all become used to? And the fact that we could have been sleeping instead of standing there listening to this crap.

I was on my way back to try and catch up on some kip when we were told we were having a team meeting. At that stage, I'd pretty much decided to give up trying to get any sleep. It was fucking pointless. We were all called together and lectured about maintaining discipline. In particular, we were told to address officers properly when we passed them. In country, we didn't have to salute officers, but we still had to bid them, 'Good morning, Sir.' Apparently, some officer had complained that he hadn't been greeted in the proper manner. Sorry, Sir, but we were tired as fuck after hours spent freezing in the cold at night or sweating our asses off by day. We had other shit to worry about other than making sure some fucking officer's sensibilities weren't offended. I stood at the back throughout the meeting smoking a cigarette and drinking a non-alcoholic beer.

I hadn't shaved in a few days, let alone had a haircut, and I got a lecture from some random staff NCO, whom I didn't know, who reminded me that I was in the Marines and I should start acting like it. That pissed me off. We were over there trying to find the pricks who were planting mines on the roads. My shave or lack of one was of little or no consequence in my opinion, but I gave a good old 'Roger that, Staff Sergeant' while thinking to myself that some of these goons belonged in the Boy Scouts. The staff sergeant reminded us that we had a day patrol the next day and we greeted the news as if it was the birth of our first-born child. So what? Could I go and get some fucking sleep now?

Ding-donging along once again – cold in the morning, hot during the day and freezing again in the evening. I started out on the morning of 30 October with as many layers as possible on my body, but by 09:30, I was stripped back down to fatigues and body armour. At 18:00, I was putting all my clothes back on. There were a lot of holes and bumps on the roads and, because I travelled backwards, I never saw them coming. Every time we hit one, there was a sudden jolt and I braced myself for the bang of a landmine. We stopped a few sheep herders later in the day who looked right through us as we questioned them. Then we searched a few gravel trucks that were crossing Neptune to get to a quarry north of Wadi Muhammadi, even though we knew it was unlikely there would be anything in them. For one, there were never any attacks in that sector and, second, that was mainly due to the fact that the guy who owned the quarry was probably a pretty influential rich man by Iraqi standards. He was wise to the fact that if there were problems in that area, then his trucks wouldn't be allowed to operate. I suppose there was some sort of an unspoken mutual agreement. In the evening, another team found a big IED – consisting of several 155 mm artillery rounds – on one of the routes near the base, primed and ready to go off. They had EOD come out and it was destroyed. One that size would have obliterated anything passing by. It was a sobering thought as we headed back to base.

Chapter 20

Halloween. As a kid I had always enjoyed Halloween, but in Iraq, there wasn't much going on in the way of trick or treating. I had been thinking of dressing up as a US Marine, but apparently everyone else had the same idea. We did have some fun, though, with a new video camera that had arrived for me. I got some good footage of the desert and of Baghdadi as we passed through it and when we spotted some donkeys at the side of Neptune, the lads got out of the vehicle to pet them while I recorded the scene.

We were on our way to check out an old, abandoned Iraqi military airfield which lay off Route Saturn farther south. I was kept busy making sure the civilian vehicles stayed well back from our convoy by waving my left arm while holding my machine gun at the ready. A click or so along the road, we made a right turn and headed out on a small paved road onto the runway, which had been bombed to bits by our pilots during or before the invasion. The place was covered in old ordinance. We patrolled there every now and again to see if we could catch anyone trying to salvage explosives to make IEDs, although the

Romero and I pose under the Stars and Stripes.
We erected the flagpole, and raised the flag, shortly after
we arrived but, about an hour later, were told to take it down
as it would offend the Iraqis. I went back to my rack,
got a Jolly Roger and we hoisted that instead. Then, a
major came over to us and asked us what the fuck we were
doing and gave us a fifteen-minute lecture on the barbarism
of pirates. As he walked away, I shouted after him, 'Sir,
does that mean you want us to take it down?' He replied,
'You know what to do, Marine.'

Massive Marine Corps Sea King helicoptors on
the airstrip at Al Asad air base.

'La Guente' –
Sargeant Harry, myself, Mendez and Romero.

Stolen Iraqi National Police equipment which was recovered in a civilian vehicle search by Marines. Insurgents frequently posed as National Police which complicated security. In this recovery, many AK-47s and RPKs were seized.

The sun sets as we head off on another endless night patrol on Route Saturn.

The dusty main street of the town of Baghdadi – the scene of many of our patrols.

A series of pictures taken of an EOD team detonating
an IED that has been discovered hidden alongside
one of the military-only roads.

EOD sends
out the
robot ...

... which
detonates
the IED in
a controlled
explosion
and ...

... the
crater left
behind.

Two days before Christmas, we were surprised and delighted
to be issued a couple of beers. We drank them in our squad
bay and my rack is obviously the one under the Irish Tricolour.
It is the same flag I have flying outside my house today.

I am in the middle
of this picture,
kneeling in front
of an anti-tank
landmine that
we were lucky to
find in complete
darkness.

Driving
through a
palm grove
overlooking
the River
Euphrates ...
some parts of
Iraq could be
deceptively
tranquil.

This photo of me was taken as I sat in my turret waiting to go out on another mission. It was taken 9 January 2005 – a couple of hours before the worst moments of our lives.

This is the helicopter that came down low and dropped a huge net containing toys for the kids at the little school in the middle of the palm grove.

A Humvee at a security halt. This one is actually the 'Hooah' vehicle from the psych-ops team. A loud-speaker system that broadcast information about the election is set up in the turret.

Myself (second from the left) and several members of my squad, just minutes before we left FOB Hit after completing our final mission.

Vick's boy runs to embrace his dad when we
arrived back in Austin, Texas.

This is me sitting on a rock beside my kayak on Town
Lake in Austin after I got back from Iraq.

insurgents appeared to be so well armed I doubt they had to scrounge around for bits and pieces to make bombs.

The destruction to the airfield was impressive. The runways were covered in craters, some of which were more than fifteen metres across. We were admiring the damage when we got a flat tyre from a piece of shrapnel which was probably from one of our own bombs.

We didn't even have the proper equipment to change tyres and as we struggled with a fucked-up jack, we heard over the radio that one of the other squads from our Austin unit had been hit by a suicide bomber. A vehicle had been driven into their checkpoint and detonated and several of our Marines were critically injured. Bastards. We were just absorbing the news when we heard six loud bangs in the distance. Reports started coming in that the FOB at Hit, which was only five or six miles away, had been mortared yet again.

By now, we were all on edge, and we scrambled to change the tyre and get back to base. We were on Route Neptune, heading north to Baghdadi, when we spotted an Iraqi police car up ahead. We decided to stop them and see what they were up to, as they had no business being on this military-only road.

We were angry after hearing about our boys and when they pulled over, our dismounts all jumped down and roughly got the two policemen out of their car. They ordered them to put their hands on their heads and took their weapons. Almost all of the lads had had a run-in with cops at one stage in their lives and they took a perverse pleasure in searching the policemen and scaring them. The two policemen were surrounded by a gang of dirty, anxious Marines and from the looks on their faces, they obviously thought we were about to kick the shit out of them. It turned out that the policemen weren't the brightest crayons in the box and after subjecting them to a rigorous search, we let them go and told them to stay off the road.

Back at the main gate at Al Asad, some Marine was handing out lollipops and wishing everyone a Happy Halloween. We thought that was pretty cool of him. We pulled into the Ranch and asked about the Marines who had been hurt earlier that day. They were going to be OK, but it was a sharp reminder that the war was getting closer all the time.

The following day, we were on another night patrol to insert more snipers at known mine and IED sites along Route Neptune. There had been a lot of activity in our sector and it was hoped that sending out three or four snipers would solve the problem. At one point, a guy called Reilly dismounted from the highback when we stopped to drop off one of the snipers, as was standard operating procedure, but in the mix-up, his vehicle moved away, leaving him standing by the side of the road. His vehicle commander radioed back to us to pick him up as we were bringing up the rear. The only problem was that nobody told Reilly. I could see him through my night-vision goggles standing in the middle of the road not knowing what was going on. He couldn't see us and he obviously thought his Marine buddies had just left him behind like an unwanted puppy. Another patrol passed by on the road and Reilly was desperately trying to get them to stop as we looked on, laughing. I could see him waving his hands as if to say, 'What the fuck, man?' as they drove on into the night. Poor Reilly, he was pretty relieved when we finally got him on board and we joked with him for a long time afterwards. I have to say, though, that as I laughed along with the rest, I felt a cold shiver of fear run through me at the thought of being left out there in the desert all alone. When you were in the truck, you were with your mates and you were safe. Out there in the dark, you were on your own.

The rest of the patrol was uneventful, just another long night out on the cold road. As usual, I was thinking of home and about the things I wanted to do when I got back. We started playing one of our favourite games to take our minds off things – we asked each other what we would do if we could go back home for three days with unlimited money. It was easy for most of us – we'd get so messed up on the first two days that we'd have to go to hospital on the third day to recover.

I was looking forward to morning chow back at the base with a nice cup of Barry's tea. I'd had my ma send me over some teabags from home and wherever I went, I tried to remember to carry a few around in my pocket. I was pretty much the only tea drinker I knew in the Corps and the lads would look at me in disgust when I added creamer powder and sugar to my tea. They couldn't understand how I could drink a hot cup of tea, especially when it was 120 degrees Fahrenheit outside.

Later that evening, to nobody's great surprise, we were sent out yet again on what promised to be another seemingly never-ending night patrol. This shit was getting old and something was going to have to give. We were dog tired and it was hard to remain focused. I feared we were letting our guard down.

As we were going through Baghdadi on Route Saturn, a vehicle came up behind us at top speed. I shouted at the top of my lungs at the driver to get back while I trained my weapon on him. He got the general idea and was slowing down when another goon came along and overtook him. This guy was flying down the wrong side of the road towards us while I was shouting, 'Fuck off! Fuck off!' I racked my weapon to condition one with the bolt to the rear, the safety off, and braced myself. I was just about to light him up when, less than forty metres away, he jammed on the brakes. The car screeched and started wobbling all over the road as he tried to regain control. He got the message and stayed back, but then started following us at a safer distance. I was watching this idiot like a hawk as we went through the town. When we took a turn, he followed slowly behind, obviously tailing us. I was thinking, For the love of God, this guy must want to die tonight. I radioed in his details and continued to watch him until he fucked off around the next corner.

We stopped in the square at a housing complex by the school. I provided security from my turret while the dismounts got out for a quick walk around. About an hour later, we were back on Neptune when we heard over the radio that the Seabee team we had escorted to the water crossing a few weeks back had been fucked up by an anti-tank mine. Apparently, it was pretty serious and there had been injuries, but little else was known.

The following night, we were assisting army Special Forces and Marine Force Recon, who were conducting a raid on an internet café in Hit. They were acting on a tip-off that there were some bad guys down there and there was a serious briefing, as they expected trouble. With Special Forces involved, there was always potential for things to get interesting, and additional units which we would escort were on standby to bring back prisoners and to get the wounded out if things went wrong. We stopped about half a mile away and watched as the raid kicked off with a few flash-bang grenades that were designed to stun individuals rather than kill them. We waited for bursts of gunfire, but there were none. The Special Forces guys got on the radio and said the raid had been a blowout. There was nobody at the café but a few scared locals who had been happily surfing away online when the grenades went off. Obviously, someone had given us the wrong information and we ended up looking like assholes, but at least no one was hurt.

We headed back towards the base and were just in the gate when my Humvee broke down. We had to tow it back to Motor T and were issued a back-up vehicle that was in even worse condition than the one we had been using. The turret locking device consisted of a bent piece of metal that was tied on with a bit of string, but whenever we hit a bump in the road, the rod came flying out and the turret spun wildly around in circles. I couldn't believe it. I managed to rig up something better, but it was a small victory. The vehicle was a death trap. It had obviously been Frankensteined back to life too many times and everything about it made us uncomfortable. The fact that we could see the road slipping past beneath our feet through the holes in the floor convinced me we were getting fucked over but there was little that we could do about it – the powers that be didn't give a shit.

Chapter 21

A few days later, on 4 November, we were driving through Hit when we saw for ourselves the results of an ambush on a police station.

The entire station had been utterly devastated by RPG fire and was blackened and empty. We didn't know the fate of the Iraqi policemen, but it was obvious from the evidence around us that whoever had survived had fled and wouldn't be coming back. What little law there had been in the town – and there wasn't much to begin with – was gone, and any progress we had made in taking back the city had been wiped out.

As if to prove the point that we had lost the high ground, a few days later, Second Squad was escorting a Civil Affairs Group (CAG) into Hit when they were ambushed. The CAG was kind of like the military equivalent of a PR team whose job it was to go around telling the civilian population we were there to help them and that we were all friends. Then they would report back on their findings so they could be incorporated into the strategy on the ground. On this particular day, they were going into the town to set up an office at the town hall to conduct reimbursement operations for locals who had lost family members or property through hostile actions. Now, you have got to love this shit – they were going into enemy territory where we had no presence and where there wasn't even a single police officer still alive to announce to the citizens that, at a certain time and a certain place, the Marines were going to be handing out money.

Of course, the insurgents were waiting for them and the squad was immediately ambushed. Heavy gunfire was exchanged and they were lucky to get themselves and the CAG team out of there without any really serious injuries. Captain Fantastic did get himself hurt though, something to do with falling on his knee. He would not be coming back, so we were now without our platoon commander. The mission had been a recipe for disaster from the get-go and although the boys went out as ordered, they were nearly killed for their troubles.

A few nights later, we were staking out a train station that was located close to Route Neptune. It was suspected that the station was being used to observe military traffic on the road, as there was always staff hanging around, but we had never seen any trains pass through. Just after dark, we pulled up behind some high ground where we wouldn't be seen while the rest of the patrol moved off into the night, leaving us behind. They moved on a click or so up the road, making it appear that the entire patrol had moved on. I stayed behind in the turret with our new vehicle commander, Sergeant Kent, while Romero and Mendez trekked off to a better position from where they could observe the train station. They stayed in constant contact with Sergeant Kent while I relayed messages to the other vehicles over the main PRC-119 radio. We sat quietly in place for over an hour, but there was no suspicious activity, so we called in our guys and told the rest of the patrol to come back. A few minutes later, they roared past and we started the engine and fell in behind them.

We had gone just three or four miles down the road when, without warning, there was a loud bang. I spun around and saw a huge plume of smoke rising from the ground near where the lead vehicle had been. It looked like they had been hit by a large IED. I felt instantly sick to my stomach. My best mate Vick was in that truck. In a situation like this, there were security measures to avoid being hit by a secondary explosion, but things got a little confused. Instead of following our immediate action drills, everyone started talking on the radio at the same time. I was frantically scanning around waiting for a secondary device to go off. We were stopped near a railway overpass, the perfect position for a trigger man to hide, so I kept the machine gun trained in that direction as we moved up to assess casualties.

The Navy Corpsman was by the wrecked Humvee, looking bewildered. He didn't even have his medic bag with him and he was just standing there like he didn't know what to do. The guys were already popping out of the vehicle, a little shaken but otherwise OK. The side of the Humvee had several holes in it from the shrapnel burst, but it was still roadworthy. I got a thumbs-up from Vick and it was good to see his goofy head still bobbling around in the turret. Satisfied that he was all right, I turned my attention to finding the bomber.

It was a little late by now, I was thinking, as it had already been several minutes since the explosion and he was probably already on his way home, laughing his ass off. Sergeant Kent was firing illumination rounds from his 203 mm that lit up the night sky. We moved cautiously towards the railway line and drove under the bridge with our dismounts out in front looking for landmines buried in the dirt. On the other side of the bridge, I noticed a stationery vehicle about a kilometre off to the east. I racked up my weapon and requested permission to take the shot when Sergeant Kent told me to hold my fire. Under the rules of engagement, we couldn't open fire unless we had a positive ID. In other words, we had to wait until the terrorist was standing in front of us with a coil of wire in one hand and a battery in the other before we could do anything about it.

He took off in a cloud of dust and we barrelled off road after him. We made it all the way to the public road and hammered across the dirt with me bouncing around the turret, but we had no chance of keeping up in our battered vehicle and we soon lost him. We pulled over and one of the lads popped a flare to show our position to the others. I was so pumped up to kill that I didn't realise how tightly my hands were gripping the machine gun.

While we were stopped, a car approached. It was unusual for vehicles to be out on the road at that hour of the night, so we were immediately suspicious. We had our Humvee facing the approaching vehicle and, at a signal, we suddenly turned our headlamps on full while I popped a flare. Romero and Mendez put their rifles to their shoulders and took aim as I ordered the vehicle to stop. Our adrenalin was up and we weren't in the humour to take any shit. There were two people in the car and we screamed at the other occupant while the lads pulled the driver out. We had him face down in the road and Romero and Mendez searched the car, but it was just a very frightened man and his wife. It could well have been our suspect for all we knew, but without any evidence, we had to let them go. We sent them on their way and when another car came along, we stopped and searched that too, but it was obvious that we had lost our target. Convinced that the attacks had been co-ordinated from the railway station, we waited until reinforcements from another patrol unit arrived and then the lads stormed in to search the building. The few frightened railway staff were huddled on the ground, where they were interrogated. While we were inside, another gun truck was moving into position to provide support when it hit a big hole. The collision snapped off half the shaft on the front of the vehicle and the wheel just fell the fuck off. The guys were all mildly injured with just cuts and scratches, but now we had a vehicle out of action. We stayed put to provide security while everyone else headed back towards our position to regroup. We sent a team back to the Motor T in Al Asad to get a tow truck, but it took them over an hour to return because they weren't ready when the lads got there. I was really spooked. With the word out on the street about what was going on, we expected an attack at any minute. The Motor T finally got through to us and we hooked up the damaged Humvee. We were all a little bit nervous on the way back as a result of what had just happened and were waiting for an IED or landmine to go off but, eventually, we got the downed vehicle back in the gate.

It was after 05:00 when we all arrived back, tired and badly shaken up. We had just been hit by our first IED and some of the guys who had been in the vehicle were still dizzy and couldn't hear very well. Despite the shitty night, we had an hour of patrolling left to do and we were ordered to go out and finish it.

Chapter 22

After the drama of the night before, the following day – 7 November – we were promised a short day patrol but, as always, we were wary of such promises.

Off we went down the dusty roads on our day patrol, passing through a Marine Vehicle Control Point on the highway before heading east on nothing more than a goat trail. It wasn't a route usually taken by coalition forces and I was sitting in my turret wondering if that meant there was a better or worse chance of hitting a landmine.

After about twenty minutes of navigating the almost impassable track, I felt like Marco Polo on his quest to the Far East. The short trip was well worth it, though, as we moved down a hill towards a little town that was half hidden in the palm trees. The town, for a change, was striking, with sun-baked stone houses piled on top of one another and small goat pens made from branches and bits of wire. It was called Al Muhammadi, or something like that, and as they hadn't seen a coalition presence in some time, we attracted the immediate attention of the entire population. The older kids were hanging out all the doors and windows while behind their parents' cloaks, the younger ones peered at the strange sight. The adults themselves stared and some even waved cautiously.

Somebody had found a bag of toys that had been left in the armoury for some reason and the cargo pockets of our cammies were full of stuffed rabbits and ducks. We started throwing them to the kids as we passed slowly along the street. I felt really stupid when I threw one overboard and it landed in a mucky puddle. The kids running to catch it laughed and gave me a look as if to say 'you gobshite'.

At one point, we came to a stop. The town seemed pretty friendly, but I was scanning the rooftops and alleyways for any potential threats. By now, there was a crowd of children beside our vehicle trying to catch the toys. I looked carefully at each one of them, alert to the fact that someone could use one of the kids to carry an explosive device towards our vehicles while we were distracted. Then I noticed one small girl standing about twenty feet away on her own. She was about four years of age and was dressed in traditional Iraqi clothes. I felt sorry for her and I took out one of the last bunny rabbits from my cargo pocket and threw it as hard as I could so it would land at her feet. It bounced right off her head and landed on the ground. She started crying and the other kids were quick to snap up the toy. It upset me and I shouted down to my vehicle commander to get the fuck out of there, but we didn't move. The whole crew had seen what happened and they were laughing their asses off while I sat there, embarrassed. An older kid, who I presumed to be her brother, came along and put his arm around her, leading her away. I half expected to see a pissed-off parent shaking his fist at me, but none showed up.

Finally, we started moving off and my crew members were still laughing uncontrollably, which made me feel worse. Corporal

Townsend in the vehicle behind ours got on the radio and informed us that the girl appeared to have Down Syndrome. I felt like a right jackass.

We continued on with the patrol, stopping now and again to search a few isolated shepherd huts along the way, before gradually making our way back out into the desert. We spotted some civilian vehicles travelling on a military-only road so we decided to give chase. I was pretty sure the occupants were scared witless when they looked in the rear-view mirror and saw four tactical vehicles with guns mounted on the roof coming after them at fifty miles an hour. The cars stopped on the road ahead and our dismounts got out and cautiously approached them. I could see from my turret that they appeared to be just families with kids, but we were treating it very seriously, as there had been a series of IED, landmine and suicide bombs in that area in recent weeks. While the dismounts talked to the adults, two Marine Cobras circled overhead and asked if we needed any air support.

The vehicles checked out OK and once we established that they were just a few folks who had tried to take a short cut, we let them go. We headed back to base, making a few more stops along the way to check out possible IEDs, but they turned out to be little more than pieces of trash by the roadside.

When we got back, there was mail from home. I received some clippings from my mum taken from the Irish newspapers and a very special friendship bracelet from a young girl in Texas. I'd been getting letters from an entire class of sixth graders and had written back to them. The letters from the children were great and were very calming to read. They reminded me that there was still some goodness left in the world. The bracelet was handmade from red, white and blue wool. This little girl told me it would bring me luck and that she would pray for me. I tied it onto my wrist and vowed not to take it off until I was safely out of Iraq. It was a touching gesture and I wrote her back that very evening to say thank you.

The next day, we were aware that major military operations were kicking off in Fallujah and Ramadi but I, for one, was guessing that it would be another typical day for us, stuck out in the boonies. As it turned out, we were to babysit some Iraqi Special Forces soldiers out on patrol. It was to be an organised day trip to prove that we could work together and that we were one big happy family. It was also a face-saving exercise since the day before, an Iraqi National Guard (ING) unit had accidentally shot at one of our units which then, not knowing or caring who was firing at them, returned fire. It was all over in seconds, but not before one of the .50 calibre gunners fired eighty rounds of ammo which riddled the Iraqi vehicles and even knocked a machine gun off its stand. This all took place outside a military housing complex where the guards were based and, apparently, one .50 calibre round had gone through several walls and through a room where Colonel Fijada, who was in charge of all the local guard units, was sleeping.

Somehow, in all this confusion, nobody got killed and we teased the guys from the other squad when we saw them afterwards. When the so-called Special Forces unit showed up, there were only seventeen of them. The rest had already quit and, even as they were walking down the road, we could see others taking off. Apparently, they had decided that the military wasn't really for them.

I was introduced to a first sergeant who would be riding out with us in our vehicle. He was the liaison officer between the Iraqi unit and ourselves for the day and was a pretty cool guy. He admitted right off the bat that he didn't trust them as far as he could throw them. He told me that the unit had started out with more than seventy volunteers but that since the commencement of their training, the rest had dropped out. They had been paid around five hundred dollars in cash every month, which was an enormous amount of money in Iraq. After the first month, most of them had taken the money and run. They probably joined the insurgents the very same day after we had so generously helped to train them to fight.

With large military operations underway down the road, we were to conduct a show of force with the Iraqi soldiers. We rode out to the town of Baghdadi along Saturn and came to a halt just south of Al Asad road. I was keeping the traffic well back from behind the convoy while we stopped to let our dismounts and the Iraqi soldiers get out to ride the rails. This involved a column of troops moving on foot on both flanks of the vehicles as we made our way slowly along the street. Together, we passed through the town for several hundred metres, walking past folks in little stores and stands who were selling oranges, dates and meat. One driver who wasn't paying enough attention got too close behind us but a loud shout and an arm signal did the trick and no one lost their temper, their car or their life.

We mounted up and headed to the local police station, where the cops came out to greet us. They looked very happy to see us. They stood there in their oversized uniforms and Saddam moustaches repeatedly shaking our hands and saying over and over again, 'Welcome America. Welcome America.' After what had happened to their brothers in Hit, I'd say they were pretty fucking delighted to have us around. The Iraqi soldiers were going out on foot patrol, as someone thought it would be good to have the Iraqi people see their own troops out on the streets. But as they left the relative safety of the police station, the looks on their faces were priceless. God love them, they were terrified. I didn't much envy the Marine advisers assigned to go with them either. Now those guys had balls!

We remained behind at the police station in constant radio contact, ready to back them up in case they took fire. Loads of kids had gathered around us begging for money and sweets; one even wanted a smoke. Most of them were pleasant enough, but the bigger boys could be right pricks. One kid came over and started smacking the smaller ones over their heads with a stick and forcing them away. Then he had the cheek to come over and stand in front of me saying, 'Mister, Mister, you give me Pepsi.' I wanted to give him a kick in the bollox, but as it probably wouldn't do much to help us win any hearts and minds, I told one of the Iraqi coppers, who wasn't much bigger than the kid himself, to tell him to fuck off.

As we stood guard, I was thinking that maybe it was a good idea to have the Iraqi troops out on the streets. Perhaps I had been too skeptical of their ability and hadn't given them enough credit. Maybe this initiative would be the start of a new sense of direction and part of the resolution to the entire problem we were facing in Iraq.

Then, in the distance, we heard three loud bangs, one after the other. We radioed battalion for information, but all they could tell us was that there were no controlled blasts scheduled in the area. While this was going on, our dismounts had decided they'd had enough excitement for one day and were getting back into the vehicles.

We moved out to look for the Iraqi patrol and when we found them, they looked pretty relieved. We still didn't know what had caused the explosions, so we continued farther into the town and down narrower streets, expecting trouble around every corner. This was a deliberate confrontational tactic to provoke the enemy into fighting and I'll admit that, sometimes, we were desperately trying to get them to react. We were sick of being a moving target up on the roads and would have loved a chance to take these fuckers head-on.

But it wouldn't be that day. The patrol ended without further drama and we were back to base in time for evening chow.

The next day, we rode out with a translator and a Marine intelligence operator who reminded me of James Bond. He was way too softly spoken and polite to be hanging out with the infantry. When I asked the translator where he was from, he replied with a smile that he was from Michigan. He was actually from Iraq, but had lived in the US for twenty-five years.

We were on our way back to the police station where we had been the day before, but – no word of a lie – when we got there, we found it half-blown to pieces. It looked like the building had been hit by at least six RPGs. Outside, the squad cars were riddled with bullet holes and were burned out. The police stations were being targetted and systematically destroyed in each of the towns where we tried to impose our presence.

Some of our dismounts had gone in to check the building. When they gave the all-clear, I got someone to sit up in the turret with my machine gun while I followed another Marine into the building with my M-16, rifle at the ready. There was no sign of the policemen we had been speaking to only the day before, but the floor was strewn in paperwork that appeared to be important. I shoved as much as I could into a box and took it with me.

There were a lot of people standing around outside watching us as we left. I felt sure that they knew who had attacked the police station, although nobody was volunteering any information.

I showed the intel Marine the documents I had picked up and he got the translator to read some of them. Not only were they the policemen's personal files, but there was also information on known scumbags in the area. The intel guy said we needed to go back and get the rest of the material and a request was radioed to Battallion HQ, who told us to continue on with our mission. The intel guy was shaking his head. He said he appreciated me picking up the documents, but who knew what sensitive information we had left behind. There were details of the policemen who had disappeared during the raid and now maybe their families were in danger. But what could we do? We had to move on.

Further along the road, we stopped near a tiny town beside the River Euphrates. We set up a security position on the bank of the river and the children immediately started to congregate around us again. There was one kid in particular who caught my attention. He was the first Iraqi person I had ever seen with a shaved head, although it looked like it was a botched home-made job. When he spoke, he appeared to have some form of mental illness, but he also knew a few English words. He pointed towards a man coming down the street and said, 'Ali-Baba.' Some of the guys took him seriously and were about to stop the man for questioning when the young Iraqi turned around and pointed at a goat and said, 'Ali-Baba.' He was obviously disturbed, so we left both him and the other guy alone.

We had set up a roadblock on the access road to a narrow wooden bridge that was the only crossing over the river for miles. We were still allowing civilian traffic to cross the bridge, but only after we had searched their vehicles. There were a few Marines out in front, stopping the vehicles as they approached the wire, and we were taking no chances. This was when the job got very dangerous. I had my finger on the trigger guard, as did all the other machine-gunners. The guys who had to actually search the vehicles were the ones most in danger at that point. We were fully aware that the insurgents had no problem in killing themselves if it meant they could take a few of us with them, so the fact that those who were approaching us were, for the moment, sitting calmly in their cars didn't ease the tension.

All this time, the kid with the shaved head was still hanging around, even though we had told him to stay back and go home. At one point, he decided to help out and he stopped a car that was coming up to our checkpoint. To the astonishment of the Marines, he started searching the vehicle as he had seen them do it. We decided that the guy shouldn't be out there on the street and no where near our checkpoint as it was too dangerous and we made him leave.

Some time later, four toddlers, no more than two or three years of age, walked up to my vehicle holding each other's hands. They were beautiful little kids and my heart sank to see them. Here we were, heavily armed foreign soldiers parked in our massive green army vehicles on the street where they normally played. The kids looked up at me and smiled, showing off their gap-toothed grins. I pointed to a donkey in the field beside us and said 'donkey' in English and made a 'hee-haw' sound, much to their amusement. I repeated the word a few times and every time I made the silly sound, they laughed louder. They started shouting, 'Don-key, don-key,' and that made me smile. Then I got carried away. There were animals everywhere so I pointed them out and did the same thing for the goats, sheep, cows, dogs and chickens. It was hilarious and we were all laughing hysterically until I remembered that it was dangerous for them to be standing so close to me. The last thing I wanted was for them to be hurt if someone took a pot shot at me. I gave them some sweets and they walked off in the direction that they had come from, still holding hands and looking back at me and waving.

I felt really bad for those kids. Everything was a mess. The place could be so ugly at times, and yet, there were some really nice people hidden behind the ugliness. I didn't enjoy the feeling of being one of the occupiers who was patrolling these neighbourhood streets. I really felt for the people and understood their frustration at our presence and the situation itself. I hoped that we could somehow turn things around and leave the place better than it had been. It seemed a tall order, but it was at moments like that when, despite everything else that was going on, I really hoped our efforts would be worth it.

Back at base, we went through the usual routine of cleaning our weapons before we went to sleep. We were listening to some tunes on the armed forces radio network and during the advertisement breaks, there were sponsored messages from the corporations that were making a lot of money from this gig. They told us we were doing a wonderful job and to remain strong. Fucking propaganda. I stuck my middle finger up and pointed it in the general direction of the radio. 'Switch it off,' I told Vick and then laid down on my rack.

Chapter 23

10 November marked the 229th birthday of the Marine Corps, but for me, it was just like any other day out in the desert of Iraq.

I woke up at 07:00 and it was already bright out. I was surprised I had stayed asleep for so long. If nothing else was going on, there was still the noise of F-16 and Harrier jump jets screaming down the runway that would normally wake us up.

I had been thinking about morning chow when we were all summoned to the briefing room. There was a big flap on. We were on our way to the city of Hit again but, along the way, we had to cordon off a children's school in the small town of Um-Tibet. We had been told by intel that the school would be empty but, of course, when we got there, it was still full of six-year-olds and their teachers.

This was a difficult situation. There was nothing more likely to cause fear and suspicion among a population than to surround the local school where their kids were playing. Sure enough, the children's parents got wind that we were in town and soon they were congregated around the school as we were setting up security. Their stares bored into our souls as we ordered the teachers to evacuate the children from the building. It reminded me of a scene from a Second World War movie, with us playing the Gestapo rounding up the little Jewish children to be taken away. Some of the kids were scared witless and crying, but many others were eager to see the soldiers and get some sweets or soda from us. Our dismounts entered to secure the rest of the building and to ensure there were no terrorists hiding behind a desk trying to steal chalk from the blackboard.

One of the officers asked the principal if they needed anything for the school, in an effort to placate him. I'm sure all the teacher wanted was for us to go away and leave them alone, but he accepted the few boxes of pens, pencils and writing pads that had been offered to bribe him in return for his affection.

While we were giving the kids an early day off school, some of the Recon guys travelling with us went off on their own little patrol to familiarise themselves with the town. They got on the radio a few minutes later to report that they had stopped a suspicious vehicle. During the search, they'd damaged the boot of the car and the driver wanted some compensation – they wanted to know how that worked. They were told to offer him a pack of smokes and a can of Pepsi.

A few hours later, we left to continue on our mission to Hit. As we slowly rolled out, some of the kids crowded behind our vehicles begging for Pepsi – obviously the taste of a new generation – and I watched the crowd carefully. We had just pissed off a lot of people and, as the last man, I was waiting to get a stone or something worse sent my way. I had to shout at some of the kids who got too close and were trying to take stuff from the vehicle. I got myself in a knot, screaming and watching, expecting someone to take a shot.

We arrived at Hit. The sign on the way into the city said 'Welcome to Hit' in Arabic and English, but the English translation had been struck through. It reminded me of an Iraqi version of IRA graffiti written on a wall in Belfast during the Troubles. I couldn't help but reflect on the irony that, as a kid, I objected to the presence of the British army in Northern Ireland, yet here I was playing a similar role to that of a Para patrolling the streets of Belfast.

Everyone was staring at us as we drove through the town. It was a lot different from the other places we had been in. Here, there was open hostility and some of the people looked like they wouldn't be afraid to try something, even if it meant their own death. We headed towards the heart of the city, keeping our eyes open the whole time, scanning the rooftops, the alleyways, windows and doors, trying to spot a potential threat before it materialised and keeping all traffic well back.

We drove around on high alert looking for our objective – the town's fire station. This place was seriously dodgy. There was a reason why there were no other Marines or Iraqi police in the town. Romero was so pumped he was carrying an AT-4 rocket on his back. When we found the fire station, we set up a security perimeter around it and handed out some information leaflets to the locals. Everyone seemed eager to get one, but then they ripped them up in front of our faces and threw the pieces up in the air. I smiled back at them and applauded one guy. It caught him off guard and he made a stupid expression before walking away

We stayed in that position for what seemed like hours, becoming increasingly anxious to get the fuck out of there. The longer we stayed, the more time it gave someone to go home and get a plan together on how best to kill us. There were a lot of young men standing around within a stone's throw of our positions and they didn't look like they wanted to bring us out on the town. I couldn't really blame them; we were in their city and they had nothing else to do other than stare at us. We glared at them as they made cut-throat gestures with their hands. One in particular was staring at me and walking around to other groups of men and whispering in their ears, so I took a picture of him with the digital camera we carried and had my dismounts search him. He had nothing on him, so all they could do was tell him to leave the area.

Finally, the job was done and the dismounts climbed back aboard the vehicles. Soon we were on our way toward the square, where we would take another route out of town – we could expect to get blown to pieces if we went out the same way that we had come in.

It was pretty tense the whole way out. I fucking hated being the last man, covering our backs as we pulled out of a potentially hostile town.

We got out of there in one piece, but I think we were lucky there hadn't been an incident. I breathed a sigh of relief as we left the city behind and thought that at least it was another notch on the rope for me, one more day closer to home.

We would spend the next few nights dropping off snipers at intersections on Route Neptune on our patrols, where one or two IEDs or landmines were being found every day.

The routine was seriously starting to get to us. At night, we lived in a world of ghostly green illumination as we stared hard at the road ahead, trying to spot a landmine or a roadside bomb before it tore us to pieces. The constant vigilance wore us out and plummeted us into a state of hypnosis. We were zoned out and unable to concentrate on anything other than the ongoing quest to identify a potential threat before it found us. It was the most head-wrecking, draining work I can imagine.

On 11 November, we found a freshly dug hole in the middle of the road that was particularly suspicious. It looked like somebody had been disturbed in the act of planting a mine, so we set off looking for tyre tracks in the dirt. We just ended up going around and around in circles until all we could see was our own tracks in the sand.

We were frozen half to death and the sheer boredom numbed our brains to a state of near-vegetation. It was getting so cold that I was wearing as many clothes as I could find. I even pulled dirty T-shirts out of the laundry to put on over the clean ones. Despite having gloves, I needed to keep my hands between my legs to stop them from freezing. It was important to keep the circulation in my feet going too, so I did a sort of dance routine to keep the blood flowing. I called it the 'Daler Dance' and it was my answer to Michael Flatley. I had been trying to grow my hair out and sported an effort of a beard for a while to add to my insulation, but that wasn't how the Marines wanted it and I was constantly told to have my hair cut to US Marine Corps regulations.

Throughout the patrol, we tried to talk to each other to keep ourselves sane and awake, but it was harder for me up top. The voices of my team-mates were drowned out by the roar of the diesel engine, which I had grown so accustomed to it was almost soothing, and the strong wind at my back as we moved along the empty desert roads.

The night turned to day and as we rolled back in the gates, I put a smoke in my mouth to celebrate the fact that I was still alive. My body was shivering in the freezing cold. I wanted a shower and a bed and couldn't decide which was more appealing. A half-warm excuse for morning chow awaited us back at the Ranch, but first I sent out an email to explain to everyone at home that I was OK and nowhere near Fallujah; there were reportedly twenty-two Marines already dead up there. I thought about those guys and prayed for them.

I was also thinking of my ex in Austin because it was her birthday, but after spending over an hour in line waiting for a phone, I only got her voicemail. That got me down and I spent some time randomly kicking stones and pondering my life choices. I really didn't want to be there any more. We seemed to be getting nowhere. Every day I heard of another dead Marine – from a landmine, an IED or a random sniper attack. These people hated us and we weren't winning any hearts or minds. It all seemed so pointless, but I resolved to try to stop thinking about it so much because the fact was I was there and the war, if that was what you would call it, wasn't going away anytime soon. I needed to think positively and ignore the questions in my mind that called me to doubt my purpose. Then it was time for another patrol.

I asked the squad leader if I could switch out with Vick to be the lead gunner in the first vehicle. He said it was OK with him as long as Vick didn't mind. Vick had had a lucky escape when his Humvee was hit by the IED. I thought it was about time we swapped places. As the lead gunner, he had the highest chances of being killed. It wasn't fair to have my good mate up there on his own having all the fun.

The problem was that his vehicle commander and I didn't see eye to eye on some levels. I thought he was a bit lazy, while he thought he was God Almighty because he'd made corporal. In the Marines, when you're promoted to corporal, it's kind of like joining an elite section of society. In fact, it was considered such a high honour that it enabled you to sleep on patrols and discard rubbish on the floor and make someone else pick it up. It would have been funny if it wasn't so frustrating and dangerous. Despite failing to pass the annual fitness requirements, he got promoted partly because he had taken some home study courses. That was the way it went. One of the basic requirements for promotion is to read some textbooks like *Personal*

Finance for Marines. The system isn't based solely on merit, leadership ability or intelligence. You just took a test based on the book and off you went. Most of the time, the guys didn't even read the book, they'd just get a copy of the answers and spend two minutes filling in the little circles on the answer sheet. A lot of the other guys didn't care to much for the books and focused more on doing their jobs professionally rather than trying to get promoted, and they made excellent man servants who put up with the elite.

But what could I do? I had made the move and was now assigned to his vehicle. Although the transfer was supposed to be indefinite, I ended up switching back after a few weeks. In the meantime, the only option was to do as he said and not to speak my mind.

After my first patrol in my new position, His Almighty ordered me to clean out the vehicle. I peered inside and there was a pile of rubbish around his seat. The fucking audacity of this guy – now he had me picking up his rubbish for him. I asked the other guys in his crew if this was part of their daily duties and they told me that they had to do everything. By the time we had finished restocking water and chow, the guy was already asleep. Great leadership there, boss, not exactly George Washington on the River fucking Delaware.

On 17 November, we had two main stops – one at a water treatment plant and the other at a sewage treatment plant, both in the town of Baghdadi. To look at it, you would never have guessed they had any services in that one-horse town but as it was a Sunni town, it was well equipped because Saddam liked to look after his own, or so it seemed to me anyway.

We were greeted with the usual stares and frowns that we had become accustomed to. Some of the kids gave us the thumbs-down, which pretty much let us know they hated the sight of us, while the younger ones waved out of innocence. The men would just stand farther back, watching our every move. They didn't wave or say anything; they didn't move at all. They just looked at us, almost through us, it seemed, while the women quietly disappeared. The main street of the town was filled with tiny little shops selling everything from sweets to household goods. There were workshops and repair yards dotted along the road and whenever we passed, the welders and mechanics downed their tools and stared. Only the dogs acted like everything was OK. It was an eerie feeling, like when you walked into a bar and everyone turned around to look at the stranger standing in the doorway.

We had to step up our vigilance when coming into a town and we couldn't relax for a moment – God only knew what was hidden around the next corner. The gunners constantly kept their eyes on the rooftops, the alleyways and windows as we passed down the roads and lanes.

We visited both sites as planned, and the CAG team got out and visited with the workers. I remained in my turret keeping watch and wishing they would hurry up. I was pissed off in that lead vehicle. The commander somehow managed to spend more time on patrol passed out asleep than awake. I couldn't believe that my patrol leader let this shit fly. I wished I was back with my own guys. Despite our differences, we worked well together as a team.

Back at base later that day, I decided to clean my weapon before I ate. I was just about finished when my new vehicle commander came over and told me he wanted to inspect my weapon. I told him it was fine, but he insisted and I had to dismount it and take it down from the roof so he didn't have to get up on the truck to look it over.

I laid it on the hood and he opened it up, rubbed his fat finger along the inside and showed me the results. Yep, there was grease on the inside of my machine gun. I'd just put it there. Machine guns needed grease. I kept that weapon in tip-top shape and everyone knew I spent more time cleaning it than anything else. We had an argument about it, but I failed to convince him and so I found myself sitting up on top of the vehicle removing all the grease. After filling his belly at the chow hall, he came back over to reinspect it. He ran his finger along the inside once again and this time it met with his approval and he fucked off. Two minutes later, I was reapplying the grease and was right back where I'd started, except now it was too late for chow and that pissed me off no end.

A couple of days later, I found out that some of the other guys from our unit got hit with a landmine in the neighbourhood. The force of the blast caused their Humvee to flip over onto its roof. The gunner was in critical condition and had been medivaced to Germany. It really sucked to hear that and we prayed that he would make it.

We were hearing that the Marines were getting hit as often as six times every day in this one province alone. We were hurting badly, but there seemed to be no plan to do anything about it. The emphasis was still on keeping the supply routes open so we could deliver construction supplies to the big bases we were building in Iraq. Once again, I found myself questioning my reasons for being there. I had come to Iraq to fight, to get revenge on the terrorists who had attacked America. This was not what I had signed up for. We were relagated to the role of a glorified police force that was trying – and failing – to bring security to the region. I wasn't helping the Iraqis and nobody else seemed to be either. There were no police left in Hit, Karabash, Habbaniyah, Haditha or any of the other towns around there and we didn't even enter those places any more. Sometimes at night, when we were sitting out on an operation, you could hear gunfire in the distance coming from the cities. It was beyond me what was going on, but one thing we knew for sure was that the people there were on their own.

The following night, we were out patrolling again but any enthusiasm we had left for this job was gone. All that Rambo mentality had been left behind at the airport in Kuwait. We had no ambition to resolve any issues now. It was just a matter of passing the time and all our will power was concentrated on staying alive until we got to go home. We tried to stay focused on the job. The preparation for each patrol was the same. We'd sit through another long briefing before walking out to the vehicles. As the crew climbed aboard, I mounted up on top with my machine gun. Almost in a trance, we would go through all the checks and make sure everything was good to go.

We tested the radios, adjusting frequencies and calling in our call signs. The gunners examined their weapons, ensuring they were clean and lightly lubed and checked they were fully functional by dry firing them. The drivers examined the vehicles' fluid levels, the fuel and temperature gauges. Do we have enough ammo? Do we have enough water? Enough food? How about smokes? Count the signal flares and check the thermal-imaging system. Are there spare batteries for the night-vision equipment? More smokes, water, Cokes and, of course, a shovel. You name it, and we had it on board.

We were ready to roll, but it was only when the engine started that we snapped fully awake. I put everything that was happening there and any thoughts of home out of my head. As we approached the front gate, we loaded our weapons. At that point, it was game on and only God knew what would happen next.

Driving along Route Neptune on another night patrol, it was difficult not to get complacent, because we knew that when we did, it would be our last day on this planet. I kept a sharp lookout for suspicious shapes on the road ahead, but it was getting harder to see what might be waiting for us. The road wasn't designed for the huge convoys of trucks that went up and down it all day and night and it had deteriorated further now that the wet and cold weather had pushed in. Entire sections of it were fragmented, cracked or simply washed away and this worried me, as it created the prime conditions in which to plant a landmine. At that rate, it would soon become impassable.

Eleven hours later, and another patrol had come to an end. It passed without any incident and that was a victory in its own right. We were all extremely tired and hungry, but that was good. It meant we were still alive.

Chapter 24

21 November 2004

Way to go for the heroic freedom fighters fighting the Yankee oppressors in Iraq this week ... They abducted and then shot a sixty-year-old Irish woman, Margaret Hassan, in the head. She had spent thirty years helping the poor in Iraq. She was also married to an Iraqi man.

It would appear that these savages believe it is not only the Americans who are oppressing them, but also elderly aid workers who are actually trying to help their children. Tell me I'm wrong when I say we are not dealing with a rational foe here.

I am being moved to a forward operating base somewhere in the boonies in a few days' time – I'm not supposed to tell you where it is, not that it really matters, as it's so remote you couldn't even find it on a map.

As I don't expect there will be any phones or email out there,

I won't have access to the outside world anytime soon, so this will be my last message for a while.

Graham

We were told to begin packing our gear as we would be moving out to a place called Haditha Dam in a few days. I didn't know much about it other than that it couldn't be good. It's in the middle of nowhere and facilities were bound to be sparse. On the plus side, more than half the company had been up there since they replaced another unit that was being sent to Fallujah, so at least we'd be a happy family once again and I'd get to see some of my mates.

We were more upset to find out that some Air Support Marine personnel would be moving into our living quarters. We had been ordered to sell all our acquired electronic equipment to them, as we wouldn't be needing it where we were going, but the idea of these rear-echelon fucks getting an easy bargain out of us before we were kicked out angered me. When one guy knocked on my door and offered me twenty dollars for our microwave and television, I told him I would rather put my fucking K-Bar knife through them than sell them to him. He gave me a weird look and told me I wouldn't get a better offer, but I told him to fuck off out of my face. I had bought that gear with my own hard-earned money out on patrol and rather than let him have it, I got a strange satisfaction from driving my knife repeatedly through the front door of the microwave.

The following morning, we were out bright and early on patrol. Along the way, my squad leader called me on the inter-squad radio I had strapped to my head and told me to fire a flare at a vehicle that had pulled out into middle of the road ahead of us. I stood there in the turret with a smoke in my mouth and waited until we caught up to the car, then I calmly aimed the flare at it and fired. It went off like a rocket and flew straight over the guy's roof. He immediately panicked and drove straight off the road. The flare whooshed past and almost hit some poor innocent fella carrying a few bags of fruit and nuts. It impacted about fifty feet away from him and burst like a firework into thousands of bright sparks and trails of green smoke. I'm sure yer man soiled himself. We roared past and left him lying in the dust with all his oranges and dates rolling around. I felt a little bad, but at the same time, I was responsible for the lives of the Marines in my vehicle and I was going to do whatever I had to do to protect them. If that meant spreading the message aggressively, so be it.

Further along, we pulled up outside a small town as a funeral procession made its way through the streets. We didn't want to interfere or get surrounded by all the people, so we stopped and watched from a distance. I couldn't help but wonder about how that person had died. I hoped it wasn't as a result of our handiwork, because we were already unpopular enough as it was. If the mourners decided to get angry, we'd be in a bit of a pickle.

Two Marines from a Human Exploitation Team (HET) who we had brought along dismounted and went ahead to talk to the locals so they could ask them about their problems and if they had clean water and electricity, and so on.

As usual, a bunch of kids grouped up near our vehicles and started asking for sweets. They could speak pretty good English, which was always surprising, as I had been led to believe that these people were very poor and had no education. We tried to keep them as far back as possible from the truck, as it was a huge target and I'd have hated for innocent kids to get hurt if we were attacked. We also had to be careful because one or two of them would chance their arm and try to take something from the truck. They would even try to pull stuff out of the pockets of the Marines who were dismounted, holding security. I knew guys who'd had everything from sunglasses to knives just walk off on their own. No big surprise there, I guess. I know I would have jumped at the chance to nick a few grenades or a rifle when I was a kid.

We had razor wire strung out across the road and as we watched, one poor old man came walking along who obviously hadn't seen it. We were all shouting at him to stop, but he walked into it and cut up his fingers as he tried to untangle himself. I bandaged him up as best I could and we let him on his way.

When the HET team was happy they'd accomplished everything they needed to do, we mounted up in the vehicles and headed back to Al Asad. It was raining heavily as we approached the base and the temperature plummeted. I had forgotten to bring any rain gear and got a good soaking huddled up in the turret.

A few days later, we were up at 04:45 for the, by now, standard pre-patrol briefing. This was the same every day, except this time we were told to be on the lookout 'for a man wearing a beard and dressed in Iraqi clothing' who intel had reported as dangerous. Great. Armed with that knowledge, we could set off and arrest every second male in the country.

It wasn't until later that morning that somebody realised it was 25 November – Thanksgiving – although we didn't really have that much to be thankful for. As an Irishman, Thanksgiving never meant that much to me anyway, but I felt sorry for the lads as their thoughts turned to home and sitting around watching American football and eating home-cooked food with their families.

Our route took us through some guy's farm and as we drove across his fields, we approached a series of irrigation pipes that had been carefully laid out. We debated about going around so we wouldn't damage them, but our orders were to carry on, so we drove over them, flattening them. We more or less ruined the entire irrigation system and all we could do was shake our heads at the thought of the poor farmer's devastation when he saw what had been done. Later, when we passed some goat herders on the way back home, we gave them some water, a couple of MREs and shook their hands. We got our pictures taken with them, hoping they weren't the same guys who owned the farm we had just trampled on.

Back at base, we were told our orders had changed and we would be moving out to FOB Hit at 04:30 the following morning. We were ticked off because there was a Thanksgiving party down at the chow hall. While everyone else was busy tucking into a real turkey dinner, we were lugging all our gear onto the vehicles and ended up with nothing to eat.

By first light the following morning, we were mounted up on our vehicles ready to move out to our new home. I would miss Al Asad. Even though it wasn't much to look at, I had grown used to it over the past three months and we had made it our own.

We were travelling north to conduct a forward security sweep ahead of a convoy of equipment that was moving up to the FOB to support our unit. Put simply, this meant driving along to flush out any hidden insurgents or roadside bombs. Despite the many layers of clothes I was wearing, including four undershirts that were all filthy dirty, I was shaking with the cold in the morning air.

We had been told to keep a lookout for a red Opal vehicle on the roads. That was pretty funny, considering every fourth or fifth vehicle we passed seemed to be a red Opal. I rolled my eyes at how stupid the order was and as we made our way along the public highway, I pointed out each one until everybody was sick of hearing me shout,

'There's another one. And there's another one right there. And there's another one.' Eventually, they told me to shut up.

I was back in my usual position maintaining security to the rear and was using colourful language and hand gestures to keep back the cars that were following us. Up ahead in the lead vehicle, Vick had a much harder job to do, as he had to deal with all the traffic approaching from the front. He was waving the drivers off the road onto the hard shoulder as we approached and most of them immediately understood that they had to get out of the way. We were on high alert, as Sargeant Harry, one of our former squad leaders had been hit the night before. He was blessed that his vehicle actually had armour and everybody got out with just a few bruised limbs and egos. I was relieved to hear he was OK, but the fact that he had only escaped with his life because his vehicle was armoured was a salutary reminder of our own poor protection.

When we arrived at the FOB in Haditha in front of the resupply convoy, we quickly refuelled, turned back and headed south to FOB Hit, as the plan had changed. We were only a mile or so away from FOB Hit when we were told not to approach, as they had just taken enemy fire. Some welcoming committee, I thought to myself. Not a good sign. As we drove around waiting for the all clear, we spotted a pick-up truck pulled over to the side of the road. As we passed, I noticed that two men were sitting comfortably in the cab while in the bed of the truck their two women huddled up, freezing. I shook my head, laughing at the Iraqi men's idea of chivalry.

After getting the green light, we proceeded into FOB Hit, where we made ourselves as comfortable as possible. It hadn't improved much since our last visit. The food in the chow hall was basically the contents of an family-sized MRE splashed onto a plate. I had no idea what I was eating, but it filled a void. Then we were assigned our new quarters, which was basically the same large room we had stayed in before with slabs of concrete to sleep on. It reminded me of a morgue and at one time I think it may have been, but we were grateful that it at least had electricity.

The following day, 28 November, we escorted a Civil Affairs Group (CAG) team into Baghdadi, where they visited a medical clinic. We were positioned on the south end of the street, where we scanned the surrounding rooftops and the road for possible danger. We had wire out about fifty metres in front and this was the kill line. If a car drove past that point, I was to shoot as much and as fast as I could to stop him before he got to us. There wasn't much margin for error and I hoped I would have enough time to take out an attacking vehicle.

I was distracted by the usual gang of kids hanging around our vehicle when, from around a bend in the road, a vehicle came tearing along way too fast. Within a split second, all of my crew, including myself, had our weapons raised to our shoulders and aimed at the car. We were about ready to pull the triggers when the driver realised the danger at the last moment and jammed on his brakes. He skidded to a stop only metres away from the kill line. The only thing that kept that guy alive was the fact he reacted as quickly as he did. A second later, and we would have wasted him and I would have killed an innocent man. He threw his arms up and started shouting at us in Arabic while we kept our weapons at the ready. Eventually, he backed off and turned around.

The CAG team emerged from the clinic some time later, reporting that the mission had been successful, and we made our way back to base. Along the way, one of our vehicles got stuck in the mud. It was sunk so deep that the base of the vehicle was flush with the ground around it and you couldn't see half of the wheels. We didn't want to risk getting another Humvee bogged down trying to pull it out, so we waited until a heavy military convoy came along and asked them for help. They used one of their seven-tons, a beast of a truck, to get our Humvee out. After thanking them, we were on our way again. An hour later, we heard that the very same convoy had been badly hit by an IED. There was no word on casualties, but I wondered if it would have been us had we not been delayed.

Back at the FOB, I was almost done cleaning my weapons and was looking forward to some well-earned sleep when the lads walked in and told me we had to go find some guy's pistol that had gone missing while we were out on patrol. In Iraq, you could buy a pistol like that for $20, but because it was American government property, we had to retrieve it. In disbelief, we mounted up to look for it, so exhausted we were stumbling around like we were drunk.

We were going along this track and that track in the dark, scratching our heads and wondering where we were. At night, it was an entirely different-looking world and we had a hell of a time trying to find the exact routes that we'd taken earlier that day. I almost fell out of the turret, I was that tired. The lads let me get in the back, and put a replacement up in the turret. I slept like a dog as we bumped down the road.

A little while later, one of the lads fell asleep behind the wheel and nearly drove off a fifty-foot bridge which had no side barriers. They woke him up just as the vehicle was a few inches away from going over the side. They would have had no chance if they had fallen that far and there would have been another six folded flags for the folks back home.

This shit was getting dangerous and it was fast becoming time to call it a day – and then vehicle number two broke down. We radioed back to the FOB and requested permission to tow it in. Finally, somebody saw sense and agreed to let us come back. We were on our way when we got word over the radio that some guys from our own company had been hit by an IED while out on another mission. We knew all of them well and we were dejected to hear that some of them had been badly hurt. Two had suffered shrapnel wounds to their heads and faces and had been medivaced out. When the survivors arrived back on base later, we listened to their accounts, which were pretty graphic, and then sat there in disgust at the situation, hoping that the two lads would be OK.

On radio watch the next morning, I sat writing letters to my mother and ex-girlfriend, who was good enough to still write to me. Writing to them really helped me stay in touch with reality. It helped me escape the rut of being a nobody in a situation I just couldn't figure out. As I sat there, I thought a lot about my life and all the good experiences I'd had, both big and small, and hoped I would live longer to experience more. When your life is on the line, you tend to think about some of the best moments and some of the regrets too. I recalled the buzz of getting picked up at Heathrow airport by a driver in a suit holding a placard with my name on it and how I quit that job; my first kiss and how I messed that up; my first fight, which erupted over some kid calling me fat even though I wasn't; and my first pint in a pub with my oldest brother.

They were just dreams now, part of a distant past that was once my youth. I didn't know what I was any more. I didn't know who I had become or what I was doing. In a way, every day was just like the last and there was nothing but these memories to keep me going. I wondered what it would be like to go home and live a normal life. I hoped that some day I might fall in love, maybe have a dog and even a kid. I dreamed of fishing off the coast of Ireland and of smelling the sea and tasting the salt from the sea spray. Funnily enough, more than anything else, I fantasised about sitting in my parents' kitchen eating a bag of chips from the chipper around the corner and drinking a nice cup of tea.

After a while, I tried to think about something else because dwelling on the memories of home was bringing me down. I was glad to be distracted by the lads starting to wake up. We waited for the chow hall to be done with 'officers only' hour so we could go eat some rubber morning chow. The officers ate at different times to the enlisted men so they didn't have to share the same room with our stinking bodies. When we walked in, we were told by the so-called cook that there were only leftovers and we would have to eat them outside as the officers were still eating. I wished I could have taken him out on night patrol and then told him he couldn't eat when he got back. I think he would have been a little more sympathetic. Later, my squad leader informed us that we were needed for a day mission to drop off some Marines to an outpost. Here we go again.

Chapter 25

We were only just back the following day and still working on the vehicles and cleaning our weapons when mortar rounds started raining down out of the sky.

The ground shook and our ears hurt from the enormous thud of successive impacts. We had heard mortar fire a lot around this FOB, but these ones actually felt very close. Without having to be told what to do, we were already running into our quarters trying to put on our flak jackets and Kevlars. I ran so fast and in such fear that I didn't notice I had scraped all the skin off my hand on the wall as I fled up the stairs.

When the mortars fell silent, a position on the suspected launch site was located and they called, 'QRF up!' We dashed back to the vehicles in a hurry, as we were now on the offensive and we were under way in less than a minute. My heart was racing as I tried to stay in the bouncing turret and load the machine gun at the same time. Maybe this would be my big opportunity to finally shoot one of these fuckers.

There was a farm located to the southwest of the FOB and that's where the mortar fire had apparently come from. The farm was surrounded by a heavy tree line and subdivided into sections by other trees and an orchard. There was also a bunch of clearings that were being prepared for the spring season.

When we got there, we were told to make sure it was clear. The dismounts poured out of the Humvees and took up positions while I and the other gunners provided fire support. The boys were moving pretty well and using good cover and concealment tactics as they advanced. They kept in constant contact with the fire teams providing cover and I listened to the orders as they moved forward: 'Fire Team One, prepare to rush … RUSH!' They called cadence to themselves to measure their advance. In their heads, they would chant, 'I'm up, he sees me, I'm down,' while they ran and hit the dirt. Then they would hold security while the flanking fire team pushed past them, repeating the move.

Beyond the orchard, the land opened out and we pulled the vehicles together in a defensive position while the boys mounted up. There was a farmhouse in the middle of the property and we headed for it. We set up a security perimeter around it when we got there and some of the Marines burst through the door and brought out the people hiding inside. They were searched and questioned as other Marines went through the house from top to bottom. Nothing was found and, of course, the farmer and his family said they knew nothing.

With the search of the farm complete, we conducted a sweep through the rest of the area before moving a little farther south, where we set up another defensive security position and waited for the higher-ups to decide what they wanted us to do. I had my binoculars out, hoping I would catch one of the bad guys making a mistake, but

I didn't see anything suspicious. Everything was quiet for a couple of minutes and then we heard two or three very loud thumps nearby. It sounded like outgoing from just over the other side of a railway line that ran along the top of a berm to the west of the farm. With our blood up, we rushed towards the berm, expecting to have the insurgents cornered.

But as we closed in, the lads in the lead vehicle realised it wasn't outgoing fire, it was incoming and that the berm was the only thing giving us any cover. The rounds started landing even closer to us, but I couldn't help but laugh as we turned tail and beat a hasty retreat. It reminded me of the scene in *Monty Python and the Holy Grail* when King Arthur and his brave knights flee from the little white bunny rabbit guarding the cave, shouting, 'Run away, run away!' We scrambled to get as far away from the kill zone as possible while another unit joined in to help look for the insurgents, but even with them on board and two helicopters circling overheard, we couldn't find them. Whoever had fired at us was long gone and was probably already sitting at home smoking his hookah pipe. After a fruitless search, we called it off and returned to base.

We arrived back at the FOB and were just sitting down to eat chow when we were mortared again. We jumped on the vehicles, expecting to go chase after the insurgents, but we were stood down before we got out the gate. Later that night, we got some bad news. Two of the lads from our Austin unit had been hit earlier that day with a huge VBIED – a vehicle borne improvised explosive device – at a checkpoint. A suicide bomber had detonated the car bomb as they had approached his vehicle on foot to search it. One of them didn't make it and the other was in critical condition, God love them. He was the first guy to die from our unit and his death hit us pretty hard.

There wasn't much talk in the squad room that night. We all just sat there and reflected on our memories of him, what was going on and our own chances of dying out there. I had never felt the need to protect the guys in the squad more. I would make no apologies and do whatever I needed to keep them alive. I had nothing more to write about before I went to sleep except to say that it was 1 December and a terrible start to Christmas, especially for that fallen Marine's family.

The next day, it was back to business as usual and we were out on three successive night missions, patrolling the endless barren roads which were frozen from exposure to the cutting wind. The patrols were long and seemed endless – the time merged into one long, uneventful experience. We got three hours' sleep after the first night and then had to spend the next day putting new tyres on the wheels of our vehicles while the mechanics sat around watching DVDs. The following night we fared better and managed six hours, but by the third, we were all on the verge of collapsing from complete exhaustion and fatigue.

7 December 2004

Hello

It's been a while, but I've been busy dodging landmines and car bombs all week.

They finally got the computers working earlier and I had almost made it to the top of the line when the place got mortared. It's almost a daily occurrence now and they come in thick and fast. There is very little warning, although they generally start at about tea-time. We suspect that's when the insurgents all knock off work at the local police station and go moonlighting for the other team.

At the moment, all I can say is that we are based in what looks like a historical reconstruction of a garrison fort from the nineteenth century. By the time we leave here, we will have learned to appreciate the small comforts such as beds and flushable toilets and neighbours who are not intent on mortaring us every day.

But anyway, just four months to go now and—

8 December 2004

Hey!

Sorry, that last email was interrupted when a few mortar rounds landed outside. As I am a stubborn fool, I refused to take cover until the message was almost ready, but then one landed a bit too close, even for me, and I scattered after accidentally pressing Send.

I was telling the lads that 8 December is a very important day in Ireland because it's when all the people from the country come up to Dublin to do their Christmas shopping. I described how all the routes into the city were blocked every year with families on their tractors. I was joking, of course, but I think most of them believed me. Whenever I tell them stories about my home, I spend more time explaining what I've just said. Sometimes, it's like we're from different planets.

Some of the lads I'm out here with couldn't find Ireland on a map of the world, but then again, I would have difficulty finding Delaware too. Most of them are Hispanic, so out of curiosity and to show a little respect, I started to pick up a few bits and pieces of Spanish, or the Texan version of it, which they call 'Texican'. So far, I've learned a few bad words and can ask someone where the cantina *(bar) is and how to order a beer.*

Anyway, better go, we have work to do and somebody has to pay the bleeding bills. So, off we go again into the desert to 'seek out and destroy the enemy using fire and manoeuvre' or, in layman's terms, to drive around all fucking day staring at the ground.

Later

Graham

Chapter 26

I was daydreaming that I was fishing back home in Howth. I could almost see myself standing on the rocks beside the Baily Lighthouse, fishing rod in hand, as the waves crashed below. It was a beautiful dream, but it didn't last long – my reverie was shattered by a Marine NCO screaming blue murder.

We shared the firebase with an Iraqi National Guard unit, but we didn't see much of them; they stuck to their side of the FOB and we to ours. There was a Marine officer attached to them and he was trying to train them on our tiny parade ground, so this was pretty much the first time I'd got a chance to see our neighbours up close.

They weren't an inspiring sight. These guys may have been in uniform, but they didn't look much like soldiers. They were called to formation, but they didn't seem to be in any major hurry to form up. One fella was washing a paper cup in a puddle of water while three of his comrades stood around smoking cigarettes. Some of them were casually strolling around while the rest were still in their squad rooms. Gradually, they made their way to the parade ground while the

Marine who had been shouting orders at them through a translator was going red in the face.

I could only assume that their culture made them pretty laid back, because I had completely different recollections of boot camp. Judging from their lacklustre performance, our efforts to train the ING so they could take over security and let us all go home was going to take some time. In the meantime, it would be the Marines who would do all the fighting.

Later that day, we were back out on the roads and Vick and I were kept busy firing flares at vehicles that got too close. It had become an effective tactic and it certainly got the drivers' attention. If someone ignored it and kept coming, we could be fairly sure they were a suicide bomber.

At the front of the convoy, Vick had fired a flare at a vehicle that failed to get off the road in time and it accidentally embedded itself in the grill of the car, a million to one shot. It went up like a rocket and the vehicle immediately came to a stop. By the time our Humvee approached, smoke was pouring out from under the hood and the driver and two of his buddies were scrambling around picking up dirt with their hands and throwing it on to where the flare was burning. There was no way we could stop to help because it was too dangerous and I tried not to make eye contact with the men, who were glaring at us over their shoulders as we roared past them at top speed. Of course, I gave Vick a hard time over that one, but I didn't push it. He was genuinely upset that he'd damaged some fella's car. It must have been hard to take, to be driving along with your mates and then have these foreigners shooting flares at you, knowing full well there was nothing you could do about it. Still, we didn't have much choice. If Vick or I hesitated, we could all be dead.

With the news of casualties trickling in almost every day, very few of us remained hopeful that we would all make it out of Iraq in one piece. Every time we returned to base, we heard of another neighbouring Marine unit that had been hit while out on patrol.

Even while we were back on the firebase, there was no reprieve, as we were continuously mortared. They were coming down so often now it had almost become routine. I should have been on edge, worrying about the possibility of getting hurt or killed, but it was pointless. I had almost resigned myself to my fate. If it was going to happen, it was going to happen. There was nothing I could do about it.

The situation wasn't helped when it appeared that sometimes our officers had their priorities all wrong. Occasionally, we would have to go over to Al Asad to pick up supplies, but we also took the opportunity to stock up on smokes and other small luxuries. In our filthy uniforms that were covered in diesel and dirt and flak jackets with all manner of apparel and ammunition attached to them, we stuck out like sore thumbs among the clean and well-groomed poster boys back at base and it attracted the attention of officers who were obviously disgusted by our appearance.

They would order us to clean up our act and so we would spend almost the entire time there waiting in line for our heads to be shaved. As soon as we were done, we would get our backsides out of the place – we clearly didn't belong.

On 10 December, on the way back from Al Asad, I popped a few flares and almost shot up one vehicle when the driver drove flat out towards us. I whipped my finger around the trigger shouting, 'Stop! Stop! Stop!' in Arabic, when he locked on his brakes just beyond what I had deemed to be my kill line. It turned out to be just some idiot who wasn't paying attention, but I was furious that he had made such a stupid mistake and had put so much pressure on me that I had nearly shot him. I was prepared to protect my buddies, but I didn't want the death of an innocent on my hands. Unless you have ever been in a similar situation, it's probably impossible to understand how difficult it is to make a decision on the spot, knowing that it will either kill or save lives.

A couple of days later, we had just finished yet another fourteen-hour day patrol. It was unremarkable, other than the fact it was getting even colder. We didn't have any decent cold-weather gear to keep ourselves warm and it made me cringe to think about the next night patrol. The following day was much the same, but when we got back, there was a treat in store – the mail had arrived. We all read our letters at least three times and then shared stories about the contents. I still had the bunch of schoolkids writing to me. Their letters were great fun and to get one from a kid who was telling me all about his pets made me feel human again. I also got a note from the little girl who had made me the friendship bracelet. She said she was worried about me and told me to keep wearing it for good luck. I glanced at the bracelet on my wrist as I read her letter and smiled – it reminded me that there was somebody thinking of me. I hoped that I would get the opportunity some day to raise a good kid like her. I vowed, once again, to wear it until I got home.

Later, we got some news that wasn't so good. There had been another VBIED in the neighbourhood. There were few details. We knew that it was a convoy that got hit, but there was no word on casualties or the unit. All we could do was pray for them.

I honestly didn't know what day of the week it was any more. I kept my journal pretty organised with dates and times, but the individual days had blurred together. All I did know was that we had a night mission later. Prior to going out, I put on every single piece of clothing I owned in an effort to keep warm. I also tried on my new balaclava. With it pulled down over my face and a rifle in my hand, I looked like a terrorist myself.

Out on the road, it was very, very dark because of the heavy cloud cover. We stopped at an intersection near Al Asad that was used heavily by military traffic – a vehicle was hit there on at least a monthly basis. Sure enough, we found another anti-tank landmine buried in a pothole. Once again, we were very lucky. It would have been impossible to spot that mine from a moving vehicle, but the dismounts had found it easily enough by sweeping the ground with their feet.

We closed off the intersecting public road that the civilian traffic used and called for an EOD team to come blow it up. It was almost 05:00 by the time they arrived and set it off. Even though we were more than five hundred metres back, the blast was so powerful that it shook our heavy vehicle. As we were close to an urban area, it must have come as an even bigger shock to the people sleeping nearby. The patrol ended without any more drama.

By 04:00 the following morning, we were back out on patrol again when the FOB came under mortar fire. Our own mortars fired back and when they finished shooting, we drove out to see if we could find anyone. We discovered another 155 mm artillery round hidden by the side of the road and called the EOD team to come out and deal with it. Things were definitely hotting up around there.

Back on the public road, we spotted a vehicle that matched the description of one on the list that intel had given us. We stopped them and closed down the immediate area while the dismounts searched the driver and his car. There were two women in the back, but protocol prevented us from searching them as it was culturally sensitive.

Further down the road, we did the same thing when another driver started acting suspiciously. We quickly sprang our traffic stop and pulled them over like we were Starsky and Hutch. We had the road closed again in both directions while we conducted the search and a long line of traffic formed. This one impatient idiot, probably not knowing what the hold-up was, pulled out onto the wrong side and started driving towards us and he didn't seem to have any intention of stopping. Six or seven Marines with rifles on their shoulders were trained on him while I swung my machine gun in his direction. We were all screaming and shouting at this guy to stop. He must have got the fright of his life and almost flipped his car over when he saw us. Himself and his wife got out and both of them were crying and waving their hands in the air. I'd love to know what he had to say, given that he had just driven at speed towards an armed squad of wary Marines.

17 December 2004 is a day I will never forget for the rest of my life because it was the first time I fired a weapon at another person in anger.

We were out on a routine patrol escorting small Marine units between the FOB and various checkpoints. The schedule was tight and the pressure was on from higher-up to complete all our tasks, so we had to skip on some of the standard safety procedures that we usually adhered to, such as stopping at intersections and bridges to check for mines and IEDs.

I was riding in the lead vehicle for a change and was screaming at the top of my lungs and frantically signalling with my left arm for oncoming traffic to get off the road while keeping the fingers of my right hand near the trigger of my mounted machine gun. For a while, everything seemed normal. The cars could see us from a good way off and were moving aside as instructed. Then I noticed two vehicles coming towards us about four hundred metres away. I began the procedure to usher them off the road and as they approached, they seemed to be complying with the order. They started to slow down and were pulling over to the side, so I moved my attention on to the next vehicles.

We were about fifty metres away from them when the second vehicle suddenly careered back onto the road, kicking up dirt as it moved back onto the hard road surface. I immediately took aim and squeezed the trigger. The heavy machine gun opened up and round after round left the barrel. I watched, fascinated, as each one, very clearly and vividly, impacted violently. I held my finger on the trigger as the vehicle careered wildly in front of us. My driver threw the Hummer over to the other side of the road and we narrowly avoided colliding with the shot-up car. I got a glimpse of smashed glass and smoke as we passed. The roof of my vehicle was littered with empty casings from the rounds and they rained to the ground when we skidded to a halt. The entire incident had lasted less than five seconds. We had already passed the danger zone and orders crackled over the radio to hold firm while the rest of the patrol closed down the road to deal with any further threat. I was trying to catch my breath. I didn't know if I had just killed someone. I had no chance to see into the vehicle, as everything had happened in an instant and at such close range. I remembered that some of the rounds had appeared to go through the windscreen, but beyond that, I was clueless. The only thing I knew right then was that we were still alive.

The two patrol vehicles behind me had stopped a safe distance away. The dismounts had jumped out and were approaching the smoking wreck, their rifles raised to their shoulders. I lit up a smoke in my shaking hands and put it into my mouth while keeping an eye on the rest of the traffic, which we had stopped a safe distance away. We were all well aware that it was a common insurgency tactic to detonate a secondary device to catch units which had already been dealt a blow off guard.

The search team closed in and reported that there was a family in the shot-up car and they needed the Navy Corpsman. Instantly, I felt sick and couldn't breathe. I threw away the cigarette and forced myself not to look around. As the minutes passed, I prayed to God that I hadn't killed anyone.

The radio crackled again and I fought a sudden surge of nausea. 'No injuries requiring further medical attention, situation is under control.' 'Thank God,' I whispered to myself, as I sat there looking down the road in the opposite direction. I asked the other Marines how badly the family had been hurt and they told me they were going to be OK, but it was only an act of God that kept those people alive. I could clearly see that the majority of the rounds had impacted on the hood, but one had gone through the windshield and passed between the occupants, somehow missing them all, before exiting and hitting the windscreen of the vehicle behind. Sitting in the front passenger seat was a woman with a four-year-old child in her lap. Behind them was their teenage daughter. The round had gone in through the windshield and missed their heads by mere inches. It was so close that the bullet pressure had scored a perfectly narrow and straight abrasion across one side of their heads. Glass from the shattered windshield had been sent through the passenger compartment, causing other minor cuts. The physical injuries were superficial, but I'm sure they were mentally traumatised.

The father was the only one who hadn't been injured and he wept as he stood by the side of the road. He looked on as the Marines tended to his family that had almost been wiped out because of his carelessness on the road. He told the Marines that he had being going too fast and when the car in front suddenly slowed down, he pulled back out onto the road to avoid crashing into it as his child wasn't secured in the vehicle. It broke my heart watching the corpsman bandaging up the head of the little girl. She was about the same age as my niece.

Sergeant Huerra took me aside and asked me flat out why I had shot up the car. As calmly as I could, I explained exactly what had happened. 'Sir, vehicle number two re-entered the hard-ball five zero metres away from our vehicle and it was then I concluded under protocol that it was a VBIED. I took the shot, deflected the vehicle and avoided impact.' He looked straight at me as I said it and he seemed satisfied with my answer. He patted my back and said, 'Fucking right, Dale, and don't forget that.' It was a relief to hear him say I had reacted correctly. In my mind, I had no other choice given the circumstances, but it was a vote of confidence from my boss and I was extremely appreciative that he backed me up.

The situation was radioed to higher-ups and they ordered the squad leaders to conduct an initial investigation, which basically consisted of taking a few photos and talking to the bloke who had been driving. He was standing by the side of the road with his family, crying and shaking. He was handed a piece of paper that told people who had lost property or loved ones as a result of our actions how they could be reimbursed. It was written in both Arabic and English and read:

Peace be upon you.

We are deeply concerned for your loss. It seemed as though you were going to attack the multinational forces. We know now that you meant no harm. Please remember that it is dangerous to approach military convoys or cordons. For your safety, you must observe and obey all warning signs and signals. We can properly address your loss through the local Iraqi coordination center. Please call xxx-xxx and submit the following information.

Name:

House/street:

City:

Reason for submission:

Peace be upon you.

It seemed to be a bit of a joke to leave yer man with a piece of paper with that written on it after what he had just been through, but there wasn't much else we could do. Once that was done, we drove to a nearby checkpoint and held a quick debriefing. I was still shaking as we headed from there to the FOB.

Back at the firebase, each of the lads shook my hand and told me I had done the right thing. I was then called down to the operations centre, where a major took statements and conducted a formal investigation. I had to explain what had happened, as did my squad leader. The major concluded that everything had been done by the book and that I had reacted in the proper manner. I left the room and talked to my friends and they filled me in on some of the details from their perspective. I went to bed that night thanking God that no one was hurt, but still determined to do my job as best I could to defend my buddies sitting in the vehicle below me.

Chapter 27

We'd had enough drama for a few days and I was grateful for the three overnight missions that came next. They were long, boring and cold, but I got a chance to collect my thoughts. When I got back, I resolved to clear my conscience. In light of the recent escalation in near misses and close calls, I wrote letters to everyone I could think of who I might have owed an apology to for past mistakes. For those whose addresses I didn't have, I swore I would somehow make it up to them if I ever got home.

It was really getting to me that we were in so much danger but had nothing to show for risking our lives. I wished I could say that I had helped train an effective military or police unit or even killed some insurgents, but all I had done since I arrived was drive up and down empty roads at night, just waiting to be hit, and now I had nearly killed an innocent family. It was a week until Christmas and it felt like I was locked up in prison in a distant place without a voice to shout, scream or cry.

A few days later, we were providing back-up for an army Special

Forces unit that was conducting a raid in Hit. It was colder that night than it had been in the past few weeks and the desert was covered in ice. It gave a whole new meaning to the phrase 'when hell freezes over'. We listened closely to the Special Forces' radio traffic. When they did take enemy fire, they quickly called in air support and within minutes there was a C-130 gunship circling overhead – the aircraft known as 'Puff the Magic Dragon' in the Vietnam War. When its awesome firepower was employed, it fired so many rounds that the tracers formed a continuous stream of light from the sky all the way to the target. It also created this horribly long, dark noise like a truck engine roaring as it tackles a steep hill. There was no doubt it destroyed everything in its path. After it had stopped firing, it suddenly disappeared into the night sky like a ghost and was only visible through my night-vision goggles. After that display, the Special Forces guys had no need for us.

There were only three days left until Christmas but, in Iraq, it was business as usual. Back on the firebase, there was no sign of the season apart from a two-foot Christmas tree that somebody had sent to one of the lads. I would have loved to see my family. I suspected that it was harder on them than it was on me. The news coming out of Iraq of death and injury must have been pretty much constant, but at least I knew how I was doing, while they were clueless most of the time.

We spent the next few days bouncing around in our vehicles, talking about Christmas and memories of the holidays with our families. On one of the nights, we were escorting some Marines to an isolated outpost via a public road when the guys in our second vehicle spotted wires protruding from the side of a bridge as we crossed over it. We ensured that we were well out of the kill zone and then set up a security perimeter and waited for EOD.

I was keeping the civilian traffic back about three hundred metres and the lads had the razor wire out on the road about fifty metres in front of my vehicle. EOD arrived on the scene with their security detail and took over so we could continue on with our happy little patrol. We heard later that they looked under the bridge with a robot and found two big 155 mm artillery rounds primed and ready to go off. We had cheated death once again.

When we returned to the firebase later that night, there was some beer and rum waiting for us, much to our disbelief. We weren't allowed to have any alcohol, unlike our English counterparts who got to booze it up in southern Iraq, but because it was Christmas, we were given two beers and a shot of Bacardi each. Quickly, I arranged to get another quota from a guy who didn't drink and somehow managed to get a few more until I was feeling pretty good. The next morning, I actually enjoyed the novelty of a hangover, even though it made me homesick.

Christmas Eve in Iraq, and I was walking around with my hangover whistling 'Jingle Bells' and prepping the vehicle for a night mission. It really bummed me out that I would be spending the night driving around the desert and try as I might, I couldn't keep thoughts of home and how things used to be out of my head. If I had been back in Dublin right at that moment, I would have been sitting in the Donaghmede Inn drinking pints and singing 'Fairytale of New York' with my friends. Or maybe I would have been holding my first love's hand. I missed her more than ever at that moment. Then I'd go home to enjoy the results of my mother's cooking marathon and, later, watch midnight mass on the television with one eye closed after drinking too much. But back to reality. I may as well have been a million miles from Ireland. I was in the desert in a land that was unsympathetic to my plight.

We were told to prepare for a mission to Haditha Dam for two or three days, leaving at noon. Knowing that we could be gone longer, I packed for at least a week. We all wanted to make a quick phone call home before we left, as we wouldn't be able to contact our families until we got back, but we were told that there was no time and that really hurt our morale. It was Christmas Eve, after all, and we weren't exactly being rushed into battle, but the master plan didn't facilitate even a quick phone call home. It was evident to us all that our families were insignificant to the Corps. We had all joined up voluntarily, but my mother hadn't, nor had anyone else's mother or their wives or kids, and they at least deserved a call at Christmas if it was at all possible. I guess that was part of the price you paid when you signed your life away to the military. Happy Christmas, Ma!

Christmas morning 2004, and it looked like Santa had forgotten all about us as we woke on the cold floor inside Haditha Dam. All he left me was a pair of smelly feet and a hole in my heart for home. We scoffed down some food in the chow hall before getting our brief. We found out that over the next two days, we, along with another Mobile Assault Platoon, would be out on the road, visiting six or seven towns, making surprise visits to show that we Marines wouldn't be sitting back and relaxing on our Christian holiday.

I had to stop myself from laughing out loud when the briefing officer described the mission as 'marking the start of the next step in the rebuilding of Iraq'. My only hope was that no one would get killed for such a ridiculous and pointless exercise. In the first town we stopped at, we set up a security checkpoint on the main road while the other unit went in to have a look around. Someone saw the lights on the minaret of a mosque flashing on and off and we had to presume that this was some sort of signal, so we were on high alert, our eyes scanning the rooftops and streets like hawks, weapons at the ready.

I had been tasked with closing off this one particular road and I ended up shooting so many flares that I was rapidly running out. A car stopped about seventy-five metres up the road with one man at the wheel. I was waving my arms in the air and shouting at the driver in Arabic to turn around and leave but he started moving towards me again. I decided to shoot a flare, and when that didn't work, I aimed low and squeezed the trigger of the machine gun. Five or six rounds hit the ground in front of him and some bounced up and tore into the grill of his car. He braked suddenly and put the car in reverse. I had obviously spooked him, and as we watched him backing up at high speed, I turned to my driver and said, 'Man, I hope he sees that car behind him.' Just as I said it, the cars collided. The two drivers got out and started arguing. They were waving their fists and the first fella started pointing at me. He was obviously telling the other guy about me shooting at his car on the road. I felt a little bad for yer man, but it was his own fault. I wasn't going to die on Christmas Day. He started walking towards me and I waved him back. I wasn't going to allow him to approach my vehicle on foot either because he could still have a suicide bomber's belt tied around his waist and I was already mad at him.

With the day's mission complete, we drove to Al Asad to get some food in the chow hall. Everyone was looking forward to it, especially the gunners, as we were all miserable from the intermittent rain and cold, biting wind. But when we got there, I was ordered to go back to the truck to watch our gear. I almost snapped. I was soaking wet and hungry. I stormed off and got back in the Humvee where I smoked one cigarette after another in despair. I no longer knew why I was doing this. It more or less had nothing to do with me any more. I was sitting out in the rain on my own, soaking wet, with a 9 mm holstered to my thigh, hating life. A few weeks previoiusly, I had run out of anti-depressants that, like most of America, I had been taking before

I left for Iraq, and it really bothered me. I had recently been told that I could not get a refill and, although I was no doctor, I was pretty sure that it was not a good idea to take a man who was so heavily armed off medicaton like that.

I needed to focus on something positive, but my mind was flooded with questions about what I could have been doing with my life, where I could be and who I could be with. After a while, my mates came out with food for me, but I fucked it away as I was too angry to eat. When the rest of the lads were finished up in the chow hall, we were assigned somewhere to stay for the night. We found a cold spot on the ground inside the dam where we bedded down. Happy Christmas, me bollox.

St Stephen's Day was pretty much the same – another town, another security cordon and more rain. Towards the end of the day, I felt myself drifting away and had to discipline myself to remain focused. We had completed our tour of the towns and bid farewell to the other unit when they were suddenly hit by an IED. There were casualties, but there was nothing too serious and they were going to be all right. One of the guys who had been injured, though, was my good friend Kendrix. He was going to be OK, but it was tragic – the poor guy was only twenty, not even old enough to legally drink beer in some states, and he was already another wounded boy in Iraq.

The following day, we were returning from a mission to Baghdadi when one of our vehicles spotted some wires protruding through the dirt by the side of the road at a bridge near the end of town. We set up a cordon around it and called in EOD who, as usual, seemed to take forever to arrive. We never liked sitting around near found ordinance because we knew the insurgents were close. They were also well aware that you would have to remain there for a while, so you were an easy target. When EOD finally arrived, they used a robot to disarm the device. They found on 155 mm round this time and a mobile phone. Once again, we had escaped disaster only because whoever was planning on detonating the bomb hadn't been there when we passed by. They took the IED off into a gulley and blew it up before we headed home.

When we got back to base, mystery was in the air as we got wind of a plan to kidnap some guy the next day. The word was that there was supposed to be some 'big man' travelling through a particular intersection later and we were to go hide somewhere close by and capture him.

The following day, we had just sat down in our little hides when we were relieved by another unit. When we got back to base, we were given a consolation prize of going along with army Special Forces to snatch some bad guys in Hit. We studied the route maps and mission plans diligently and were all pumped up and ready to go when they cancelled the whole bloody thing. The looks of dissappointment on the lads' faces said it all.

On 29 December, we started a two-day mission with an army psych-ops (psychological operations) team who were running around asking Iraqi civilians what they thought of us. The general consensus among the Marines was that it was a waste of time – we already knew what they thought of us. We set up random VCPs (vehicle control points) on the main roads and had the vehicles come through one by one. When they were cleared, we sent them on to the psych-ops team and their translators, who got the feedback from the population.

The following day, we drove to the outskirts of a city where psych-ops broadcast messages in Arabic to the civilians. They had this huge speaker system mounted on top of their vehicle and it was loud enough for a large portion of the city to hear. We sat there while they played their message, which I'm sure was something to do with the fact that we all loved each other and we were all friends. I'm also sure none of the Iraqis really cared what it was about.

We spent the last day of 2004 catching up on some badly needed rest and carrying out running repairs to our battered trucks. I took my turret apart and cleaned the hell out of the bearing assembly while the rest of the guys put fresh tyres on the spare wheels. Somehow that had become our job, even though there were mechanics sitting on their backsides doing nothing. It was going to be another long, cold night and word had it that it would get even colder in January.

Before we set off, we suddenly found out there was water and that we could take a shower. I honestly couldn't remember the last time I'd had a proper wash. It had been at least three or four weeks and that was only the navy version, where you wet your body for a few seconds, turned the water off, soaped yourself down and then washed it off for a few seconds with some more water. As we scrubbed the weeks of grit from our bodies, I wondered if the people at home understood the conditions the guys out there had to live in. It would have been hard, I suppose, for anyone to know what it was like to go for weeks without a single proper meal, let alone a shower or a real toilet. And that was nothing compared to the resolve it took to don the uniform each day and night and prepare for a fourteen-hour mission, one of which could be your last. That was the hardest part all right, because no matter how much of a bad ass you thought you were, it was simply a matter of luck whether or not you were blown into little postage-stamp-sized pieces in an instant. I will never forget the experience of life in Iraq and I will always appreciate what it means to have a warm bed to sleep in, a hot meal to eat and, most of all, a cold beer to drink.

Morale was raised a little after our showers, but then one of the staff NCOs called us into formation and proceeded to have a go at us.

He called us all fuckers and started ranting that we were all losing our fucking minds and operating our own programme, which was pretty accurate, since he never seemed to come out with us on patrol. He was mad that we didn't have regulation high-and-tight haircuts and that we had shabby stubble on our faces. I guess he was just trying to re-establish himself as the boss, but it never really seemed too important to us how we looked, given the constant danger we faced, let alone lack of means or time to pay attention to our grooming. We were sure that if we were killed, they would give us a nice shave before they put our corpses in the coffins. Anyway, nobody else seemed to care too much that we wore the same clothes for weeks and that we rarely got to shower.

When he was done ripping into us, he went back upstairs and pressed play on his DVD player while we continued to get ready for our overnight New Year's Eve patrol. Before we left, I got a hold of my dad on the phone and wished everyone back home a Happy New Year. He didn't really know what to say to me, given the circumstances but, for what it was worth, he wished me a Happy New Year too and told me to stay safe. I said goodnight, picked my rifle up off the floor, put on my flak jacket and Kevlar helmet, walked out to the vehicle and climbed up on top to ready my machine gun.

Out on the road, it was a particularly dark night. There was little residual light and it was difficult to see much, even with night-vision goggles. I rarely looked at my watch on night missions, as it was impossible to see the time without turning on the night light, and also because whenever I did, it seemed to make the hours drag on much longer. But some time after midnight, the lads got on the radio and were wishing each other a Happy New Year. It made me sad to spend my night out there, but at least I was with my mates and that was good enough.

Chapter 28

I spent most of the first day of 2005 in bed catching up on some sleep. I woke up later in the evening and found my ex-girlfriend in Austin had posted me a note written on a bar napkin. I was very impressed with that. It was more personal than paper and close to my heart. On the other hand, I hadn't received any response to a letter I had sent to my ex in Ireland and I was a little down because of that. I wasn't even sure she had got the letter, as it was sent to an old address and it saddened me more to think that she probably didn't know I was out there in Iraq.

We were up early the following morning to visit some little school with the CAG team. The teachers had already been given money and the CAG team was going over to make sure they were spending it on the school. My two cents said it had gone towards a new Mercedes for the man in charge, while Vick figured it had been spent on bombs and guns to blow us all up. Either way, it didn't make a blind bit of a difference. I pressed the big 'I believe' button and we were on our way. That was a phrase I had learned from one of the captains. Even though you didn't always believe what you were told, you just pressed the 'I believe' button and got on with it.

On our way to the school, we linked up with two helicopters, a Cobra and a Huey, that had come with us to provide aerial fire support. It was always a great comfort having choppers overhead, given their firepower and unique vantage point. The insurgents knew it was generally a bad idea to come anywhere near us when we had air support and it made me happy just knowing that.

Passing through Baghdadi, we received the usual spiteful stares from the locals and waves from the younger kids who didn't know any better. Some time later, we got to the River Euphrates, where we rolled into a tiny village and, once again, I was struck by how beautiful some places in Iraq could be. It was surrounded by palm trees and other vegetation – you'd have been forgiven for thinking it was the original Garden of Eden. Small, tidy irrigated fields were dotted around the lush landscape, where vegetables were growing in straight green lines. The village itself was very basic, but even though most of the houses had just one or two rooms and were made of stone, they all seemed to have a satellite dish on the roof and a television in the main room.

Well, we weren't there to be messing around like tourists on a sightseeing excursion, so I pulled my head back into the game and concentrated. I observed several men tending to their fields who stopped work as we approached, but they were more interested in the helicopters flying overhead than the ground units. We set up a cordon around the schoolhouse, which was a simple one-roomed stone structure with a little sign hanging over the front door. The lads jumped out and set up security as we orientated our heavy weapons to the outside of the perimeter, and everyone was set.

The schoolteacher came out ahead of a gaggle of tiny kids who were all between four and seven years of age. Each of them was very excited that we had come to the village and their school and they brought a smile to our dismal faces. I think we appreciated seeing them as much as they were delighted to see us.

One of the chopper pilots radioed down that they had some presents for the kids. The dismounts cleared the area and the Huey descended to about five feet off the deck. The Marine in the back threw several nets containing soccer balls and other gifts out the door and as soon as the rotor wash subsided, the kids ran out and chased the balls all over the place. It was a sight to gladden even the hardest heart.

With the visit complete, our dismounts got back on board and we rolled out of Eden and into the desert. We passed another school on the way where the older kids ran outside to have a look at us. They were soon followed by an angry teacher wielding a stick, who proceeded to smack them and chase them back inside. Ah, a familiar sight, I laughed to myself; it seemed it was the same everywhere around the world.

A couple of days later, we were up at God only knows what hour and in the best military tradition of 'hurry up and wait', we were rushed out the door without even a lick of morning chow. I wasn't really in the mood for it that day because we were only going to be on the military-only roads, which were dull, empty and dangerous. What really got to me about these particular patrols was that we were stuck out in the middle of the desert and not out on the streets of the towns, showing the enemy we weren't afraid and letting the people see that we were trying to protect them. The military roads only led to our air base and there was nobody else out there, except for the insurgents who were trying to kill us.

Just before we stepped off, we were handed an MRE box by one of the Pogues from the COC, and when I looked inside, I couldn't believe my eyes – there was a tiny puppy looking back at me. It was so bloody small, maybe only about eight weeks old, and utterly defenceless. The Pogue explained that one of the other units had found it abandoned and had brought it back. But there was a particular major at the base, who nobody exactly loved, and he had ordered that the dog be removed. The Pogue sounded genuinely upset as he explained that they had been ordered to get rid of it out in the desert, but there was not one Marine among us, tough or otherwise, who wanted to abandon it to its fate. We agreed to take the puppy, but there was no way we were going to simply drop him off in the middle of the desert. We debated at length about what to do with him. Someone suggested bringing him to one of the small towns that we passed through, but we thought the locals would kill it if they saw it had come from us. Then one of the lads remembered that the soldiers at the outer gate at Al Asad kept a dog and even a donkey as pets. When we passed by later, I begged one of the gate guards to take the puppy and see if he could find someone to take care of it. He seemed trustworthy and we were happy to leave the dog with him.

After we dropped the dog off, we were settling into the rest of the patrol when vehicle number two broke down. This shit was getting serious. We were almost too afraid to imagine what would happen if one of the Humvees broke down when things got hot. We were going to end up losing Marines, all because we had shitty vehicles. I had read in the newspapers that government officials had been quoted as saying we had some of the best equipment and training in the world. Some fairytale that was. It was criminally unjust, to say the least, that Marines were losing their lives because they didn't have armour on the vehicles. And what was worse was the fact that there were brand-new vehicles on the Al Asad base, complete with armour, that were only used to ferry officers safely to and from the chow hall. It didn't take us long to get vehicle number two back to base, as we had towed that piece of shit so many times we were getting quite efficient at it.

We called it a day at that point and I brought my weapons upstairs to clean them so I could listen to my brand-new *Dustin Christmas* CD. I had no sooner finished and was about to turn in when I had to stand my vehicle watch. I finally got some sleep before waking up six hours later to do the whole thing again.

As we were rolling out the following morning, 5 January, the gate guard got on the radio and gave us a description of a male who had been witnessed watching the FOB. We went to check it out and God help anyone we found nearby who had a mobile phone, radio or pair of binoculars on them.

We were having a look around when one of the gunners spotted a silver car exiting the area in great haste. I was almost thrown out of the turret as Romero, who was well on top of his game, flipped the heavy Humvee around and we set off in pursuit. We raced after the car, but it was more than four hundred metres south of us and getting away, so we requested permission to engage. The request was turned down by the higher-ups and we were ordered to discontinue the chase. The suspect was fleeing in the direction of Hit and command was afraid to let us follow him. We were devastated. It could have been the spotter for the mortars that were landing on us every day, although it could also have been an attempt to lead us into an ambush too. Either way, the fact that the city remained pretty much off limits because we still had insufficient manpower to secure it was another reminder of how tenuous our grasp was on that territory.

We had moved back to let our Marines conduct a foot search when suddenly we heard a BOOM, BOOM, BOOM coming from the other side of the river. It sounded like more mortars being fired, so we screamed at our dismounts to get back on board.

The front gate at the FOB radioed that they were taking incoming mortar fire to the north of our position and we set off in that direction to see if we could catch the insurgents at it. There was a thick palm grove along the banks of the river and as we approached, Vick and I requested permission over the radio to dismount with the machine guns and enter the grove. We wanted to rip through the brush to kill anything hidden in there but, yet again, we were told to hold position and not fire unless we had enemy confirmed. More mortars were launched and seconds later, reports came in of further impacts on the front gate. There could have been Marines dying over there and I was stuck in my turret looking at a grove of trees where the enemy was obviously hiding.

My vehicle commander had had enough and, together with one of the other lads, he ran through the trees to see if he could get a visual. He shouted over his shoulder that he would call me forward with the machine gun if he saw anything, but until then, I was to stay put and hold security. Before he got very far, higher-up ordered us to pull back and, bitterly disappointed, we left the enemy to live and fight another day.

We were informed that air support had been called in, but it was going to take some time to get there. In the meantime, the FOB was returning mortar fire and now shells were flying over our heads in both directions. We were instructed to get out of the area and to sit tight. We pulled back and for the next twenty minutes, we watched as the mortar duel raged on. Romero was so frustrated that he got out of the vehicle and literally took a shit on the ground in protest.

Suddenly, the firing stopped and there was silence. Forty-five minutes after the last mortar shell landed, air support turned up in the shape of a pair of helicopters. It was way too late and the insurgents were long gone.

More wasted time passed before we were ordered to carry out route security on the military-only road. We turned around in the opposite direction to the city, where all the insurgents obviously were, and pulled out. The FOB had taken a beating and initial casualty reports indicated that one Marine had been injured and three Iraqi soldiers had been seriously wounded. Enemy casualties were unknown, but more than likely were zero.

We got back some time after dark and dusted ourselves off before getting the gear down off the trucks. I checked my email and there was a message from my brother, who had just left Thailand and was now in Australia after spending some time on the paradise island of Phuket. Lucky fecker. I tried to reply to his email, but the computer was all fucked up and spat out application errors whenever I hit the Send button. I could have fixed it, or at least tried, but I couldn't be bothered. I felt like I was going insane and I no longer cared whether I lived or died. Although I had no choice in the matter, I didn't want to wake up the following morning or do anything other than sleep. I had almost stopped writing letters altogether and was just bottomed out in general. I felt like there was nothing that I could do other than perform my duties like a zombie, stranded alone in the turret, night after night. There just seemed to be no point to any of this any more.

The following morning, as soon as I woke up at 09:00, I sensed an air of despondency among the others and, sure enough, when I asked what was up, I was told we were going out on yet another overnight mission. There were sixteen of us, all in the same room, and I really wanted some time alone, so I went downstairs and rooted through the care packages that well-wishers had sent. I pulled out a copy of

Reader's Digest that was dated January 2001, but at least it was something to distract me. I climbed into the rear of one of the vehicles and tried to keep a low profile while I found the time to ease my uneasy mind. I had been getting severe headaches since I ran out of medication and I really needed a moment to sit down and clear my head. I pulled out a packet of baby wipes and tried to clean my body. It didn't get rid of much dirt, but it helped me feel a little bit better. Then I put on clean socks and brushed my teeth and that was about as close to normal as I could get for the time being.

Night patrol was busy enough, with multiple drop-offs involving snipers who were going out to combat the many mine strikes there had been recently. We were back at the FOB by 02:00 and told to stand by in the chow hall. We entered the room and warmed our bodies with lukewarm coffee and anything that had been left out for us. They had a satellite television on the wall and somebody stuck on *Sky News*. I watched in horror at the events unfolding in the Far East in the aftermath of the Asian tsunami. I thought how lucky my brother had been to have left the week before. It pissed me off when the guys wanted to switch over to American football. I walked out and sat in my vehicle alone, trying to figure out how a bunch of nancy boys wearing pads and helmets on a field could be more important than what was happening in Indonesia. It wasn't more important, of course, and it wasn't that they didn't care, it was just that watching football was their only chance to take their minds off things for a little while and so you couldn't really blame them.

I ended up falling asleep there in the back of the truck and was woken up two hours later and told we were going to take some detainees Charlie Company had captured during a raid the night before to Al Asad. I volunteered to help lift the handcuffed prisoners onto the back of the seven-tons. I was instructed to make sure that they didn't talk to each other, but no sooner had we got them on board than they all started off like a gaggle of women on bingo night. I couldn't remember the Arabic for 'Do not talk', so I just yelled, 'Shut the fuck up!' and they quickly quieted down. You could tell they were scared, but, to be honest, I didn't really care. As far as I was concerned, these were the same fuckers who had been trying to kill us.

At the same time, we didn't beat them or maltreat them in any way – we just wanted to turn them over to the powers that be at Al Asad. After that, they could do whatever they needed to do.

Chapter 29

On the morning of 9 January 2005, we had been patrolling as usual when we found some unexploded ordinance. We were told to mark the location and leave it for the EOD team. Then we were to continue north on the public road, keeping a lookout for a 4x4 headed in that direction. A chopper had called in stating that it had been spotted taking part in a terrorist checkpoint which had been stopping cars earlier and was now suspected of planting an IED by the roadside.

We headed north as ordered and had passed by a few civilian vehicles on the road when we were told to turn around and head south instead. When we completed the manoeuvre, the last vehicle in the convoy, which was mine, was now up in front.

We were racing along the road as fast as we could when our truck started having transmission trouble. Romero battled to keep it going, but the Humvee was slowing down. The driver in the Humvee behind started to overtake us. We were still slowing, so the next vehicle in the convoy moved out into the opposite side of the road to get past us. This particular Humvee was one of the highbacks and was carrying three Marines, sitting on benches in the back. Just as he passed by, I spotted a dark-coloured car coming around a bend in the road ahead at high speed. As it approached, it left the road and drove up onto the soft shoulder, then suddenly accelerated back onto the road. Everything signalled that it was a suicide attack.

The vehicle that had just overtaken mine was now between the speeding car and my Humvee. The gunner opened up and started firing rapidly while the driver tried everything to steer clear of the oncoming car, which was now swerving crazily from side to side, but what was about to happen was sickeningly inevitable. Right in front of my eyes, there was an almighty collision and the Marines sitting in the rear of the Humvee were thrown clear into the air. The car burst into flames and the two vehicles, now hopelessly entangled, spun around in a circle, spraying fuel and oil in a wide arc.

We skidded to a halt just yards away from the burning wreckage. A pall of black smoke had already blotted out the scene, but I knew it was bad. I screamed at one of our passengers, who was from another unit, to mount up in my turret while I went to help. As trained fire fighters with EMT experience, I knew that Romero and I were probably their best bet if any of them was badly injured.

As I jumped from the turret, I was anticipating another explosion. There was no doubt in my mind that there was a suicide bomber in the car that had just hit us and there was the possibility that the bomb on board hadn't gone off. All this was racing through my mind as I ran towards the wreckage. I had my medic bag over one shoulder and raised my rifle to the other as I approached the suicide bomber's car. The passenger compartment was totally engulfed in flames and I could make out two burning figures inside. I could clearly see they were no further threat, so I flung my rifle to the ground and looked around me.

Thick black smoke was pouring from what was left of the Hummer and several of our guys were desperately trying to account for everyone in it. They had already pulled Dan from the passenger side and he was lying on the ground, coughing. At a glance, I knew he was going to be all right, so I turned my attention to the three Marines who had been sitting in the back when the Humvee was rammed. They had been thrown twenty or thirty feet away from the vehicle and were lying in various positions on the road. I crouched over them and conducted triage, as I had been trained. I spent less than five seconds on each one, quickly checking to see if they had any immediate life-threatening injuries before moving on to the next. They were all pretty banged up and their faces were blackened and bleeding, but they were able to tell me that it hurt like a motherfucker, and that was a good sign. Other Marines had gathered around ready to help and I instructed them to treat the wounds as I continued to assess the situation. We had four guys accounted for. Where was the other? Then there was a shout from behind. The driver was still trapped in the burning Humvee.

Sergeant Huerra, Peter and I ran towards the burning vehicle. The flames kept us back, but we got as close as we could until we could see him. I could just make out the top of his helmet through the fire and smoke. He was slumped forward in his seat and it looked like he was unconscious. Peter and I took a deep breath, then ran back into the flames to try and pull him out, but we couldn't get near him and were beaten back by the flames. The impact had crushed the heavy door on the driver's side into the frame and it was immovable. Coughing, we backed out of the smoke and called for fire extinguishers and water. 'Water, water, get us fucking water now!' we both screamed at the other Marines nearby. Romero was already on top of it. He sprayed the flames with a chemical extinguisher, the only one we had for the entire unit, as it turned out, while Peter and I took a water can and emptied it over the Humvee's engine compartment, but it had no effect – the vehicle was totally consumed in flames.

Sergeant Huerra took over throwing the water as Peter and I tried, once more in vain, to get into the driver's compartment. Desperately, we fought through the flames and the billowing heavy black smoke, grasping the scorching metal of the door with our hands and pulling for all we were worth. We would only emerge to suck fresh air into our lungs before we ran back in again, but each time we were forced back. By that stage, there were live rounds cooking off in the car that had hit the Humvee that sounded like Chinese firecrackers. Now this was cause for extreme alarm, but nobody retreated or took cover. Not one of those guys thought of himself or his own safety that day. One of the guys from the other unit that we were out with ran forward with a fire blanket and I took it from him. Leaning in through the crushed door, I managed to get it over the head and torso of my friend inside, but try as I might, I couldn't budge him.

The other Marines were still dousing the flames with water. It appeared to be having little effect, but they kept going as if it was their last moment on earth. Our friend was inside of this burning vehicle and we could not sit back and simply watch him die. In desperation, Romero, backed up one of the other Humvees to the burning truck and set about hooking up a tow chain. We got out of the flames as Romero slowly pulled the burning truck away from the car and, at that moment, we caught a break – the flames had been fuelled by the petrol pouring from the car, so now the Humvee wasn't so heavily engulfed. We were finally able to pry our way into the driver's compartment and get to the driver. I grabbed his smoking upper torso while Peter took hold of his legs and together we dragged him out.

As we struggled, I noticed the terrific damage to the interior of the cab. The glass in the bulletproof windscreen had been fractured and the heavy steering wheel was bent all out of shape. We half-lifted, half-dragged him about twenty-five feet away from the wreck. I briefly noticed that there were small flames coming from the synthetic rain bottoms I was wearing, but I forgot all about it as I placed him on the ground. It was Greg, someone I knew very well. He was only twenty-three, a young guy and I was horrified at how badly he had been injured.

I checked his airway and, with the aid of the other Marines, cleared it of blood and vomit by rolling him over. Immediately, I could tell he wasn't breathing and had no pulse, but it had only been about a minute or two since the wreck and there was still a chance to save him. We were going to have to start CPR.

I was so grateful that myself and Romero had taken the time to teach our platoon buddies basic first aid and CPR. They were able to assist the other injured guys while we could concentrate on Greg. And here was Peter, who had never touched a patient before in his life, kneeling over his friend of all people, adamant that it would be he who would help me perform CPR.

I started the procedure by locking my lips onto Greg's bloody mouth and giving him two deep breaths. I noticed how I had to struggle to get the air into his lungs, but there was some chest rise, enough to give me hope. Peter, as if he was a trained professional, had placed his locked hands over the heart and had given the correct fifteen compressions. We were working efficiently together now, expertly performing CPR on a friend with whom we had been chatting just hours before. But there was no time for emotions at this stage – we had to succeed and we kept going. Peter and I continued with the CPR while Romero fixed up an IV and tended to the other serious traumatic injuries. I stopped regularly to irrigate the airway, as his blood and vomit kept shooting from his mouth into mine. I spat the blood out and redoubled my efforts to save him.

After two more minutes, I called for a stop to reanalyse his ABCs – airway, breathing and circulation. While he still wasn't breathing, he had a heartbeat. I asked Peter to hold off on the compressions momentarily while I continued to give mouth-to-mouth to see if I could get him to breathe on his own. But his heart started to fade and we started back with the compressions, along with the rescue breathing.

Despite the fact that we were both covered in blood from head to toe and even though there was now little chance left for Greg, I knew just by looking at the faces of the Marines around me that not a single one was ready to give up. Each one of those guys was ready and willing to do anything they could to help. They would have taken over CPR, even those who had never done it before. They had bandages in their hands and others were holding the limited equipment we had, asking me what to do. I had no doubt in my mind, not one fucking doubt, that, at that moment, any one of them would have traded places with Greg if only they could. Other Marines maintained their discipline and were holding tight security around the perimiter as they had been trained, even though they wanted to be in the middle of the situation, helping. Somebody passed word that Vick had already called in a 9-line medivac request and I could see Marines setting up the landing zone (LZ) for the chopper. I could hear other Marines on the radio relaying information on Greg's condition so that the medical facility where he would be brought would be ready for him. Sergeant Huerra was there, standing right behind us, gently offering us words of encouragement and urging us on, ready to back us up and support our every action. Rank had just left the building – we were all family out there and I will never forget it.

That day had started out just like all the other days I have written about up to this point, but it was the one when life lost all innocence. That was the moment when I was finally forced to confront the cruel and horrible truth of war and it changed my life for ever. What happened on that day put every skill that I have ever possessed to the test and tugged every emotion within my heart while challenging the very manhood, courage, love and friendship of my fellow Marines.

I was exhausted, but I was told that the bird was on the way in and was close to the scene as we kept up the CPR effort. With the chopper about to arrive, and with the intensifying sounds of the rounds cooking off in the car, now was the time to move Greg and I called for a stretcher. One of the staff sergeants from the other unit was screaming at my sergeant to just drag Greg away. I looked up at Huerra with my bloodied face and said that was not going to happen and to tell the staff sergeant to fuck off. Huerra told him we knew what we were doing and to back off and get us a stretcher.

They brought over the stretcher and we log-rolled Greg onto it and carried it to the other side of one of the Humvees and continued CPR. We had an IV in and the bleeding had been stopped by the guys applying dressings to his wounds. I just hoped that it was enough to keep him alive until we got him onto the medivac and to proper medical care.

I turned my attention back to Greg and realised that I had a serious problem. Air wasn't going into his lungs as well as it had been. I tried to reposition him so that his airway was completely open. I was aware that he had suffered massive chest and head injuries. I had to tilt his head back, but it did nothing much to help. I could hear and feel a crackling sensation as I tried to force more air in. On closer examination, it appeared that he had massive haemorrhaging in his chest cavity that had probably been caused when his body slammed into the steering wheel on impact. It sounded like his lungs were collapsing due to the pressure, impeding our efforts to get oxygen into him. To further complicate matters, he had massive upper respiratory burns.

I was fighting to push air down the trachea but I noticed that some of it was going down his oesophagus and was filling his stomach. With all the will in the world, I was trying, really trying. I was doing all I could, but there was too much working against me. Oh God, oh God, help us. 'Where is that fucking medivac?' I screamed. Then, when things couldn't get any worse, the fucking corpsman managed to somehow accidentally pull out the IV. Our medic, who hadn't contributed to any of this, had been squatting nearby the whole time. He may as well have been at the beach making sand castles. He had absolutely no field experience in heavy trauma and even when I called for an oral airway device, all he could do was stare at me blankly.

We were fucking livid and the rest of the guys were screaming at him, but I called for everyone to get back in the game. Romero attempted to get another IV in, but he couldn't, he was having a hard time. Like me, he had never had any formal instruction in administering IVs as it was above our scope of training as EMTs but he continued to look for a site and tried and tried again, but to no avail.

By now, Greg's skin colour had improved, indicating that we were getting oxygen into his body. He seemed to be fighting back, because when I stopped CPR a second time, I thought I could feel his heart beating and there was an attempt to breathe. I was hoping against all the odds that it would turn out OK.

In the midst of all the noise and chaos, I could hear the rotors of the incoming helicopter. Peter was compressing the chest and I was giving Greg my last breaths as the helicopter descended. I gave him one last kiss and stood up. I ordered the Marines standing by to pick up the stretcher and we made our way to the LZ. This would have to be quick. We needed to get him on board immediately, along with the rest of the wounded, and have that medivac out of there in seconds.

We were running towards the LZ, which was prepped with green smoke, and it felt like one of those dreams when you run and run but can't get anywhere. The bird was about sixty feet off the deck when I shouted to stop and we lowered the stretcher. Crouching over Greg to protect him, we looked away as the rotor wash blasted over us. The bird hit the deck heavily and we were consumed by a whirlwind of dust and debris thrown up by the big twin rotors. I listened to the sound of the engines as the pilot lowered the thrust and when I heard the pitch change, we were up and rushing up the ramp into the rear of the aircraft.

We got him on board and the other wounded were brought on behind us. We cleared the bird and retreated. When I looked around, I realised Romero had stayed on board to continue CPR. It hadn't occurred to me until then that there were no medics on board. They had sent in a chopper, but it wasn't a medical bird. Fuck, I was tired, but I could have continued. It was too late now. I huddled under the roar of the rotors as the helicopter ascended into the sky and my head dropped into my hands.

My heart was going a million miles an hour. It wasn't natural. It was racing inside my chest and making the sound of a small rolling drumbeat. I couldn't catch my breath. I stared at my hands, which were completely covered in blood. Did this just happen? Again, I had a sensation that I was in a dream. I looked up and stared around me. The car was still on fire and there was equipment and belongings strewn all across the road. There were the guys' helmets, some of which had pictures of their girlfriends inside, flak jackets, rifles – one snapped in half – burning sunglasses, pieces of vehicle and blackened shards of metal lying all over the road. There was no colour. The entire scene seemed to be in black and white, with the exception of the splashes of blood, which were bright red.

I was lost in shock. There was no sound. Everything was muffled, like I was underwater. I knelt down in the middle of it all and my body started trembling. I tried to focus on praying and looked off into the desert because it was only there, where there was nothing, that I could find any solace.

One of the guys, I don't know who it was, walked up to me and asked me if I was OK. I could see his lips move but I couldn't hear his voice. He put a cigarette into my mouth and lit it. I took several drags until the blood on my hands soiled the tobacco. I hadn't even started to consider cleaning it off. He helped me to my feet and hugged me.

I walked over to the car and looked inside. The two charcoaled bodies were still smoking in their seats. The driver was missing half of his head and I noticed the strangest thing – I could see into his mouth, as his lips had been burned away, and he had a nice set of straight, white teeth. As for his buddy, his intestines, if that's what they were, were laying across his lap. His head, although still attached to his body, was hanging over the back of the seat at a crazy angle. I was guessing my boy Silva got them with the machine gun before the car hit. Fuck 'em, I thought.

As I stood there, somebody else came over and handed me a bottle of water. I rinsed out my mouth and realised I was parched. For the next few minutes or so, there was a lot of hugging and back-slapping. There were few words spoken; nothing needed to be said. You could almost make out the tears in some of our eyes, but we just leaned on each other and tried to pick up the pieces.

I washed the blood off my face and then peered into the mirror on a Humvee. I will never forget the reflection I saw staring back. I didn't recognise my face and it scared me. I was only then starting to think about what had happened. As the rest of the guys started picking up all the military and personal belongings lying around, I sat on the hood of the Humvee, smoking and watching them. My helmet was gone. Then I remembered I had thrown it away because the cover had caught fire when we were trying to get Greg out. I picked up another helmet lying nearby and put it on. It had belonged to one of the guys who got hurt. It was covered in blood, but that didn't really make a difference now. I was so drenched in the stuff, it had soaked all the way through to my skin.

We were still in the process of clearing up when a radio report came in that Greg had made it to the hospital and he was still alive. It was hopeful at least. Thirty minutes later, an additional radio report came in that he had died. He was one of the nicest guys you'd ever meet, and now he was gone.

I knew he couldn't have been prouder of his buddies that day. Each man there displayed such character, it made me proud to be a Marine. These were men, real men, not some well-groomed Bacardi Breezer-drinking tools who commonly passed for men, but dirty, tired, hungry, determined bastards who had dealt with so much yet still got up every morning and did what they needed to do. There were no better people to have around you at a time like that. The car could have exploded at any minute, or one of the rounds that were cooking off could have hit any one of us, but that didn't matter to them. What mattered was that we were brothers and we had stayed together to the end.

Another unit had arrived on the scene and, soon after, a military tow truck loaded up the wrecked Humvee. We made sure that nothing belonging to any of the Marines was left on the ground, especially personal items. Then we waited for the Iraqi military to get there to pick up the bodies of the fuckers in the car. I was back at my vehicle with my buddies, but it was really hard to talk about it. I pulled my burned, bloodstained rain bottoms off and put them in a bag. All I could think about was getting the fuck out of there and putting on some clean clothes.

When the Iraqi military guys arrived, they asked us if we had some body bags for the two dead in the car. Sarcastically, I cracked to my sergeant that we should offer them a Pringles box, for the two murdering bastards were now crisps. The Iraqis went through the smoking wreck of the car and as it turned out there was no bomb inside, but it didn't make a difference. They had a collection of AK-47's and a shitload of ammunition. Good enough for me. I felt no remorse. They had killed our boy.

When everything was loaded up and the road cleared, we left the Iraqis to clean up the dead and headed back to base. We had to go by an indirect route, as command needed us to drop off the tow truck and EOD team first, like our day wasn't bad enough. We all dismounted and stood around our vehicles and listened while our squad leader talked about the day. He was obviously upset at the what had happened, but he said he was also very proud at the way things had been handled. He thanked us all individually, but, as we reminded him, it was a team effort and there had been no man more or less involved than any other. While we had been treating Greg, he had to ensure that the 9-line medivac had been called in, security set up and the LZ secured under his direction. Anything he could give us, we got. He thanked us again and we mounted up and headed back to the FOB.

When we got there, Captain Oden, an officer I had known

throughout my Marine experience, sat us down in the chow hall and had the cooks make something up for us. He gave a heart-warming speech about how proud he was of us and how well we had performed, given the circumstances. He also personally thanked each of us and told me I did a hell of a job. His words meant a lot to me because I knew he meant it. He wasn't the kind of officer to say something just because it was the right thing to say.

We broke up, and I went out for a smoke. Then I cleaned myself up. I tore off the bloody clothes and scrubbed the blood and the soot from my eyes, my hair and my body. I washed the smell of death from me and then, when I finished, I washed again. Back in our sixteen-man room there were five empty racks. It was so quiet and I was glad I wouldn't be sleeping there that night. I had been told to report to the medics, as I was wheezing from the smoke inhalation. They monitored my breathing and said they was all fucked up. Then they left me in an empty room and I lay there alone all night, replaying everything in my head. I wanted to be held. I wanted to reach out and cry or scream but, instead, I just lay there quietly and stared at a blank wall until I fell asleep.

Chapter 30

The following morning, I woke up in the empty room and it took a few minutes for me to collect my thoughts and for reality to kick in. I hadn't slept well. I'd had nightmares and woke up several times during the night in a cold sweat. I dreamed of what had happened in vivid detail and in the dream, no matter what I did, I couldn't save Greg. I couldn't run fast enough, fight the fire fast enough, pull him out fast enough – I was in a world in which everything was moving in slow motion.

I was pulling my boots on when Vick walked through the door to see how I was. We talked a little and then I told him that I needed to check with the medics to see if I could go. After he left, I walked outside to smoke. I sat there alone and looked at my hands. Despite my best efforts to clean myself, there was still blood caked into the cracks around my nails.

I went back in and the medic gave me an examination. I left with an inhaler to ease the wheezing in my chest but, apart from that, I was going to be all right. I went back up to our squad room, where everybody was awake. The guys were very quiet. We made small talk, nothing too intense, and it was hard looking at the empty cots and wondering how the other guys were. They gave us the day off; we needed it. I called home, but I didn't tell my mother what had happened. I couldn't share this with her; it would have worried her too much and I couldn't see the point in that, so I told her that everything was OK and that I was looking forward to going home.

We spent the rest of that day sitting around, trying to keep ourselves busy by reading, listening to music or talking quietly. On the one hand, it was certainly quiet and calm, but on the other, it was one of the toughest days that I have ever had to deal with. I wanted to be out on patrol – sitting around doing nothing was killing me. My mind was in turmoil and I was ill at ease. I hated the bastards who were trying to kill us. I wanted to kill each and every one of them with my K-Bar, slicing their throats from ear to ear.

10 January 2005

Subject: Don't go forwarding this around please

Yesterday I lost a friend, a nice guy, a good guy … His vehicle was in front of mine when it got hit by some Iraqi in a BMW who drove into them at 80+ mph.

We ran to the scene, expecting to be blown up at any minute, but we needed to get our guys out of there. I know people felt really useless, but we acted as professionally as we could.

I called on one mate and told him to help me with chest compressions and he knew exactly what to do, where to do it and how many times, etc., just like a true champ.

I had another guy working on his head – he had massive

head trauma – and one working on his legs. Romero had an IV going and my other mate had a medivac on its way within minutes.

Behind us 7.62 mm rounds were cooking off in the flames. We needed to move to a safer place, but we waited because we didn't want to complicate his injuries. Maybe that's not a smart thing. Maybe we should have called it and acknowledged that he was gone and there was no chance – but you cannot tell that to fifteen Marines when one of them is lying on the deck fighting for his life. That's not what Marines do, that's what makes us Marines.

We got him into the chopper and, apparently, he made it to the hospital back on the base. He died soon after from the complexity of his injuries. We did everything possible. We did the best we could with what we had. All the other four guys are going to be OK – it will take a while, but someday we will all sit down and have a beer together and talk about it. There was a lot of hugging and a lot of brave faces, but we have to start picking up the pieces and getting on with the job – we are still in a war zone and are not going home yet.

I lost a friend, but it brought every Marine out here closer together than I ever thought possible … God bless my friend and his family and hats off to my friends for a job done as well as humanly possible.

It's a sad day today, but I am proud of these guys. They are the true American heroes out here …

That's all …

Graham

A few days later, we were up at 06:00 and preparing for a day mission when Corporal Damien stood up and announced to the squad that it was my birthday. With all that had been happening recently, I had forgotten about it. He said he was playing a special song from his laptop in my honour and then he put on 'Kokomo' by the Beach Boys. I loved that song and I used to repeatedly ask him to play it. It always managed to take me away to a happy place, with its images of sandy beaches, blue skies and warm water. For the next few minutes, we listed to the song with smiles on our faces and as we donned our gear in silence, our thoughts drifted miles and miles away from Iraq.

They had given us two replacement Marines for our squad so we could recommence our duties. One of them, Corporal James, was a real special character. He had walked into the squad room the night before and taken off his T-shirt to show off his muscles. While we had been out at the FOB patrolling all day and night, eating the bare minimum and losing weight, this guy had been back in the rear, eating three squares a day and going to the gym. Needless to say, the lads weren't impressed and he was told that if he didn't put his shirt back on, those big man titties he was growing were likely to get him raped. That got a well-needed chuckle out of everyone as we got our gear ready for the mission in the morning. The other guy was Animal, a big ox of a Marine who was the type of guy you could order to run a gauntlet of machine-gun fire and he wouldn't even think twice about it. A nice guy all the same.

The commanders had decided to move Romero out of my truck and into the highback after it had occurred to them that we were the only two medically proficient guys in the entire squad and it was too risky having us both in the same vehicle. I talked with my squad leader again to stress the point that our corpsman was useless and that we needed to get ourselves a medic with some field experience. He agreed and said he understood, but added that it was impossible for the time being. He promised to put in a request. In the meantime, I didn't like Romero leaving our crew. Despite the fact that we had numerous arguments, tiffs and had even almost come to blows, we had become close enough to be brothers.

The mission that day was to escort the CAG team to another school which was literally only about five minutes up the road. Along the way, I spoke with the translator, a nice guy from Baghdad who went under the alias of Todd. He was down to earth and honest. He told me how Iraq used to be before all this 'craziness'. He said there were bars in Baghdad before the war, women went to college and they didn't have to wear a *jilbab*. He told me that where we were based was the equivalent of the Bible Belt in the USA.

When we got back, we were rejoined by Silva, who had been one of the guys injured in the suicide attack. It was great to see him and his return boosted our morale. He was still a little shaken, but he was going to be all right and, after a few more days to recover, was able to go back on patrol with us. Later, we went over to Al Asad to pick up the other two boys, who were being discharged from the medical centre. Corporal Dan, who had been pulled from the passenger seat, and a guy called Mueller, a tough bull rider who lost half a finger riding one, had both been knocked around pretty badly, but they were going to be OK after a little recuperation time. The fourth member of the crew, a guy called Reilly, had been sent on to Germany for treatment for head injuries. We heard he had also broken his nose, which was tough as he already had this crazy misshapen one. I didn't know if we would see him again until we got home.

While we were at Al Asad, we got a haircut and managed to pick up some stuff from the PX. We also got some good chow, but I ate it too quickly and as soon as I walked out of the dining hall, I threw up all over the place. It was kind of funny that the first decent meal I'd had in weeks was now all over my boots. I ended up sitting in my turret eating crackers from an MRE.

On 13 January, we were back at Al Asad to be interviewed about the events surrounding Greg's death. Like everyone else, I really wasn't in the humour, but it was generally agreed that sitting on our arses in Al Asad sure beat the shit out of bouncing up and down dusty roads all day waiting to be blown up. So, we took our positions on these long leather seats around a conference table with a lieutenant colonel asking us if we would like a coffee. There was a bunch of other officers there who knew a great deal about military law but very little about infantry matters. It was like trying to make a kid understand why daddy has to go to work. We had to go over the details again and again and we were getting frustrated at having to repeat ourselves over and over. I understood that they had to be thorough, but we were still very much in shock and having to explain ourselves and our actions in such detail was mentally taxing.

I didn't like the way they quizzed us on the rules of engagement either. At one point, I was even asked why I didn't attempt to rescue the Iraqi men in the BMW after the hit. I pointed out that they were both clearly dead and one of the officers, a military lawyer, asked me how I was so sure they were dead. I had to go into the details of how they were both in flames and that one of them had half his head missing. I added that my priority was to help the Marines who had been injured and mentioned the fact that we also feared there was a bomb in the car. The lawyer reminded me that no bomb had been found. Now, that was all fine to say sitting comfortably on a leather chair in an air-conditioned room in the relative safety of Al Asad. I tried to tell him that at the moment when the car struck, as far as we were concerned it was a suicide attack and it was safe to assume that there was a bomb on board. He stared hard at me and made a note in his book. I would have loved to tell that lawyer that I didn't care about the two scumbags who killed my buddy, but you can't say things like that. I just stuck to the facts and we got on with it.

With the meeting concluded, we mounted up and headed back to the FOB with a sour feeling in our guts. Fucking lawyers. They would have lynched us if we had put something the wrong way. Having to watch what you said while explaining what had happened to your buddy to a man who makes a living out of twisting the words coming out of your mouth was a sickening experience.

Chapter 31

There was a sudden deterioration in the weather for the last two weeks of January. The temperature plummeted to below freezing and as well as being on the alert for attacks, we had to be careful to avoid hypothermia out on the icy roads. When Vick opened the door to the room one night, he was met with biting cold wind and rain. It must have been blowing at least twenty miles an hour outside. I still hadn't been issued any replacement rain gear and I didn't have any gloves either since they had all burned up in the fire. I managed to borrow some rain gear from one of the guys in another unit and everybody put on as much clothing as possible.

It was still dark as we climbed into the vehicles in the early hours and one morning, I didn't notice that the roof of the Humvee was covered in a sheet of ice. As soon as I put my weight on it, I slid on my ass and rolled off onto the ground. It was funny as hell, although I was winded pretty badly. I sat there on the freezing ground looking up in a daze like a drunk who had been thrown out of a bar.

Vick and I forced ourselves to eat, as we were starting to look a little thin in the skin. If we were going to make it out of there alive, now would be a good time to try to eat and put some weight back on. I was also wearing Sergeant Huerra's prescription glasses, as mine were destroyed in the fire. Both pairs of my military-issued spectacles along with my own pair had been broken from being bounced into my machine gun. I'd requested new pairs weeks ago, but I was told that it could take another month or so. In the meantime, Huerra's glasses had to do.

Towards the end of January, we were all called together and told that we would be heading up north to Haditha to support our company there in the run-up to the elections. It was good news and we were all looking forward to seeing the rest of the lads again. Apparently, those boys had working showers too – living the high life, they were.

On 23 January 2005, we finished off packing a few bits and pieces for a day mission the next day, after which we would be going on up to Haditha Dam. There were other Marines coming into our area of operation from Fallujah and they would be taking over while we were up north. When we came back, they would be going home. When I heard that, it reminded me that we were all going to be going home soon. Home!

I had been writing to my family the whole time and had run out of things to say, but as my homecoming was a little over six weeks away, my spirits lifted a bit and I was able to tell everyone how many pints we would drink when I got home and where we'd drink them. I told people and myself that this deployment had enabled me to take a step back and had given me the time to examine my life and see where I was going. But I wasn't convinced that I actually believed that. I wondered if I had changed and if the people close to me would notice. I guessed that I would be finding out soon enough.

We set off the following morning in a dust storm that made everything look like it was on the set of a Martian movie. The sky was full of an orange dust that clung to everything. It was so thick that you could actually look straight at the sun without squinting. Our first mission in preparation for the elections was to escort the psych-ops team as they drove around reminding the local population that the elections were only a week away and encouraging them to vote for the future of Iraq. We rolled through Baghdadi at about five miles per hour as they spread the good word in Arabic. People came out of their houses to stare at us as we passed by. We turned around and the psych-ops guys handed out leaflets with information on how to vote. By the time we left the town, there was a trail of torn and crumpled up leaflets lying in the road behind us.

When that was done, we met up with the guys who were moving in to take over our neighbourhood and we escorted them back to the FOB. We got talking to them and they were telling us how fucked up Fallujah had been. Things had been pretty rough over there for them and it was one of those conversations where you just listen and count your blessings you weren't there.

We left for the Dam the following morning after learning that eighteen Marines had been killed the night before in a helicopter crash not too far away. We didn't know if they had been shot down by a missile or if it was a mechanical malfunction. We found out later that, in fact, over thirty had died when the huge Sea Stallion chopper had come down after it's engines had failed. One of our own units had also been ambushed during the night and had been attacked with three IEDs, along with multiple insurgents armed with AK-47s and RPGs. They had been travelling with some combat engineers and two of them were KIA straight off the bat and another two died en route to the hospital. I didn't know any of the guys who were hit, but the news was disheartening. We were being picked off without an opportunity to fight back. Our futures lay in the hands of the faceless insurgents while we continued to drive around awaiting our fate. The authorities denied access to the internet and the phone systems until they contacted the fallen Marines' families, which was normal procedure, but it also meant we couldn't tell our folks that we were all right. It was going to be an anxious few days for those at home, waiting for the dreaded knock on the front door and answering it to two Marines in their dress blues.

After arriving at the Dam on 27 January, we had a formation and several Purple Hearts were handed out to about ten guys who had sustained injuries over the course of the deployment. Then it was off to prepare for the elections that would build a better, safer Iraq. We escorted what seemed to be every single guy from Charlie Company in seven-tons to a processing plant, where they would be securing a series of buildings for use as a polling station. When we got there, the dismounts from Charlie Company cleared the buildings under protection from our gun trucks. Then a convoy of engineers with massive earth-moving machines showed up and set about working frantically to build huge berms and setting up concertina wire around the perimeter. By now, massive Abrams tanks had arrived on deck, along with light-armoured vehicles (LAVs) and in the sky above we had Cobra gunships circling around. Whoever had dreamed up this little party had gone all out and, logistically, it was superb. The various units set the position up very well and it was all done in no time at all.

We were tasked with patrolling around our new miniature firebase while this was going on and it was pretty routine stuff, even though we were on high alert. This election was the single most important event since the overthrow of Saddam Hussein. It would be the first free Iraqi election and you could be sure that the insurgents would be more than happy to fuck it all up. Just as I was thinking about that, I heard a merciless explosion and when I looked around, I could see a plume of smoke rising up from one of the diggers. Apparently, it had accidentally dug up a landmine, but the Marine driving it wasn't hurt and the machine survived too.

Everyone got back to work again, although now there was extra vigilance for landmines. A few hours later, we started to receive mortar fire from across the river. It was pretty inaccurate and the mortars came nowhere near us. Another unit was sent out to see if they could deal with them. It was starting to look like this would be one long camping trip.

30 January 2005 – polling day in sunny Iraq! I was curious to see if many civilians would show up for to vote. We were already in place by morning prayer at 05:15, but when the polls opened two hours later, there wasn't a single soul at the voting station. They sent in psych-ops along with the Abrams tanks to the edge of town to encourage the locals to come out and vote. Along the way, they found an IED on the road. One of the tank gunners was given permission to shoot it from a safe distance with his .50 calibre. He hit it and it went off with a huge roar that must have spooked everyone in the town. I'm not sure exactly what happened then, but one of the tanks reported taking some small-arms fire and they opened up with the .50 calibre again. I was busy looking through my binoculars over to the flank to see if I could spot insurgents running from the scene, but all I could see was a bunch of scampering kids running for their lives. My vehicle commander reported the presence of kids in the area and then it was all quiet again.

They made another appeal over the speakers for people to come out and vote, but with bombs going off and helicopters flying overhead, not one soul appeared. Who could blame them? We knew the insurgents had warned the locals that they would be killed if they voted. Some time later, a single figure approached the polling station and filled out his voting card. We thought, great, maybe this is the start, but then, minutes later, a mortar round came whistling down. It appeared that our one single voter had used his democratic right to calculate the distance to our position from his mortar launch site.

The polls finally closed and we were relieved that this shit was finally over. The elections had been very tense and there had been an escalation of violence in the run-up to polling day. I only hoped that this would subside and it would quiet down now.

We headed back into the FOB and asked how it had gone. Besides the one guy who came out, only a handful of ING soldiers and interim government officials, who had been trucked in to be the official overseers of the election, had actually voted. It was in some ways a complete waste of time but, at the same time, we had the polling station open and there had been an election. It was just too bad that if anyone had actually voted, they would have been found dead the next morning.

During the night, we broke down the FOB and picked up everything we had brought with us before disappearing under the cover of darkness to Haditha Dam.

Chapter 32

At the beginning of February, there was still a lot of work to be done, but word had it that our replacements would be there in early March. As we were getting short now, we were all a little edgy. There were no patrols scheduled and I managed to take a shower and change into clean cammies. I shaved my face and even put gel in my hair. I felt almost normal, like I could have been getting ready to go out for a pint.

The phone lines were open again, but it took over two hours to get my dad on the phone and we chatted about my coming home.

Vick left for four days' R&R. He had been working his ass off throughout this deployment and he deserved it. They only had one slot open, so he left alone for Qatar to kick back and relax with a beer or two. Before he left, we both talked incessantly about the trip to Europe we had sworn we would take when all this was said and done.

In the meantime, the rest of us had three night missions in a row. We tried to get some sleep, but, first, there was a gear inspection and a trip to the test fire range. By mid-afternoon, it was pissing down and that set the mood for the rest of the mission. Everybody was so down as we set off. We were already exhausted and now we were facing three more long, sleepless nights. We got through them by talking about home. We were getting close now, just one more month.

On the morning we were coming in from our third patrol, we heard that the Battalion Commander's personal security detail had hit a landmine. I knew a lot of the guys who were on that detail. The report stated that several Marines were seriously hurt but gave no names. As we were taking in the news, we got word down that we would be running another night patrol that night. The hits just kept on coming.

We finished up that patrol the following morning and guess what? We had another night mission that night. At this stage, all of the boys looked like the walking dead. To add to our misery, we still had to stand watch during the day. Each one of us had to be down there for at least an hour, so our sleep was split in half. At that stage, we were all finding it virtually impossible to stay awake and focused.

In the afternoon, we were called to escort an ambulance to the intersection of Saturn and Page, which was just down the road. A vehicle had hit a landmine at the very spot that we drove past at least twice a day. We were stood down as they got the wounded out by chopper, but since we were all ready to go, we were sent out on patrol early.

We passed a resupply convoy on Route Neptune and after about three or four minutes, I was looking backwards when I saw a bright flash in the night sky, followed by a loud boom. The convoy we had just passed had been hit with an IED. We turned around and went to see if they had sustained any casualties, but the driver, who was a civilian contractor, got away with only scratches and bruises. The rear of the truck was pretty banged up, though. We went off road to the east to look for a trigger man and found a wire all right, but when we traced it to an observation point, there was no sign of him.

The following day, I saw the crater from the mine strike the night before and it gave me goose bumps. Hitting a landmine was nothing much more than pure bad luck for the most part and we feared them more than any other means of attack. As for the other stuff – the ambushes, the stand-offs in the towns – we could have taken more direct action if we had enough personnel. The squads patrolling the area were too few and far between. I could never understand why there were thousands of Marines up in Al Asad air base who never left the wire. The war was out here, on the streets of the towns and the desert roads. This is where it would be either won or lost. We needed more boots on the ground if we were to ever take control of the country and build up an effective Iraqi security force. I had no idea who was running this war, but they couldn't really expect to win it with so few of us. In the meantime, we continued to patrol up and down those treacherous roads that were laden with explosives every day and night. Our movements had become as predictable as snow in Norway and the insurgents knew when, where and how to hit us. It was a horrible job and one for which there was no end in sight. In about a month, we would hand over the dangerous responsibility to another unit who would then start driving up and down the same lethal roads in unarmoured vehicles, and on it would go.

Valentine's Day. The guys who were married or in a relationship were all thinking about their loved ones, while the rest of us thought about what might have been if we hadn't been sent to Iraq. We spent the day out on another CAG mission to Dulab, where we gave away thirty thousand dollars for improvements to the local schoolhouse. Most of the guys were pissed off about this. As one of them pointed out, there were children in the United States who didn't have writing materials or who went to school hungry or without a coat and here we were handing over tens of thousands of dollars to a school in an area where we are being attacked on a daily basis.

Dulab in particular was known for its hostility and we had to have air support in the form of Cobra helicopters when we went there. When we entered the town, everything just stopped – there were no kids waving at us, just stares and emotionless faces. We were happy to leave, but not as happy, I'm sure, as the locals were to see the back of us so they could start spending the money on more weapons.

When we got back to the FOB later that evening, I got a hold of a satellite phone and called my ex back in Austin. I was really looking forward to telling her I loved her but, when I got through, I could sense from her voice that she had company. My heart sank as I realised she wasn't alone. I had no reason to expect that she'd ever wait for me, so I just told her that I loved her anyway and hung up. I lit a smoke and stood there with the match in my hand when – BOOM, BOOM, BOOM – mortars started raining down. Marines were ducking for cover like cockroaches scattering when you turn on a light, but I didn't move a muscle. The mortar attack didn't register with me, all I could think of was my ex with somebody else. Then I heard somebody shouting, 'Dale, get the fuck in here! Run!', and I snapped out of it and ran inside to get cover. I sat there on my rack for the rest of the day and tried to offload some of my feelings. Vick, who had returned from his R&R, put me straight. 'Fuck it,' he said, 'we're almost there. Forget about it, we'll just go home and get drunk.'

We had spent the previous week on day missions. The days were getting a little bit warmer as the spring arrived. We were enjoying the sun when we were told to pick up a Marine at a traffic control point at the intersection of Saturn and Neptune. There was a Red Cross message for him back at base, which more or less meant that somebody in his direct family had just passed away. It sucked that one of his close family had died so soon before his homecoming.

There was a night mission the following night and the FOB was crowded with additional elements preparing for a big push to take the city of Hit in the morning. Apparently, the operation had already made the news back in the States, so the element of surprise had gone completely out the window. Out on patrol, we were told to pick up an Iraqi soldier at Al Asad who had just been through one hell of an ordeal. It was quite an inspiring story. He, along with four other Iraqi soldiers, had been sent into a nearby town in plain clothes to gather intelligence. They were noticed and soon engaged in a firefight with insurgents who had surrounded them. Then they got separated. Two of them went one way and ended up getting picked up by a Marine unit who spotted them moving across the desert. Of the other three, one ended up being mortally wounded and another one was wounded in the leg. They buried the dead guy after hauling his body away over their shoulders so the insurgents wouldn't defile it, then took off into the desert, the injured one being helped along by his comrade. They trekked fifteen kilometres barefoot across the desert, only to be picked up by Marines who mistook them for insurgents. They were arrested, the injured one receiving medical treatment, and the other taken off for interrogation at the detention centre.

We arrived to pick up the uninjured one and bring him back to the firebase to rejoin his unit. He came out, a small, wiry little man wrapped in a thick, black blanket. After he was introduced to us, he insisted on giving the blanket back to the Marines at the detention centre. They were trying to get him to keep it, as all he was wearing was a ragged black shirt and pants. He must have been freezing out there but was adamant that they take the blanket back.

He could speak pretty good English, but he was very shaken up and didn't know what was going on. He asked to see his wounded friend but was told that that wasn't possible, as he was being treated in the surgical centre. The man was crestfallen and as we waited for permission to get on the road, I tried to cheer him up. I talked to him about Manchester United, who he said was his favourite soccer team, and he relaxed a little.

On the way, we offered him cigarettes, food and even some clothes, but all he would take was a bottle of water. He struck me as a professional guy, very polite and dead keen to get back to his buddies. I have to say, I took my hat off to him. So far, I hadn't seen much to inspire me about these guys, but this fella really impressed me. He sat quietly in the back of the vehicle as I manned the turret all the way back to the FOB. The only words he spoke after we arrived were, 'Thank you, Mister, thank you.'

The assault on Hit went in on 21 February and Charlie Company, along with Bravo, entered the city without taking any casualties. Apparently, Charlie Company had been lucky as a building they were occupying as a forward COC had received a direct hit from a RPG that failed to explode.

We had set up a couple of observation posts throughout the night in support of the operation and cordoned off one house that was earmarked for a visit. A patrol was ordered to make sure there were no insurgents in it and Vick had to knock on the door. Later, after the patrol, he told me how he got on. It went something like this.

Knock, knock – the door opens.

Iraqi man: 'Hello, Mister.'

Marine: '*Marhaba*. Are there any Ali-Babas here?'

Iraqi man: 'No Ali-Baba, Mister.'

Marine: 'OK, thank you, *shukran*!'

Chapter 33

I was walking up the stairs for a gear check before a night patrol when I ran into an officer I had never seen before. I was wearing a heavy Marine-issued fleece jacket and this officer started giving me a hard time and demanding to know why I was wearing it on base. I told him the simple truth – because I was fucking cold and that it had been issued to me for that exact reason. I took it off while he went on with his lecture about Marine discipline and when he was done, I went about my business. I was standing by my truck cleaning the machine gun and thinking about the audacity of that bloke coming out to the FOB with his garrison ideals and trying to exert his authority where it wasn't needed. I had my own officers and NCOs who were out there to do that job.

Some time later, the same guy came over to me again and this time he started pulling me up about the angle of my cover on my head. I couldn't fucking believe it. I grabbed my rifle in my hand, loaded a magazine, cocked it and then just walked away. He called me back, but I ignored him and carried on. I had done everything I could for the military. I had experienced pain, hunger, sleep deprivation, fear and horror. I was almost at breaking point. I needed to get away. I found myself with one of the corpsmen minutes later and told him I was coming very close to losing it. I needed to talk and figure something out before somebody got hurt. I handed over my weapon, as I felt it was dangerous for me to have it. He was understanding and sent for Captain Oden, who was in charge of my company at the FOB. The captain came in to see how I was. He sat down with me and I admitted I wanted to kill that officer. He actually thanked me for being honest and admitting that my head was wrecked. He organised for me to be sent to Al Asad the next day to talk to a combat counsellor and promised he would put the officer straight and tell him to leave the guys alone. It made me feel a bit better but, that evening, I was pulled from the overnight patrol, which didn't sit well with me. I wanted to be out on the road with the boys, but the patrol commander reminded me that I was outside myself and needed to take a timeout so that I could get back soon and continue my job. I walked back to my room as my guys rolled out the gate without me.

The following morning I went with another patrol to Al Asad to see the doctor. Accompanying me was a corpsman whose job it was to make sure I was all right. I had given them my M-16 the night before, but I insisted on having it back as I was sure as shit not going outside the gate without it. At Al Asad, I met with a doctor at the combat stress clinic. I had never sat down with a shrink before and instead of having my blood pressure checked and sticking out my tongue, I was sitting there telling him about the way I was feeling. He listened carefully and after a while, he gave me the scoop. I was experiencing the classic symptoms of combat stress and post-traumatic stress disorder. It didn't mean much to me, but it hit home when he told me he wanted to keep me in Al Asad. I refused. I needed to finish this thing with my mates. We were almost there now and if my boys were going to spend the last few weeks out on the road, I was going to be with them. No glitch in the brain, which to me wasn't a serious injury, was going to keep me from that. He agreed reluctantly that if I felt that strongly about it, then I could go back on condition that I reported back in one week for a check-up. He finished up by telling me that I needed to go over to the chow hall in Mainside to get some ice cream. Now that was an order I had no problem with and when it was my turn, I demanded an extra large serving, just as the doctor had ordered.

When I was brought back to the FOB, my own squad was suiting up, ready to go out. I jumped from the vehicle and ran over to my squad leader and told him I was going out with them. He didn't want me to go, but I pleaded with him. I didn't want to be sitting back there with my 'crazy head' while my mates were out on the road. Two minutes later, I was back behind my machine gun, apologising for leaving her with another man the night before. It was a long, uneventful night patrol, but it was just good to be back out there with my team, where I belonged.

On day patrol the following morning, I was still pissed off about a lot of things there, but we were only days away from finishing our missions and going home. We took an army EOD unit out who were equipped with two vehicles that were straight out of a science-fiction movie. They were mad-looking machines that had all kinds of devices attached to them to detect mines and IEDs. They were supposed to be bomb proof, but there was no way I wanted to try them out to see if that was true.

They were accompanied by two Bradley fighting vehicles that were loaded with army soldiers, who we referred to as 'Hooahs', an all-purpose expression in the army. We patrolled along the roads at little more than walking speed while their bizarre contraptions scanned for explosives. It wasn't long before we got a call to go into Hit, where four 155 mm artillery rounds had been found along with a mobile phone detonation device.

There were still a lot of Marines in the city since the assault, but as we rolled in, the streets were deserted. Apart from a squad or two manning a traffic stop, it was like a ghost town. We set up security a safe distance away from the IED site while one of the mine-sweeping vehicles drove up and the crew set a charge in place to safely detonate it. As they retreated, they gave a three-minute warning. Moments before the detonation, I ducked my head down inside my vehicle because even though we were more than three hundred metres away, you could still catch a piece of shrapnel. When it went off, it shook the vehicle violently. It was a pretty intense IED and I was glad the insurgents didn't have the opportunity to detonate it. Once that was taken care of, we continued along with the mine-sweepers for the rest of the day, driving at a painfully slow pace, talking the whole time about our approaching homecoming.

Back at base, there was mail waiting for us and it was exciting to be reading letters from our loved ones, knowing that we would be with them again soon. We had a night patrol earmarked for later that evening, but it didn't faze us. We could count on our fingers the number of patrols we had left until the deployment was over.

We were out with the Hooah EOD team again, scanning the main roads running through Hit. We only had one of the mine-sweepers with us, as the other one had broken down. This forced us to clear one side of the road before we had to turn around and sweep the other. It took a long time and increased our exposure as we slowly moved along in the open. Adding to the danger was the fact that there was still only a tenuous grasp on the city and it was unclear to us where the friendly forces were. We would have to be very careful not to mistake our own forces for insurgents.

Progress was slow and we tensed up as we passed through positions where other units had been ambushed just days ago. The scars of battle were clearly visible. The streets we patrolled consisted of buildings that were three to four storeys tall and some of them were pockmarked with bullet holes and blackened from RPG strikes. The neighbourhood was run down and the paint on many of the buildings was peeling away. Bags of trash lay along the sides of the streets where people had obviously thrown them from their windows. Some of the buildings had no windows and others were boarded up. There were very few people on the streets. Two young girls were playing nearby though. I had a Frisbee that had 'Say No to Drugs' written on it. I threw it to the girls, who picked it up and ran back inside their house. I think the message written on the Frisbee was probably the least of those poor kids' problems.

We hadn't gone far when the mine-sweeper out in front told us to stop and move back as they had spotted an IED containing three 155 mm artillery rounds by the side of the road. We backed up while they disarmed it. They took it with them, as they couldn't blow it up in a built-up area. Then we simply moved on as if it was just another minor inconvenience at the office.

We hadn't gone much farther when we stopped again. The dismounts clambered down out of the vehicles to have a look around. Peter was kicking some dirt randomly when he uncovered a yellow wire. He bolted back to his vehicle and yelled at the driver to get out of the kill zone. Dismounts scouted around the vicinity at a safe distance to see where the wire possibly led to while the mine-sweeper dealt with the device.

Eventually, the EOD team uncovered a steel box containing PE4 explosives, three more 155 mm artillery rounds and two plastic bottles of gasoline. The combination of the plastic explosives, the artillery rounds and the gasoline could have had horrific results had it gone off. The EOD guys told us they had never seen such a device used in theatre before. The insurgents were obviously evolving and improving their methods.

As the EOD team prepared for a controlled explosion, we reflected on how lucky Peter had been. He had been standing only a foot away from the home-made bomb when he stumbled on the yellow wire.

We moved on again only to be halted some five hundred metres farther along the road when the mine-sweeper uncovered yet another batch of 155 mm rounds. The street was riddled with them and they had been planted with the intention of causing the maximum amount of damage.

We spent the rest of the afternoon disarming one device after another as we slowly crawled along the road. It was frightening to think how well prepared and well armed the insurgents were. They were definitely stepping up their game and I felt relief that we would be out of there soon.

I had a night patrol later in the evening, but first I had to go back to that bloody combat stress clinic at Al Asad. This time, the doctor pissed me off no end. He was nothing like the doctor who had seen me the week before. He got me riled up to the point that I told him that I was done talking to him and I walked out of the door, despite his protest.

On my way back from the doctor, I ran into some of the guys who would be replacing us. They told me that most of them were already on the ground in Iraq and were just waiting for orders to move to the FOB to replace our battalion. They were curious and they bombarded me with questions, just like we had when we'd arrived. They looked very young and although they were excited, you could tell that they were a little on edge, as they had no idea what to expect. We were waiting in line for a burger and their sergeant told them they were only to eat the healthy options, but when I explained that they wouldn't see the likes of this food for months on end, he relented and let them at it. I left them chowing down on burgers and hot dogs, drinking Cokes and licking ice cream from their lips.

Waiting to go out on patrol that night, the talk was all about the replacements and the fact they were there already. It could only be a matter of days now and then our tour would be done. Sergeant Kent didn't want me to go out, as he said I was too tired, but I was too excited after meeting the replacements and I didn't want to stay behind. I spent the next twenty-six hours out on the road.

It was another lovely day in Iraq, out on the road – though it had to be one of our last and I could almost taste the creamy pints of Guinness and feel the civilian clothes on my back as I bounced around the turret listening to the music from the iPod down below. It was a late addition to make our lives a little more comfortable and I have no idea why we didn't have one all along to be honest, as it worked wonders for us. You could barely hear the music over the roar of the engine, but it was loud enough to take the edge of the boredom.

We stopped and talked to some shepherds who were walking in the direction of Al Asad. They were only teenagers and we joked about giving them twenty dollars for a sheep to have a BBQ. The cheeky kid wanted a hundred. I'm not sure of the going rate for a sheep back at home, but a hundred dollars seemed a little steep for Iraq. We passed on the offer. On our way to base, you could sense everyone's happiness and when we got back, I looked into booking a holiday in the

Canary Islands. Later, a small convoy arrived in the FOB. It was the advance party of Marines from the replacement unit and as they stopped and dismounted, all the Marines came outside to cheer. The new Marines got off their trucks to a standing ovation and a chorus of whistling. They were the reality that we were going home soon.

In the meantime, the show had to go on. We were to travel up north and link up with a unit that had retrieved the body of the Iraqi soldier who had been killed a week earlier. We rehearsed a respectful handover procedure for giving his body to his Iraqi comrades, then headed out on a patrol. The nights were getting noticeably warmer again and I breathed a quiet prayer of thanks that we wouldn't have to endure another freezing night. We set up an observation post near one of the military-only roads. I hadn't had much opportunity to get out of the vehicle lately, so I offered to take up a position fifty metres away with my rifle and thermal-imaging camera. There were two of us out together and I radioed back every ten minutes to report our status.

'Black 3, this is Sneaky Squirrel [my self-appointed call sign for the operation].'

'Send it, Sneaky Squirrel.'

'Sneaky Squirrel is incredibly bored. How long will he be here?'

'Unknown duration, Sneaky Squirrel. What is your status, over?'

'Completely bored, over.'

'Roger that.'

'Sneaky Squirrel, out.'

After what seemed like an eternity, they called us back in. As we mounted up, I asked how long we'd been out there. I was surprised to learn that my entire sniper career had only lasted about an hour and a half. Obviously, I didn't have the patience to be a sniper.

Chapter 34

We woke in our darkened quarters and tumbled out into a sea of activity at the firebase. A load of the new guys had arrived. In their clean cammies and fresh-looking faces, they stuck out a mile. They were being given classes on everything from IED detection to last-minute cultural and language training. As we watched them with smiles on our faces, it reminded me of when we arrived seven months earlier. How different we looked now in our filthy, torn uniforms with the name tapes and rank insignia missing. We were no longer the green Marines. Later, we were sent to Al Asad to pick up the rest of them and there was lots of shouting and running around, counting off of weapons and bodies while we stood beside our vehicles waiting for them to finish up and to get onto the seven-tons so we could get on with the day's mission.

As we were leaving Al Asad with our convoy of new Marines, one of the guards we had got to know well from the many times passing through the gate shouted out, 'New meat for you guys, huh?', and one of our lads replied, 'Hell, yeah, we're out of here, man!' As we drove off out into the desert, we heard him shout one last time, 'Well, drink one for me at home, would ya?' That brought a smile to everyone's face.

The next day, we were heading south with some of the new guys to show them the ropes. As our dismounts were scanning an intersection for landmines, Vick had to fire a warning shot at a car that wouldn't stay back. It was a precision shot and he managed to cleanly blow out the tyre from about a hundred metres away. The driver quickly turned around and got the hell out of there. We shrugged and got on with it, but I noticed that the replacement guys looked nervous.

While we were out on the road, Charlie Company was with another one of the fresh squads on a foot patrol near the FOB. They had stopped the traffic on a public road to enable the patrol to cross when they encountered a suicide bomber. The guy had driven a car loaded with explosives at the patrol, but he detonated it prematurely and blew only himself to pieces. He didn't kill anyone else – but he sure scared the hell out of the new guys. We agreed later that the suicide bomber should be given a Darwin Award for his heroic effort in only killing himself.

By the time we got there, the foot patrol had engaged a second vehicle that had rushed at the Marines. They ripped the driver apart with gunfire and the car crashed and overturned. Several men of military age, who had suspicious material with them like binoculars and mobile phones, crawled out of the wreck. We suspected that they may have been a unit sent to conduct a battle damage assessment in the wake of the initial suicide attack.

The remains of the bomber and his vehicle were scattered everywhere. There were bits of flesh and bone strewn across the ground, just like scraps from a butcher's table. I could make out various bits and pieces from the body, parts of his head, feet and hands. The lumps of meat were blackened from the blast and the birds were already landing to take advantage of the free meal. We set up a security perimeter while the mess was cleared up before we got the new Marines back inside the safety of the base. But it wasn't over yet. Suddenly, there was a loud explosion. We looked over at the gate to the FOB, where we could see the smoke from a mortar round that had exploded in midair. The pricks had set it to detonate above the ground, a highly effective way of ensuring maximum damage. Only one mortar exploded and not a single Marine had been killed or seriously hurt in what was obviously intended to be a co-ordinated attack.

Finally, after the area was cleared, we escorted the dismounted Marines inside. They were visibly disturbed by the events on their first day out – and who could blame them? The insurgents must have been wise to the fact there was a transition in progress. They knew there were new guys on the ground and were obviously trying to take advantage of the situation and kill an easy target. If any good came out of that day, it was that the new guys had learned a quick lesson in what to expect for the rest of their tour.

On 9 March, the rumours were flying high that our night mission later that evening would be our last. Rumour had it that we would be there until 15 March and then we would be going home. The new guys were still getting classes and while I was cleaning my machine gun, I listened in on their lessons. They were being told that they were required to wear seatbelts and that Humvee drivers needed eight hours of sleep before driving a vehicle, all garrison-type education that was impossible to practice out there. It was the same scripted bullshit that we had received when we arrived and as we had learned, it had nothing to do with reality.

We brought a bunch of them out with us on night patrol and let one of the new guys drive for his first time. He did all right and between himself and his corporal, they asked a lot of good questions and got some good advice in return.

Our new driver, Munoz, who had replaced Romero, was almost falling asleep on the way back, so I took the wheel while he sat up on top in the cold morning air to wake up. As we rolled back to the FOB, Sergeant Hughes in the lead vehicle confirmed that we had just completed our last mission. We drove our battered Humvees through the gate for the final time and I said my last Hail Mary. We'd completed our mission in Iraq. It was over.

Part 3

COMING HOME

Chapter 35

It's hard to explain how I felt when we were finally done with our last patrol. Part of me couldn't believe that I was still in one piece. I think I really didn't expect to still be alive. The more immediate sense was one of relief. The endless night and day missions were a thing of the past and, for the moment, I didn't have to think about patrolling, IEDs, suicide bombers or landmines.

The handover process started as soon as we came back in through the gate. I told the Marine who was getting my M-240G to take care of her as if it was his only child. He looked at me nervously while I gave him a quick crash course on how to maintain and love her. Some hours later, when the official transfer of duties was complete, I finally got to do something really important. I called my mother and told her the good news. It only rang for a second when she picked up.

'Howya, Ma, it's Graham. I'm coming home! Go out and have yourself a drink tonight and sure, I'll see you in a few weeks.'

She was overjoyed and set about thanking God and a host of

saints. It made me feel better to know that my mother could relax now, safe in the knowledge that I would be home soon.

Then I dragged my heavy boots up the stairs to get some rest, but it wasn't easy. There were fourteen of us in the room and we were all giddy and couldn't stop talking.

With the deployment over, all we had to do was pack our belongings and wait for the freedom bird to bring us back to the 'land of the big PX'. With nothing to do, we had a lot of time to think. I started thinking about my enemy, the people who had been trying to kill us. We were led to believe that the majority of the insurgents were fanatics who had crossed over the borders of Iraq to join in the *jihad*, but I suspect that many of them were actually local men who couldn't tolerate the occupation of their country by a foreign power – a bit like the Irish.

We referred to them as terrorists, insurgents or religious nuts and considered them nothing better than a rag-tag bunch of unorganised, illiterate scumbags. That may be true, but these guys were also clever. They were always watching us, alert to our every move. They knew everything about us. They had brought the fight to the most renowned military force in the world. They had struck hard blows. They had killed and maimed our finest and disrupted, if not destroyed, the process of transition to democracy. And they still controlled the towns and cities of western Iraq. It was hard to believe that just a few miles outside a base with over ten thousand Marines, there were towns where we had absolutely no presence, where the law on the street was dictated by the insurgents.

Meanwhile, the Iraqi people were still living in fear. They couldn't defy the insurgency and hope to live because we had failed to protect them. We came out and showed off our fancy weapons and just like cockroaches, the insurgents simply ducked out of the light. But as sure as anything, as soon as we were gone, they popped their heads back up again. We couldn't pretend we had brought anything under control when the only time we travelled in relative safety was when we were heavily armed, and had overhead helicopter support.

Soon I would sleep in relative security, but those innocent people out there would sleep with uncertainty, caught right in the middle between a vicious insurgency, a foreign occupying force and a weak national government that may as well have ruled from ten thousand miles away.

I had seen all of the police stations and Iraqi army posts in my area of operation systematically destroyed while we endlessly patrolled the empty supply routes to our bases. I suspect we all felt a lot of frustration, but we had done our bit and now all we wanted was to be reunited with our families and forget all about it. I can't remember who said it, but one of the lads told me he was going to a hypnotist when he got back to see if he could get the last year erased from his memory. If it worked, I would gladly follow him down that road. It was time to get out of there and go home.

On 12 March 2005, we mounted up on the seven-tons for our lift to Al Asad. I had never seen so many happy faces in all my life and when the engine started, we roared in delight. As the trucks started to roll, we waved and cheered at the Marines who now occupied the FOB.

Our ecstasy was short lived when the convoy stopped suddenly. A suspicious device had been found along the route that we were going to be taking. It was a little embarrassing, considering that we could be heard cheering for miles around and now we were just sitting there in silence, having moved just a few yards.

It turned out to be nothing more than a plastic bag with a water bottle in it and soon we were on our way again except this time, there were no cheers or whistles. We were afraid to jinx ourselves. Along the way, some of the Marines kept their rifles pointed over the sides of the trucks in case a suicide bomber had a go at us on our last trip on the open road. The rest of us crouched down in the bed of the truck, behind the protection of the steel walls, and tried to ease our anxiety by talking about girls, beer and football.

Back at Al Asad, the entire company was once again reunited. We were assigned to one of the huge tents and there were seventy of us in there swapping war stories and boasting incessantly about what we were going to do when we got home. Some of the guys got into serious card games. Vick was doing really well, but another guy, Ambrose, who was actually a good card player, had a terrible card face that would cost him a lot of money, so he was sitting there with his gas mask on.

A few days later, I was walking to the PX in the afternoon when I stopped to watch some Marines playing ball on the football field. I looked a little harder and couldn't believe what I saw. It couldn't be; no fucking way. I walked closer and stopped one of the Marines. 'Hey man, what are you playing there?'

'Gaelic football,' he replied.

'Are you fucking serious? Where did y'all learn to play that?'

He told me his officer was from New York and that he played Gaelic football for a team. He had his Marines play it in Iraq as a way of keeping fit. I explained that I played and he invited me to join them. I laid down my rifle and went onto the field. I only played for a few minutes, but it was a fantastic experience.

I had hoped to be home by the time St Patrick's Day came around, drinking pints and enjoying a parade somewhere, but we were still at Al Asad waiting on our flight home. When I woke up, though, the lads all wished me a happy St Patrick's Day and that cheered me up even more.

Later that morning, we had to sit through a bunch of classes that were meant to help us with our transition back into society. Apparently, the process of returning to the world could be a tough one. We listened blankly to the stories of how returning soldiers and Marines had been arrested for kicking the shit out of their wives and girlfriends, and worse.

At 16:00, they called a formation together and several names were read out. Mine was one of them and Romero's was another. We were receiving some form of award for our actions in dealing with our injured brother in January. I asked the first sergeant if Peter's name was on the list. He checked and said it wasn't. I felt bad for Peter – he had done as much as anyone else that day, but he wasn't getting any recognition.

They called us to attention and the group of us that were receiving awards was marched out in front of the entire company. Major O'Reilly, the company commanding officer, presided over the ceremony. I liked him. His ancestors came from Ireland and had fought in the American Civil War. He carried in his pocket a beautiful silver snuff box inlaid with painted green shamrocks that one of his relatives had with him in the Civil War.

The Company First Sergeant read through my award citation that described the events and my actions on that grave day. Then the major pinned the Navy and Marine Corps Achievement Medal to my chest. It's not the highest award the Marines have – actually, it's the lowest – but that wasn't important to me right then. It was a symbol of how we had all stuck together when we needed to. My only wish was that there could have been a squad citation instead. It meant a lot to me all the same that Major O'Reilly, a proud Irish-American, was pinning the medal to my chest on that day of all days.

So, that was St Patrick's Day 2005. No beer, no parade and no party. There wasn't even any Irish music. But I had been recognised for something I had done and that made me proud. My war was over. I had done my bit and had done it well. Later, I read the write-up that came with the medal over and over again. It didn't seem like it was something I had participated in. I think I had to shake about a hundred hands that evening and to top it all off, we got the news we had all been waiting for. We were flying home the next day.

As we were packing up, we were ordered to put all our stuff on the ground so they could go through it to make sure we weren't taking any illegal items with us. They were looking out for body parts such as ears and fingers that people may have been trying to keep as souvenirs, personal weapons, stolen Iraqi gear and, the funniest one, porn.

A staff sergeant picked up a *Playboy* magazine that my brother had sent me and said it was contraband and couldn't be brought back to the US. I laughed and told him to take it, but then he said he needed to pat us down for a body search. Vick refused to be searched and was taken away for a talk. I saved the staff sergeant a trip by following them around the corner. I wasn't going to be searched like a common criminal after serving the United States in Iraq all bloody winter. I told the staff sergeant that I would rather die on the spot than submit to being frisked. I told him it was unnecessary and that we shouldn't be treated in such a humiliating manner. He was actually quite understanding and we agreed on a compromise that we would empty our own pockets and let him look through the stuff. I apologised and asked him to understand that I was severely stressed and needed to get my head sorted out when I got home. He patted me on the back and let me go on my way after a half-hearted glance through my stuff.

We waited in a holding room until well after dark and then walked out onto the flight deck in a single file. The aircraft's engines were already turning and the noise blasted away our voices. This was it. We were on our way home.

With our bodies tightly packed into the aircraft, they closed the rear ramp and we felt the aircraft moving. Everybody had their cameras out, the flashes were continuous as we took photos in the dark. The pilots gunned the engines and it was so loud that nobody even tried to talk any more. The pilot disengaged the brake and we were hurtled down the runway. He pulled the nose up and the aircraft soared into the sky. We cheered in the back and shook hands with the Marines sitting on either side.

I think most us soon fell asleep on that flight. I know I certainly did because I was dreaming of sipping cocktails on a Caribbean beach with Alicia Silverstone when I was woken by the thump of the wheels touching down at an air base in Kuwait. We were no longer in Iraq; we were truly safe.

From the aircraft, we were taken by bus to the same base that we had staged in at the beginning of the deployment. We spent a day there trying to eat as much food as possible so we could start putting on some weight. Vick and I were talking about a trip we planned to take together to Ireland and the Canary Islands. He had never heard of the islands before. I was telling him all about the Irish tradition of going to Spain on your holidays and spending the entire time in an Irish bar when I ran into a girl from Dunshaughlin in County Meath. She was selling Celtic coats of arms and Celtic swords at the base to returning troops, who she knew had a lot of money to spare. It was nice to talk face to face with someone else with an Irish accent. I was worried that after spending almost a year surrounded by Texan accents, I would come back talking like J.R. Ewing.

We didn't stay too long in Kuwait. We were bussed to the

international airport the next day, where we saw the United Airlines 747 that would bring us home. After loading our own bags into the hold of the aircraft, we walked up the steps, took our seats and stowed our M-16s on the floor.

I was hoping that we would have a stopover at Shannon on the way back, as rumour had it you could get a drink at the bar in the airport, but after take-off, the captain informed us we would be landing at Frankfurt again.

After a brief layover, we were once again on our way and several hours later, the captain came on the intercom to announce that we were now officially in United States airspace and to welcome us home. There was a huge cheer throughout the aircraft. It felt good to finally be back in the USA.

We touched down in California and as the aircraft taxied to the hangar, two fire trucks came out on deck pumping water high into the air in a fire-department salute.

We boarded more buses and as our convoy made its way to Twentynine Palms, a local radio station followed behind in a mobile broadcasting truck telling everyone that another battalion of Marines was coming home. The trip was exciting, to say the least. People were standing by the roadside waving miniature US flags and clapping as we drove to the base. Outside one town, a cowboy on a horse galloped onto some high ground and saluted from the top of the hill. People were running out of shops and bars to welcome us home and standing by the sides of the roads, cheering and waving.

When we finally arrived at Twentynine Palms, we were offloaded on the parade ground, where a welcoming party of women was waiting for us. I assumed they were ladies who worked on the base or wives of officers, but we just stood there awkwardly, not knowing what to do. They stepped forward and hugged each of us over and over again and told us well done. After about ten minutes of that, we were back on the buses to be brought to our quarters.

The first thing I did was make a deal with Vick to cover for me while I ran to the PX to get beer. As soon as they let us go, I took off like Jesse Owens. I was standing in line when another Marine asked if I had just come back from Iraq, and when I told him I had, I was moved to the front. I was disappointed that there was no Guinness left, but I stocked up on Murphy's and Heineken and ran all the way back. When I found Vick, we both cracked open our cans, shouted, 'Sláinte', and took our first deep mouthfuls of beer.

It was a great first evening back. We took off our cammies and walked around drunk in our one set of civilian clothes. After drinking many, many beers, we called it a night. As we crawled into bed, Vick insisted on taking the bottom rack. I warned him that I always fell out of bed when I was a kid, but he laughed and said I was full of shit.

Twenty minutes later, I woke up on the ground. The lights came on and there I was on the floor, holding my head, looking very confused. I was unhurt apart from a huge lump on my forehead. I sat there looking at Vick, who was bursting his shite laughing. 'I fucking told you so,' I yelled at him.

We spent almost two weeks at Twentynine Palms and on our last weekend, Vick, Peter and I rented a car and took it on the road to Hollywood, where Peter used to live. We went shopping at a mall to increase our civilian wardrobe, but we could barely afford anything. Some of the loveliest ladies that I'd ever seen walked by, but the only person who talked to us was a male clerk who worked at one of the department stores. He was looking at us closely and asked if we were in the military. When we confirmed that, yes Sir, we were Marines, he squealed with delight and invited us to a party, as long as we wore our cute little uniforms. We politely declined and after buying what we needed, we were out the door. After seven months in the desert, that place was an alternate reality. Back outside in the sun, I noticed that the palm tress lining the sidewalks were nicer in Hollywood than they had ever been in Iraq.

A few days later, we left California for our final homecoming in Texas. The plane was full of guys who were pumped up about seeing their families for the first time in almost a year. As the aircraft descended into Austin, we had our faces pressed against the windows identifying all the city landmarks like the UT Tower, downtown, Interstate 35 and Town Lake. Yeah, it was all just like we had left it a year earlier.

The Austin Police Department met us with a motorcycle escort to bring us back to Camp Mabry and we took off through the city behind the cops. Unlike California, there was nobody out on the streets to welcome us back. Nobody really knew that we were coming home except for our friends and families and that was OK with us. We just wanted to see our loved ones. As we neared the camp, though, we could see the front fence was covered in painted cards and flags welcoming us home. We drove in through the gate and the soldiers and camp civilian employees were lining both sides of the streets, saluting or waving little flags. When we pulled into the naval reserve centre, though, we were absolutely overwhelmed. There were what seemed like thousands of people cheering for us. The last thing we had to do before we could go to our families was hand in our M-16s. The buses parked around the back of the building out of sight of everyone else, where we let go of our beloved rifles. Then we were marshalled into platoon formation and marched to the cadence of the police department's pipes and drums out onto the parade ground. There were a few brief words from our commanding officers and then we were released into a sea of arms.

Vick's kid was there with the rest of his family and it was really good to see him hug his son. My friends showed up, along with my car, which I was going to drive off in. I gave my mates a quick hug and told them to turn around and get the fuck out of there. Ten minutes later, we were sitting on our old bar stools in Razzoo's, knocking them back. Vick and his family showed up later and we drank and sang long into the night.

Chapter 36

I gave myself a week or so in Austin before I made plans to go back and see my family. I hadn't booked my flight back to Ireland, as I'd had no concrete idea when we would be relieved from active duty. Finally, the day came and Vick and I were once again on a plane together although, this time, there were no weapons, no uniforms and no fear. We were just a couple of regular Joe tourists taking a trip to Ireland.

My heart was in my mouth as we touched down at Dublin airport. I had forgotten how beautiful my home country could be. It was a perfectly cool, damp Irish spring day. I waited impatiently in the baggage-reclaim area, knowing my family was waiting just minutes away. When we got our bags, I walked as calmly as I could through the green channel and rounded the corner and there they were – my parents, brothers, sister and all my nephews and nieces. I gave my mum the biggest hug I ever had and moved on to everybody else. Now I was really home, in my town, in Dublin.

Back at my parents' house, Vick and I were tucking into an Irish breakfast while my family watched the video footage I had taken in Iraq. I could tell from their expressions that they really had no idea what I had been doing over there. We talked for hours and later we drank many pints in the Donaghmede Inn while Vick and I told our war stories.

One thing I noticed in the pub was that I was no longer referred to as 'Graham'. When I was introduced to people I was 'yer man here fought in the fucking war'. It was kind of embarrassing. I just wanted to have a quiet pint, but I found myself sitting there trying to explain to curious listeners what it was like in Iraq.

It was all fine until someone would start talking about the politics behind the war. I had to remind them that I was just a solider and that soldiers didn't make policy, they only enforced it. I accepted that I knew I might be forced to do things I didn't agree with when I joined up and that I had made a conscious decision to join, fully aware of that fact. But whether the war in Iraq was right or wrong had nothing to do with me. That was something that needed to be addressed to the public who voted the people who ordered it into office.

Most people in Ireland were pretty cool about it, though, and they respected my desire not to talk about it when I told them I was just trying to relax at home and didn't want to think about the war, Iraq or the Marine Corps.

One night, Vick and I headed into the city. We were refused entry into a couple of clubs and when Vick tried to explain to one bouncer that we were from out of town, the bouncer wasn't very polite about telling us where to go. For a split second, the thought occurred to me to send the arrogant prick crashing to the ground, but we were out for a good night, not a prison sentence.

Eventually, we got into a nightclub in Temple Bar and were downstairs drinking our pints and watching all the goings-on. Vick, not being from Dublin, was mystified as to why we hadn't been allowed into the other clubs. We were sober, well dressed and had identification. In Austin, you could go to a club wearing a pair of sandals and shorts if you wanted. I tried to explain that we were now in a different world, one where we were considered scumbags because we had our tight haircuts and looked like beaten dogs.

We were talking away about this when a guy to my left started arguing with his girlfriend. He had her up against the wall and was hurting her. I looked at Vick and he must have seen that look in my eye because he started shaking his head, knowing full well I wasn't able to do nothing about it. I turned back around and, by now, this guy was choking his girlfriend and her face was turning red.

I put my pint down and told him to quit it and he told me to fuck off. I swiftly elbowed him in the head and sent him to the floor. With that, several other guys came at me from all directions and I soon had my back against the wall. Fists were flying and the only thing I could do was go on the offensive. I went straight at them with every gun firing. Vick, meanwhile, had flanked my attackers and was elbowing and punching them from behind. I was hitting from the front and soon people started dropping on the ground one after the other. Then it started to get out of control – even the girl who I had tried to help was trying to bite me. Other elements engaged and were now fighting each other. I'm not sure if they knew who they were actually supposed to be attacking, but I took that as my cue to get out of there. I grabbed Vick and we made our escape up the stairs as three bouncers barged past us to the mêlée. We calmly got out onto the street and walked back over the River Liffey, going over what had just happened and counting our injuries. I had a small black eye and both our hands and arms were covered in blood that wasn't our own.

We continued drinking a few beers on the northside, laughing that both of us had been in way more serious brawls in Texas, the kind of ones where you expect someone to come out shooting.

The following morning, we were sitting eating breakfast and my father asked me where I got the black eye. Vick embarked on a melo-dramatic and theatrical account of what happened. According to him, I had stood up in the middle of the club and declared at the top of my voice, 'I am Lance Corporal Graham Dale of the United States Marine Corps, unhand that female immediately.' It was total bullshit, but I had to laugh when my dad pointed out I had just spent a year with the Marines and only got a black eye when I came home to Dublin.

The following day, we went on the holiday to Spain we had talked about for so long and it was great, although we had some strange arguments when we first got there. While Vick wanted to go to the beach, I found I had zero interest in going near the sand. I was sick of sand. So he spent a lot of his time doing what you are supposed to do in Spain while I sat in the Irish bars in the shade, making sure I didn't get sunburned.

The holiday soon came to an end and I bid farewell to my family once again as I went back to the States. After I got home to Austin, to my astonishment, I ran into the same problems I'd had when I tried to get my job back before. Despite the fact that it was supposed to be protected by federal law, IBM refused to rehire me. I contacted the ESGR, a federal agency charged with looking after troops on their return from active duty, and a lawyer was assigned to my case. I waited for three weeks until he finally called me back and told me that technically, IBM had no responsibility to hire me. I couldn't believe it. I was back to square one again. I hadn't been sitting around idly waiting for them to get back to me either, I had been actively looking for other work, but I couldn't even get a phone call returned. One potential employer said that I had been out of the industry for too long while I was in Iraq and that I was no longer a desirable candidate. I managed to get some shifts driving an ambulance that paid enough to just about cover the rent, but it didn't go very far and soon I was broke. I was very frustrated. Once again, I had been let down by the country I had gone to fight for and now I didn't even have enough money to eat.

It would take the employment agency I was with more than two months before they found me a job in San Antonio. It was a ninety-six-mile journey from door to door, but I decided to take it in the hope that something closer to home would come up. I had written a letter of complaint to the ESGR some time later and a top-level woman eventually contacted me to tell me they had been mistaken and that IBM did have an obligation to rehire me, but I felt that if I had to force my way back in there, it wouldn't be long before they would find some reason to get rid of me.

In the meantime, I was back stealing MREs from the base when I went there on drill and eating them at home or sitting in my car on my lunch break because I was too embarrassed to let anybody know that's all I had. I felt lower than shit. If I had known I was going to be unemployed when I got back, I would have saved my money, but I didn't and the meagre wages I'd made while I had been in Iraq had already been spent on my two-week holiday in Europe.

Eventually, I was forced to quit the San Antonio gig when the price of petrol went up to three dollars a gallon. I would look at homeless people by the roadside on my way home. I now knew how war veterans had ended up on the street. I was about to become one of them and it was only when I got a disconnection notice from the electricity company that I swallowed my pride and mustered up the courage to call home and ask for help.

Afterword

The year after I came home from Iraq was one of the hardest of my life. My parents had to bail me out as I spent months trying to figure out where, who and how I was both physically and emotionally. I found myself aimlessly wandering around local bars and dives looking for comfort or maybe some sense of resolution, I'm not sure.

I eventually found a computer job that would support me and I became somewhat refocused on life once again, for the time being at least. I was getting on top of things when just five months after I got home, I was plunged headlong into the chaos of another catastrophe. A few minutes after six o'clock on the morning of 29 August, a Category 3 hurricane with sustained winds of two hundred kilometers an hour made landfall near the town of Buras-Triumph, Louisiana.

Soon, I was watching the devastating aftermath of what the world knows as Hurricane Katrina on my television. I watched in horror at the scenes coming out of New Orleans where hundreds of thousands of people were trapped in the floodwaters that swallowed the city after its protective levees broke. Once more, I found myself pulling on my boots, prepared to respond to another national emergency.

I had started to work part-time with the ambulance company on the weekends when a request came in from FEMA, the government body that was overlooking relief efforts, to send help. They were dispatching eight ambulance crews from my company to relieve the EMTs and paramedics who were already on the ground and I volunteered to go without hesitation. I packed enough provisions and uniforms to last for at least a week after politely asking my employer permission to miss a day or two of work. I locked the door of my apartment in Austin and headed for the company's headquarters downtown to once again face an unknown challenge.

It normally took eight hours to drive to New Orleans. I had made the trip before as a tourist and stayed in a hotel on Canal Street but this time, it turned into an epic journey as we were slowed by the massive military convoys and queues of emergency vehicles from services all across Texas and beyond that were responding to the crisis. Adding to the chaos were the large number of Louisiana residents who mistakenly thought that they would be allowed to simply drive back into New Orleans, which had been declared a disaster zone.

As we inched out way down through the Louisiana swamps along Route I-10, we passed hundreds of vehicles that had been abandoned by the fleeing residents when they ran out of fuel. The obvious signs of panic were an early indicator of what to expect.

We arrived at the staging area in Baton Rouge and were told to get some sleep but found our way to a triage centre at the Louisiana State University complex. We spent a busy night helping out at the university, where we were emotionally distraught by the sheer number of people requiring aid. It was the next morning when we got our first uninterrupted view of New Orleans in the distance.

It was a vision straight out of hell. Huge columns of smoke billowed from buildings across the city and what seemed like a hundred helicopters, both civilian and military, were crisscrossing the sky in all directions. As I looked over the skyline of this once majestic city which was now burning and under water, I could not help but think of my time in Iraq. There were soldiers out on the streets riding around in Humvees and armoured personnel carriers armed to the teeth. Police officers and state troopers were backed up by the armed forces and no one could venture far before being stopped at a road-block manned by police or military units. I would spend the next four days dealing with a tide of human tragedy – an experience that reminded me of some of the worst days in Iraq.

I found myself working at the Convention Center as a triage co-ordinator for the evacuation of civilians from the downtown area. At one point, I had to call on the commanding officer of an air-force unit to radio in an emergency medivac for an elderly woman who was suffering from severe chest pains.

As the chopper descended and we prepared to lift her, I was suddenly back to that terrible day in Iraq getting ready to carry Greg to the chopper. The image came suddenly with the dust and debris swirling around me and, shocked at the intensity of the memory, I glanced down at my clothes expecting to see them covered in blood. I tried to shrug it off as we had a job to do and soon we were off the ground. I continued treating the woman on board the chopper with the other medic on board and she survived but I saw much death and destruction in those few days. And fear. On more than one occasion, we were warned by the police not to stop for anyone as ambulances were being looted and even shot at. It was shocking that this was happening in the United States.

What I witnessed in New Orleans affected me deeply. It made me realise that I was still haunted by my experiences in Iraq. After I came home from the desert, I had found it difficult to reintegrate into society and I often spent long periods at home on my own locked behind closed doors. I couldn't sleep and I was always on guard. Loud noises startled me and I avoided driving whenever possible because I found myself glancing around nervously, waiting for something to happen. I tried to date girls but I felt disconnected from them because I just could not summon up the interest to listen to anyone else's problems. Whether black shoes went with the white top or the red shoes with the yellow top was of no consequence to me. Every relationship I got into was sure to fail and each inevitably painful experience separated me further from reality.

After about a year, I was sent to the Veterans' Administration by the Marines because I had lost all interest in my uniformed life, and it showed. The people there worked with me and I started seeing a psychologist who gradually helped me out of my mental rut. One of the first things she did was confirm the diagnosis by the doctor in Iraq that I was suffering post-traumatic stress disorder.

I also found out my ex, who still lived in Austin, had got married and that hurt deeply but there was nothing that I could do and, in a way, I was happy for her. Everything around me had moved on. I felt like I was no longer a participant in society and that I was merely looking at life, witnessing it from a window in another world.

I began to see better days though. I had started to attend Fire Academy and got a new job. I started to hang out with new and old friends again. I began running every day – and completed two marathons. I bought a kayak and took a new interest in life. Every so often, I met up some with of my Marine buddies and we would grab a beer and shoot the shit. It was a comfort, being able to talk to someone who had been through the same things as me. I also made contact with my ex in Ireland who I still care so much about. I was so glad to be able to talk to her.

One day, completely out of the blue, I realised exactly what I needed. When I was growing up, I had a dog, who died when I was eighteen. So, I went out and found a dog that suited my personality and was a reflection of who I was – I didn't settle on a bulldog or a pit bull but on a Chihuahua, and I called him Killer. Killer did for me in one day what all the doctors and counsellors had been trying to do for a year. He licked me on the face, pissed on my floor and chased his tail around in circles. He made me laugh and gave me something to care about, quickly becoming my right-hand man – and he has been ever since. That dog was the best therapy I could have got.

In the summer of 2007, I was thinking about all of this as I sat against a wall, having a smoke after drill. I had just spent three days with my Marine reserve unit, just like I do for one weekend every month. As usual, I had been cursing the idea of having to spend my precious time off running around Fort Hood with the Marines but a little part of me always looks forward to seeing some of the people I would consider to be my greatest friends. Despite the fact that we like to fight each other, make fun of each other and do nasty things to each other, we are closer than men could ever be in the 'real world' and we'd still give our lives for each other.

We share the same problems, the same fears and the same hopes. We talk for hours about anything and everything – politics, life, family – but, invariably, we always end up discussing the war. It sets us apart from the new guys – who pray they will get the opportunity to go to Iraq. They have not yet been overseas and they want to go kick some ass and make their names – they are the believers in our unit.

But the Iraqi war vets I know are more reserved. There are those who earned the Purple Heart after being wounded in combat and bear the physical scars from the war on their bodies but all of us have the scars on our souls – the ones that itch and keep us awake at night. Some of us receive psychological treatment from the Veterans' Administration, but others are too afraid to seek help and there are others still who we know are getting help but who would never tell you about it for fear of being treated differently both by society and the military.

We would not mind so much, I guess – and perhaps it would be a little easier to live with – if the scars had been inflicted after fighting a conventional war that had clear goals and front lines, where the object was an easily defined cause – like freeing Europe from the Nazis or even defending a small country like Kuwait from aggression, but that's not what we did. We spent seven months driving up and down dangerous roads in the desert, hearing about friends getting blown to pieces on a regular basis, and baffled by a government, people and a media that continuously debated the principles of why we were there in the first place. In fact, we were simply just some normal guys, placed in extraordinary circumstances who were murdered on a daily basis by people who hated us. We were angry that the Iraqi people did not want our help, but we were even angrier that we had to force our help down their throats.

We were told that we were doing good things in Iraq. The message was that every American life lost was worth it. And that sounds great as you watch from the sidelines, but I have been to Iraq and I do not know what the hell 'it' is. As far as I am concerned as a Mr Joe Nobody, 'it' is not worth the high price that is paid when it's the blood of a man whom you have served with and, in doing so, have loved. Yes, we are fighting men. We signed up to fight and, if necessary, die for America but I cannot help but think when I really get myself down that, sometimes, this war reeks too much of oil and freshly printed dollar bills and Halliburton, Blackwater and oil company contracts – and it's all covered in the blood of my friends who had their lives cut short.

Maybe I am wrong; I really cannot tell. I am bombarded by media reports from all sides, and official statements and general opinions. I'm confused. I only know about my experiences, and they are enough to deal with.

On the one hand, I have the military telling me that we did a great job; on the other hand I have the media telling me that it is all about money. And here I sit in between these opposing views only really knowing and believing what I have seen for and experienced for myself.

It's weird, people sometimes still meet me in the street and thank me for what I did, while at the same time reminding me that they do not believe in why we were sent over there in the first place.

We will always be Marines and should the call ever come again, we will answer it. We took an oath to defend the United States but there are those dark times when some of us cringe at the idea of correlating the defence of our home with our role in the occupation of Iraq. It seems that the general consensus now is that invading Iraq was not the greatest idea, but there is little anyone can do about it.

So we served our time – but at what cost? Some got the 'Dear John' letters from their women while they were still in country; others have been divorced since they got back. Plenty of guys came home and fitted right back into society with not too much difficulty, but there are many more who have had a much tougher time and who still linger in turmoil to this day.

They are the ones who cannot go on dates and who don't like to go to crowded places. They find it hard to trust others. These are the guys who sleep with their eyes open and drop their beer when someone makes a loud noise in a bar.

As I sat, smoking my cigarette, I thought about where we had been – and when we might be sent back. I paused to look around the training ground and wondered where the three boys from my unit would be standing if they had not been killed.

After formation, I sat in a classroom where we were told that we were going to watch taped footage from CNN which actually had a camera crew out on that patrol on the night of the ambush when the boys from our unit in Haditha were with the engineers who were killed. Some of the guys who had been ambushed were in the room.

It sounded like a stupid idea to me, and I think I was right. We watched the firefight in this special CNN report, which went on for about ten minutes. The programme then switched gears from the action footage to showing the families of the Marines who had died. It interviewed their kids, their wives, their moms and dads, who all talked about how the fallen Marines had lived their lives, how young they were and how much they were missed. At one point, I almost burst into tears as it touched me close to my heart. I was ashamed, worried that the others would notice I was upset because, as a man – and even more importantly as a Marine – I am not supposed to show such emotion but when I looked around, I could see that the other vets in the room were feeling the same. I also noticed that the new guys were not really paying attention. They were chatting away to each other during the programme or doodling on pieces of paper.

They had not endured the same experiences of loss, anger and frustration. They still believed that war is a video game and that, sure, when the game is over you can just hit the reset button and off you go again. They uphold the boot camp notion of a Marine being the best fighting man in the world, 'kicking ass since 1775'.

It sounds like a marketing slogan and it is but, in reality, we are made of the same stuff as everybody else, and roadside bombs do not discriminate. No matter how tough you think you are, you can be blown apart just as easily as the next guy on the street.

The CNN report ended some time later and we walked outside for a smoke and discussed the purpose of being told to watch it. The good thing about being so close to your buddies is that you are in a group that is honest and open about anything and pretty much everything. If you think that the cartoon chick from *Who Framed Roger Rabbit?* is hot, well, you can tell the boys and you'll laugh when they tell you you're sick.

We all agreed that watching the footage was completely unwarranted. There was no point to it as there wasn't even a discussion about what had happened. As we talked, I knew I was not the only one who almost shed a tear in that room, that was very clear.

We all agreed that the new guys were not affected because they didn't yet appreciate the reality of war. We understood why – they were young and innocent and we hoped that they would remain that way.

As we were standing there, though, rumours began spreading like wildfire – all Marines who had not been to Iraq were to be sent there that summer with another unit. Apparently, the other unit was under-manned and needed reinforcements. This, in itself, spoke volumes – the kids were no longer joining up. It's hard enough being a young college student without having to worry about going to an unpopular war tainted by controversy.

Some polls indicate that over sixty per cent of people in the US do not support the war. As Marines, we will tell you that we are all motivated and ready to go anywhere, any time and we will do our jobs, but when the number of troops drops like this it's their way of telling you how they really feel. Young men have a lot of opportunities these days, and joining the Marines is the last thing a nineteen-year-old man thinks about. This is the generation of well-kept kids who looked on from the back seat of their parents' cars at the veterans of the Vietnam War who gather on street corners in the midst of the wind and rain holding up pleading signs for cash to folks on their way home from school. Why would they want that? They want to go to school and meet girls and drive a big car like everyone else.

Soon after, we were sitting in another room, officially being told about the deployment, when I noticed that something had dramatically changed. Now, it was the vets who were chatting away among themselves about an array of light-hearted topics, from Britney Spears and her dramas to why we should not have to learn Spanish in Texas. As for the new guys, well, they looked like five-year-old boys waiting for a tetanus shot – pale, silent and motionless. They stared at the wall as if there was a television there.

I tried talking to some of them because I could see how scared they were and they told me that they were frightened. I could not help but feel sorry for them. These eighteen- and nineteen-year-old boys were going to Iraq. Some of them might come home mangled and deformed and some of them might never come home at all.

The day after the deployment was announced, news came back about one of our other new guys who had volunteered to go to Iraq with another unit. He was a typical all-American kid, a real nice guy. He had been cut to pieces by a roadside IED. God love him.

I know that I will not sleep well tonight because of the ghosts that torment my soul, but I also know that I am not alone. Tonight, there will be many other young guys lying awake in their beds praying, thinking, worrying and questioning.